Historical European Martial Arts in Its Context

Single-Combat, Duels, Tournaments, Self-Defense, War, Masters and their Treatises

by

Richard Marsden

Historical European Martial Arts in Its Context

by

Richard Marsden

Copyright 2016, All Rights Reserved

ISBN 13 978-0-9847716-7-7

Edited by Cara Patterson
Formatted by Henry Snider
Cover Art by Henry Snider

Without limiting the rights under copyright reserved above, no part of this publication, except images that are public domain or under creative commons, may be reproduced, stored, or introduced into a retrieval system, or transmitted in any form or by any means (electronic, mechanical, photocopying or otherwise) without the prior written permission of both the copyright owner and Tyrant Industries, except in the case of brief quotations embodied in critical reviews.

Dedicated to Phillip, Pam, Jennifer and AJ Marsden

Father, Mother, Sister and Wife

Contents

- i   Preface
- 1   Single-Combat
- 9   The Judicial Duel
- 31   The Private Duel
- 63   Self-Defense
- 81   Tournaments
- 99   War
- 127   Weapons
- 143   The Masters and Their Treatises
  - 146   Italy
  - 162   Holy Roman Empire
  - 175   England
  - 182   France
  - 188   Spain
  - 192   Netherlands
  - 195   Poland
- 199   Conclusion
- 205   Bibliography
- 221   Index

Preface

HEMA[1] stands for Historical European Martial Arts. The goal of HEMA is to recreate the lost European martial arts of the past. These martial arts are generally directed at one-on-one combat, or small group fighting at the most, and not for massed formations of men. The HEMA movement as a whole spans as far as one wants, ranging from pre-recorded history to roughly World War I. However, the standards accepted by the HEMA community measure the reconstructed arts by their source material. The more sources, the more likely the historical art is being practiced accurately. The fewer sources, the more likely the art has errors in its recreation.

Using sources as a measure, HEMA can be narrowed down to times and places that have treatises on the use of martial arts, first and second hand accounts of their use, as well as artwork and surviving weaponry in what is known as archeological experimentation.

Some societies were more literate than others. Some had fencing treatises. Some had firsthand accounts. Alas, some have very little to go on at all.

Viking martial arts of the 10th century, for example, lacks clear sources of any sort. While Viking sagas depict combat, these poems were written not to teach martial arts, but to teach history and entertain. They were also written centuries after the events they described took place, or the events within are purely mythological. It is possible to pick up a recreated Viking shield and sword and experiment, but with so little to go on it is easy to be led astray. Two separate groups could take up a sword and shield and come up with vastly different ideas on how the Vikings used them. This is because they have so little to work with.

Italian rapier of the 17th century, on the other hand, is blessed with a great amount of sources. There are numerous fencing treatises, firsthand and secondhand accounts, and artwork, as well as related sources from the 16th century and the 18th century acting as bookends to help readers understand the material from the 17th century. Two separate groups could take up a rapier and, with the many sources available, would likely look very similar. This is because of the great amount of resource material to work with.

Place can matter as much as time. The German tradition of longsword of the 15th century has plenty of source material called *fechtbuchs*, while the English tradition of longsword from the same century has only a few sources, including highly interpretable poems.

Sources often provide the "how" of things but not the "why." A rapier treatise may spell out the lunge and dozens of techniques, but it may be sparse when it comes to when it was proper to draw steel and use it. Self-defense might be one reason, of course, but why is it that the great majority of rapier plates depict men with equal length weapons opposed to one another? The answer can be found in the history behind HEMA. Very often, the masters themselves spelled out why they wrote their works.

History provides context to the social rules of combat, and these social rules of combat can help students of HEMA better understand their arts.

---

[1] The acronym HEMA was coined by Matt Easton of Schola Gladiatora.

History provides the backdrop to the arts, giving them life. The martial arts of Europe were not created in a void. Context can be found in Europe's attitude toward dueling and self-defense as well as in the wars that were continually ongoing. National character also influenced how the arts were practiced and why.

Vast as HEMA is, this work focuses on the history behind the arts and the known treatises, starting with *MS I.33*, a German treatise on sword and buckler from the early 14th century, and ending with the small sword of Domenico Angelo in the 18th century.

MS I.33 is the earliest European fencing treatise, and Angelo's treatise covers the last sword commonly worn by civilians in Europe. Anecdotes from before and after these time periods provide further insight into the use of the sword and other weapons.

An additional reason for writing this book was that in my years in the HEMA community I discovered that a scant few were versed in both the history and the techniques of the treatises, but that many were familiar with the treatises alone and knew nothing of the context behind them.

My hope is that this book helps those unfamiliar with the history come away with a greater understanding of that which they study, while those already versed in the history behind HEMA come away with a few more anecdotes to share in their teaching of others. My goal is to put HEMA in its context.

Richard Marsden and John Patterson, founders of the Phoenix Society of Historical Swordsmanship.

Single-Combat

Alexander the Great killing Porus in front of their armies in single-combat. The event never took place, and Alexander the Great and Porus certainly looked nothing like medieval jousters, but medieval and Renaissance art often placed historical events into their times.[2]

The duel, judicial or otherwise, is not unique to Europe, but is something that Europeans developed elaborate customs for and is the base context of HEMA. Nearly every treatises is set in the context of a duel, either explicitly or implied. There are of course exceptions, and some treatises double as both a guide on dueling and self-defense, but in general, HEMA treaties depict men with equal weapons facing off against one another. The depictions of mixed weapons or facing multiple opponents or women fighting men or exotic weaponry, like sickles, were more supplemental than they were central to the known treatises.

Early origins of dueling tie into battles between champions of armies in what was called single-combat.

Since biblical days, with David and Goliath, all the way into the 19th century when the British were campaigning in India, it was not unusual for champions of opposing armies to face one another. These were duels, though usually not as ritualized or organized as the judicial and private duels that came later. Single-combat was also not a part of any legal practice, but its customs were rather uniformly understood, even between vastly different cultures.

Sometimes they were dramatic encounters taking place between two armies before battle commenced. Other times, single-combat occurred during the middle of a battle when a champion would stride forth and demand a challenger. Another encounter might be when skirmishers, mounted or otherwise, came upon one another and lone champions presented themselves for battle.

The first century Roman historian Quadrigarius described single-combat between a Roman soldier and a Gaul, which led to the Roman's name being amended. While the original history is lost, Livy and Gellius, centuries later, gave likely romanticized versions of the encounter.

> Meanwhile, a certain Gaul came forward—naked except for a shield and two swords, and bedecked with a torque around his neck and arm-bracelets. He surpassed all in strength, size, the vigor of youth, and courage. At the height of the battle when both sides were feverishly striving against one another, he began to signal with his hands that both sides should stop fighting. The fighting paused and, as soon as it was quiet, the Gaul shouted that if anyone desired to fight him in single-combat, then he should come forward. No one dared on account of his size and savage appearance. Then the Gaul began to laugh and stick his tongue out.
>
> As soon as he witnessed this, a certain Titus Manlius—a youth of noble birth—was grieved that such a shameful insult should be suffered by his country, and that no one from such a great army should step forward to challenge the Gaul. He, as I said previously, stepped forward and did not allow that Roman courage be shamefully debased by this Gaul. Taking up a shield and a Spanish sword he stood against the Gaul. Both sides anxiously watched the meeting on the bridge. As I said earlier, they were arranged thusly: the Gaul, according to his training, was prepared with his shield at the ready; Manlius, trusting more to his courage than to his skill, pressed forward and struck shield against shield, knocking the Gaul off-balance. While the Gaul attempted to steady himself, Manlius again struck his shield with his own and muscled him from his place. Then he slipped under the Gaul's sword and drained the blood from the Gaul's chest with his sword. Then he immediately struck his right shoulder and did not relent until he had overthrown him, never allowing the Gaul a chance to strike back. When he had defeated him, he cut off his head and removed the bloody torque and put it around his own neck. From this action he and his posterity are called the Torquati.[3]

Medieval German literature takes special note of single-combat and often uses it as a literary device. In the *Rolandslied*, twelve times a Christian leader is challenged to single-combat as the opposing armies prepare for war. The said leader obliges, and afterwards general battle ensues.[4]

---

3   Aulus Gellius, "Stories From Aulus Gellius," Translated by Dustin Simmons, accessed May 10, 2015, http://dustinsimmons.blogspot.com/2013/02/kill-gaul-get-name-titus-manlius.html

4   Rachel E. Kellet, Single-Combat and Warfare in German Literature of the High Middle Ages, (Leeds: Maney Publishing, 2008), 109.

Knights watch as single-combat takes place. The unspoken tradition was not to interfere once the two opponents agreed to do battle. Many illuminated manuscripts depict kings engaged with one another in single-combat, even if this did not occur.[5]

In 1380, according to Russian legend, a Russian monk, Alexander Peresvet, and a champion of the Mongol Golden Horde, Cheluby, fought single-combat before their respective armies. They killed one another in the first exchange. Painting by Victor Vasnetov.[6]

The tradition of offering single-combat continued. During the Hundred Years War, according to the chronicler Froissart, a French knight rode up to an English garrison. He called out to the sentry,

> Who is your captain? Tell him the knight Languerant challenges him. Your captain is a good and valiant knight, for his lady's sake he will not give me a refusal. Should he reject my challenge, he will be dishonored and I will everywhere expose his disgrace.

---

5   http://www.strangehistory.net/2013/11/15/the-last-single-combat/ Public Domain Art. May 18 2016.
6   http://www.bryanskobl.ru/region/history/img/peresv_b.jpg 1914 Public Domain Art.

The English captain could not let his honor and that of his lady be disgraced and so met the French knight, killing him in single-combat; such was the duty and consequences of chivalry.[7]

At the siege of Cherbourg, the combat was fierce and dreadful, when a French knight called out to the English, asking to fight their best. An English champion strode forth and for a time, the battle stopped. One on one, the champions engaged each other. When one of them was slain, the battle recommenced.[8]

Sometimes, single-combat had a ritualized aspect to it, making it similar to a judicial or sanctioned duel, even though enemy armies were involved.

In 1487 warring Austrian and Venetian armies were camped close to one another near Trentino. A Venetian, Antonio Maria di San Severino challenged the Austrians to send forth a champion to face him in a knightly battle. He said he wanted to re-create the single-combat of antiquity, citing Greek heroes like Hector and Achilles. A bounty was also offered should he be defeated. A Swabian knight, Johann von Sonnenberg, took up the challenge and matched the bounty, offering a thousand guilder, his horse and harness should he lose.

To keep the duel fair, and prevent treachery, both sides exchanged hostages. Barriers and stands were built between the Austrian and Venetian camps. Inspectors from both sides ensured the dueling grounds were suitable for both parties while Antonio and Johann both had *Greiswart*, or Keeper of the Sands, who acted as seconds and judges. The presiding lord was Roberto d' Aragonia di San Severino and Gaudenz von Matsch, who warned the spectators not to speak on pain of death. The terms of the duel were also arranged. Whoever called out "Katarina" would lose the fight and the winner would be richly rewarded.

The two mounted horses and fought with lances, but quickly, the fight was taken to the ground and resulted in wrestling. The two armored knights fell upon one another and Johann was able to lift up Antonio's armor from around his waist. Johann drove his dagger into Antonio's body and thighs until the Venetian knight called out to Saint Catherine and forfeited. The single-combat was over and both sides returned to their camps to continue their war, while Johann earned the victor's spoils.[9]

There was an almost universal nature to single-combat in war. In the 1520s, according to Guatemalan folk-lore, one of the native chiefs, Tecun Uman, sought out the Spanish commander Pedro Alvarado during a battle. The two met, and according to the local legend, Tecun Uman, who had never seen a horse before, could not tell the difference between Alvarado and his mount. He used a wooden sword with an obsidian edge to decapitate the conquistador's steed. Alvarado, in turn, used his lance to kill the native chief.[10] Like many examples of single-combat, especially between leaders, the veracity is questionable. However, the idea of leaders fighting it out was appealing, even if it rarely came to anything.

Charles V, Emperor of the Holy Roman Empire, was embroiled in endless turmoil both domestically and abroad. He thought a quick way to end his war with France was to challenge King Francis I to a duel in 1526.

---

7   F. Kottenkamp, The History of Chivalry and Armor, (Mineloa: Dover Publications, 2007 org. 1857), 39.
8   Ibid 40.
9   Jens P. Kleinau, "1487 the Duel between Johann Waldburg-Sonnenberg and Antonio Maria d' Aragonia si San Severino", accessed May 30, 2016, https://talhoffer.wordpress.com/2015/06/19/1487-the-duel-between-johann-von-waldburg-sonnenberg-and-antonio-maria-d-aragonia-di-san-severino/
10   V.G Kiernan, The Duel, (Oxford: Oxford University Press, 1988), 59.

Baldassare Castiglione, author of the *Libro de Cortegiano*, a book on court etiquette, was close with Charles V and witnessed the event. Following rules and rituals, the two monarchs exchanged written challenges called a *cartello*. Castiglione sent copies of the two *cartello* to a friend in Italy and remarked on the affair,

> His majesty (Charles V) is so eager to fight that I shall not be surprised if the duel takes place.[11]

Indeed, Charles was quite serious and he bid Castiglione tutor him on the use of weapons and stand by him during the duel as his second.

Others were not so sure. Maximilian of Transylvania said,

> I was greatly amused to hear of the challenge between these two monarchs. It is quite a tragedy, although I expect the result will be more comic than tragic. Meanwhile people talk of nothing else. When kings go mad, the people suffer."

The King of France refused to see Charles V's herald, and the negotiations for the duel broke down. Charles was deeply concerned that Europe might see him as a coward, and so he pressed the issue, but was eventually convinced by the grandees of Spain that he had done all he could and his honor was secure.[12]

Thus the single-combat between kings never took place and the Hapsburg Valois wars went on until 1559.[13]

In 17th century Sweden, an elderly Charles IX thought to end his war with Denmark with single-combat against King Christian IV. As Charles put it, they would settle the war with one fight in the manner of the ancient Goths. Just as the duel between Charles V and Francis I came to nothing, the two Scandinavian monarchs did not meet in combat either. Still, there were accounts of single-combat taking place in the Renaissance and beyond.

When the Duke of Orange was besieging the city of Florence in 1530, a rather unusual request came from the besieged. They asked that two champions of Florence be allowed to fight two Florentines in the service of the Duke. The Duke agreed and four Florentines met outside the city to fight with swords, wearing no armor. Landsknecht mercenaries acted the part of a living barrier for the combatants.

Brantome, who heard the story from another, said the men fought valiantly, but one of the pro-Florentine men was wounded and told to surrender by his opponent. Unable to continue, he reluctantly did so and his partner gave up as well. Hands were shook and the defeated party was allowed to return to their city while the victorious Florentines were celebrated by the Duke of Orange.[14]

---

11 Julia Mary Cartwright, Baldassare Castiglione the perfect courtier: his life and letters. Volume 2 (Toronto: University of Toronto Libraries, 1908), 391.
12 Ibid 392.
13 Stephen Banks, Duels and Duelling, (London: Shire Publications, 2012), 48.
14 George H. Powell, Dueling Stories of the 16th Century: From the French of Brantome, (London: 1904), 40.

Modernization of European armies in the 16th century made single-combat less common, though still plausible. Ben Johnson, playwright and duelist, claimed he once killed a Spaniard in single-combat in 1582 in front of the opposing armies. He went on to say he stripped the man of his possessions, as was his right.[15] However, the occurrences of single-combat became rarer in Europe as the 17th century approached.

Further dampening the prospect of single-combat was the sheer risk, not to the lives of the champions (this was always at risk), but to the state. The Swedish King Gustavus Adolphus led his armies to repeated victory in the Thirty-Years War, earning Sweden a serious military reputation. However, at the Battle of Lützen in 1632, the king became isolated after leading a cavalry charge. He was surrounded by Imperial cavalry and killed. Protestant forces won the battle, but at the cost of the Swedish king. Gustavus had no male heirs and his loss was a profound blow to the Protestant cause. It was also a sign that the days of kings leading their armies from the front, and perhaps engaging in single-combat, were largely at an end—at least in Europe.

In the 19th century, British colonial soldiers repeatedly encountered Indian armies who would send forth a champion, and the British, in an unspoken ancient tradition, would oblige. While in days of old, generals, or even kings, might engage in such duels. In the 19th century, it was up to the lower ranked officers and common soldiers to mimic the ancient tradition.

Captain Bellew recounted the tale of a British sergeant who was more than happy to seek out single-combat.

> Speaking of single-combats, which rarely occur in what may be paradoxically termed civilized warfare, a man who dearly loved fighting for fighting's sake, and eagerly sought every opportunity of gratifying his propensity, was a sergeant of the 27th Dragoons, a splendid swordsman and during our contests with the Mahrattas used constantly on the line of march to ride out when he could and seek every opportunity in engaging an enemy hand to hand and when he found an antagonist, he would go to work *con amore*[16] and soon demolish him.
>
> On one particular occasion, a Mahratta darted from a cloud of horsemen hovering about the flanks of the army, caracoled his horse, flourished his lance in the air and seemed to toss a haughty defiance in the teeth of the British.
>
> This was a glorious opportunity for the fighting sergeant and at him he rode. But the skillful agile Mahratta, evading the stroke and collision, wheeled his horse about and in turn becoming the assailant, bore down full tilt, lance in rest, on his English foe.
>
> Cool as a cucumber, the sergeant received him, averted the point of the spear with his sword and again spurring up, strove to cut down the Mahratta.
>
> But the latter, by sudden duckings and doublings, evaded the charge and the sergeant's thirsty blade cleft the air. And then he again attempted to bore a "tunnel" through the sergeant, but neither could harm his advisory; and at length, fairly exhausted, they drew up as if by mutual consent and eyed each other for a few moments in mute admiration and astonishment.

15　　V.G Kiernan, The Duel, (Oxford: Oxford University Press, 1988), 59.
16　　With love.

> "You're a damned fine fellow!" said the sergeant.
>
> "Shabash, Bahdur" [Bravo, Brave One!] exclaimed the Mahratta; and the former raised his hand to his head salutingly and the Mahratta flung him a proud, but gracious salaam.
>
> Each then wheeled off his horse and departed; each had found in the other a foeman worthy of his steed.[17]

Sometimes it would be the British who would initiate single-combat. Major General Strange commented on one such an engagement during the Sepoy Rebellion of 1857.

> Up rode Hodson by himself. Within two or three hundred yards of us was a body of the enemy's cavalry and what Hodson was dying to do was lead the Lancers against them. Orders, however, were to stick by some nearby guns.
>
> Hodson, disappointed in this, started off toward the canal. He had gone a very short distance when he found himself confronted by one of the enemy with a shield and tulwar.[18] I shall never forget Hodson's face as he confronted this man. It was smiles all over. He went round and round the man who was in the center of the circle dancing *more Indicio* (Indian method of fighting including feints) doing his best to cut Hodson's reins. This went on for some time, when a neat point from Hodson put an end to the performance.[19]

Even common sailors understood the ancient and respected nature of single-combat. William Martin, a private in the British army, recollected such an occurrence during the storming of a Sepoy stronghold.

> Just before we left the building, some sailors came upon one of the last of the rebels. One of them stepped out and attacked him. It was honor bright; no one interfered, but looked on while the two fought. The Sepoy was a good swordsman and wounded the sailor in the sword arm.
>
> "Had you there, Jack," said one of his comrades.
>
> Quick as thought, the sailor shifted his cutlass to his left hand; this was something the Sepoy was not prepared for; and before he could guard, the sailor cut him down, remarking as he did so, in an answer to his comrade, "Yes, by God, he had me, but I have him now!"[20]
>
> Single-combat was usually an informal duel, one in which if the army's champion was victorious, it showed some form of divine favor in the battle to come. In terms of spontaneous moments of single-combat, it was a chance for those involved to demonstrate their skill and bravery. However, by the middle ages there was a ritualized aspect to single-combat which would be shared in judicial dueling and in tournaments.

---

17   D.A. Kinsley, Blades of the British Empire, (Lulu: 2012), 94.
18   A slender curved blade commonly used in India.
19   D.A. Kinsley, Blades of the British Empire, (Lulu: 2012), 142.
20   Ibid 167.

John Patterson of the Phoenix Society of Historical Swordsmanship with a longsword.

The Judicial Duel

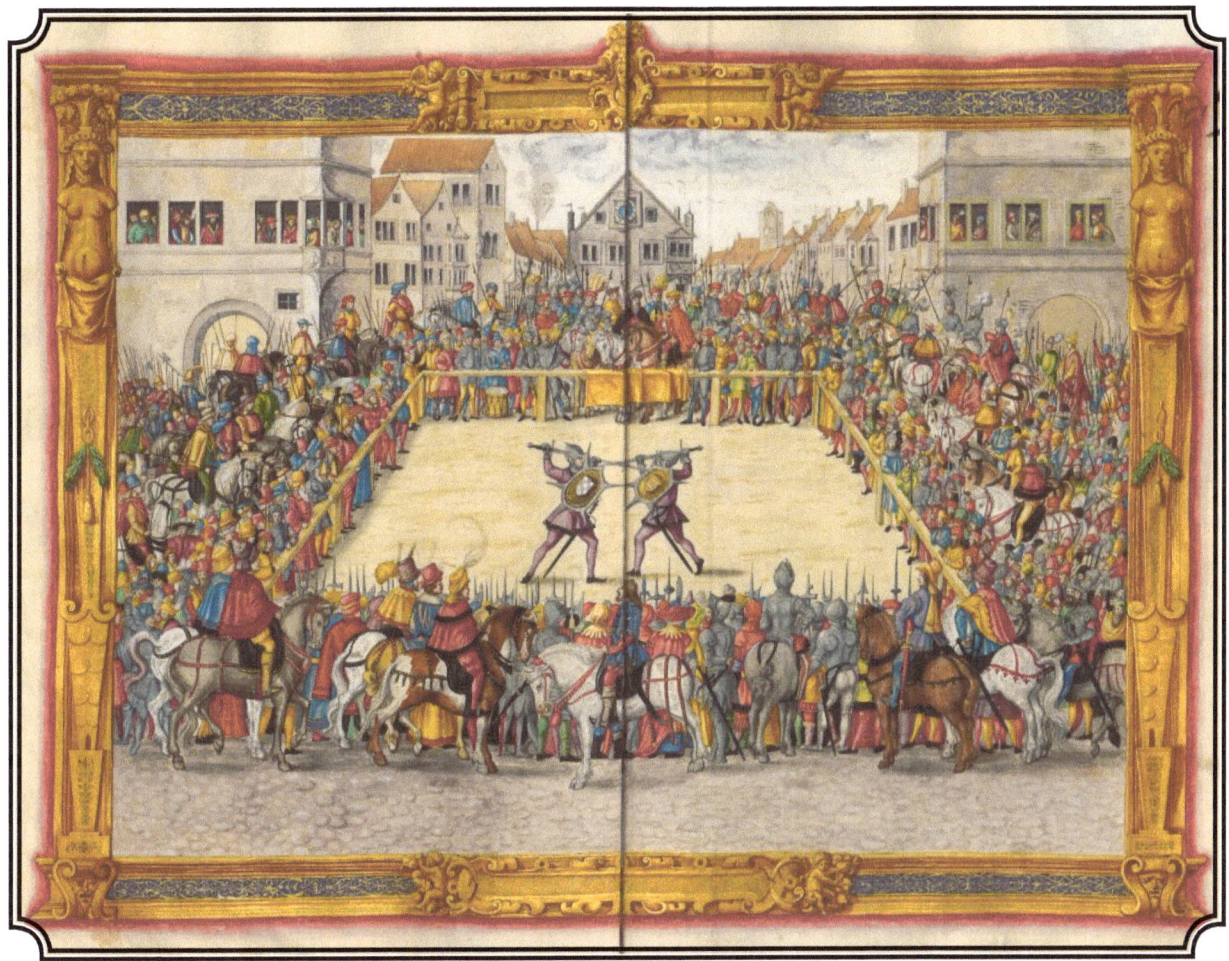

A judicial duel taking place before an assembled crowd between Marshal Wilhelm von Dornsberg and Theodor Haschneacker in Augsburg 1409. Dornsberg's sword broke during the duel, but he managed to wrestle away Haschenacker's and kill him with it.[21]

When the Western Roman Empire fell in the 5th century, the Germanic inheritors and invaders brought with them their laws, which included rules about interpersonal violence. Romans, such as Tacitus, described them as fiercely independent, where every warrior had and valued a high level of freedom. Each man was a king in his own right.[22] Men who disagreed with one another could legally fight out their differences, something Roman law did not allow for. Furthermore, in ancient Germanic law, whole families could legally fight one another, and vengeance was their sacred right.

Salic Law, established by Clovis of the Franks during the 6th century, further codified ancient Germanic law on interpersonal violence and tried, with some success, to limit familial warfare and transfer it to courts where fines handled many issues. Through a process known as compurgation, a defendant

---

21   Bayrische Staatsbibliothek Cod. icon. 393 Mair, Circa 1544 Dbachmann Public Domain Art.
22   Henry Charles Lea, Wager of Battle, In Superstition and Force: Torture, Ordeal, and Trial by Combat in Medieval Law, 95. 3rd ed, (Philadelphia: Bodleian Library, 1878), 14.

could take an oath, and so long as several upstanding people believed the oath, it was binding.[23]

While Salic Law limited familial violence with compurgation, the practice of using oaths was open to abuses. A popular man with many kinsmen could commit a crime knowing his family would accept his oath of innocence, while a friendless man could not gather the people needed to verify his oath and so was doomed to be guilty due to his unpopularity. Despite this inherent flaw, the taking of an oath with a set number of guarantors remained a legal option in France, Sweden, Denmark, Poland and Germany even into the 19th century.[24]

A counter to the weakness of compurgation was the right to fight out legal matters. This right was called a wager of battle, trial by battle or judicial combat. Its roots started early in European history.

In Old Swedish law, it was acceptable for men to settle their differences outside of town, and the same Scandinavians brought forth *holmganga*, a ritualized fight between two parties in a ring that had German tribal equivalents.

Charles Buschmann and Adam Simmons of the Phoenix Society of Historical Swordsmanship demonstrate with the sword and buckler. This combination of weaponry was popular in early judicial duels.

In Bavaria, two parties arguing over an estate would meet before a court. As with compurgation, oaths could be given, but as a way to force an issue, the accuser could state that his opponent was lying. By doing this, the accuser was stating that only battle and God's judgment would proclaim the truth.[25]

---

23 Ibid 43.
24 Ibid 64.
25 Ibid 75.

Even into the 18th century, these ancient methods of settling disputes were acknowledged as the foundation of fencing. Henry Angelo, introducing his father's works of 1763 in *L'Ecole des Armes*, succinctly summarized the history of fencing.

> When the Goths introduced the custom of single-combat, the art of defense became a necessary study: it was confined to certain rules and academies were instituted to train up youth in the practice of them.
>
> The moderns having adopted the small sword in preference to the ancient arms…

The small sword that Angelo noted the 'moderns' had adopted.

Just as compurgation could be abused, the same went for judicial combat. The Lombard Laws of the 8th century introduced regulation and restrictions on legalized combat and thus introduced a more formal system of judicial dueling.[26] King Rothari in Pavia in 643 had laws written in Latin that included judicial dueling, but also required that in the case of a woman, some evidence had to be provided. Future generations added further stipulations such as fines for the vanquished rather than death.[27]

When Charlemagne conquered large portions of Western Europe in the late 8th century he took existing judicial dueling laws and modified them. For example, Charlemagne made the judicial duel mandatory in the case of perjury, but removed the Lombard punishment of amputation of a hand.[28]

Judicial dueling had value as a means of limiting violence, not necessarily encouraging it. During the First Crusade in the early 11th century, John van Ackle of Holland had the misfortune of having the same coat of arms as a German noble. The German noble tore down Ackle's insignia from his camp, and Ackle promptly confronted not the German noble, but rather Godfrey of Bullion, the leader of the Crusade.

Godfrey decreed only a judicial duel would suffice to determine who could wear the coat of arms. The two entered the lists and did battle. Ackle killed his opponent and had avenged himself of the insult of having his coat of arms torn down. His victory in the duel won him the right to wear it forevermore.[29]

What very well could have been two knights and their accompanying retainers battling it out in the Christian camp was mitigated to just the two of them fighting.

Europeans largely adopted judicial dueling for the same reasons they accepted compurgation, despites its faults. Both were a means of clamping down on murder or, worse, family vendettas that could bring ruin to a country. Two powerful Spanish families, the Monroy and Solis, argued at a wedding party in 1464, leading to a multi-year conflict throughout the country.[30] Italy was plagued with such vendettas that could last for generations, and clan warfare in Poland, Scotland and Ireland was rampant. Judicial dueling was a means of bringing some order and limitations to violence that was seen as inevitable, but perhaps manageable.

When the Normans invaded England in 1066, they brought with them the judicial duel, which was not seen, by them at least, as an introduction of barbarism. Quite the opposite, the Normans saw the judicial duel as a civilized way to deal with familial warfare.[31] The English were having none of it, though, and William the Conqueror exempted them from judicial dueling, though his descendants re-introduced it.[32]

The judicial duel was a legally sanctioned conflict, overseen by the state—and sometimes the Church—and intended for the noble classes. Given that God's favor was being invoked, and everyone was a subject of God, the judicial duel was theoretically open to all.

---

26 J.B. Bury, The Invasion of Europe by Barbarians, (London: 1928), Chapter 15.
27 Frederick R. Bryson, The Sixteenth-Century Italian Duel, (Chicago: University of Chicago Press, 1938), XIV.
28 Ibid XV.
29 Henry Charles Lea, Wager of Battle, In Superstition and Force: Torture, Ordeal, and Trial by Combat in Medieval Law, 95. 3rd ed, (Philadelphia: Bodleian Library, 1878), 76.
30 V.G Kiernan, The Duel, (Oxford: Oxford University Press, 1988), 32.
31 Stephen Banks, Duels and Duelling, (London: Shire Publications, 2012), 6.
32 R. C. Caenegem, Legal History: A European Perspective, (London: Bloomsbury Academic, 2004), 91.

The commoners could participate in sanctioned duels, though they were performed differently than the judicial duels of their social betters.

In Burgundy, during the mid-14th century, a law stated that any man who killed another could claim self-defense and remain unpunished, but that anyone could challenge him to a judicial duel. A tailor, Mahout, killed a man and claimed his privilege.

A relative of the deceased, Jacotin Plouvier, accused Mahout of murder. The local authorities arrested both. A judicial duel was arranged in which each would be armed with a club and a triangular shield, though, as men of lower birth, they would have to carry the shields upside-down.

The Duke watched the proceedings, but the trial was officially in the hands of local magistrates. A large crowd gathered and unrest nearly prevented the duel from taking place. Once quiet was established, the men fought. A gibbet stood nearby, awaiting the loser of the contest.

In a brutal fight, the men used their clubs to bash and crush bone. Plouvier threw Mahout to the ground, tore out his eyes, then, holding him aloft, tossed him out of the wooden barrier and into the hands of the executioner.[33]

Women could engage in a judicial duel, though they rarely did. More often, a champion was chosen to fight in a woman's place. Several manuscripts depict women fighting men in a duel including— Paulus Kal's *fechtbuch MS KK5126* and Hans Talhoffer's *fechtbuch MS Thott.290.2º*. In Talhoffer's work, the woman is armed with a primitive flail, in the form of a stone wrapped in cloth, while the man is in a waist deep hole armed with a club. In Denmark, if the man missed hitting the woman three times, she was innocent.[34] While an unusual set-up, judicial duels were driven by social status on the one hand and a desire for fair play on the other.

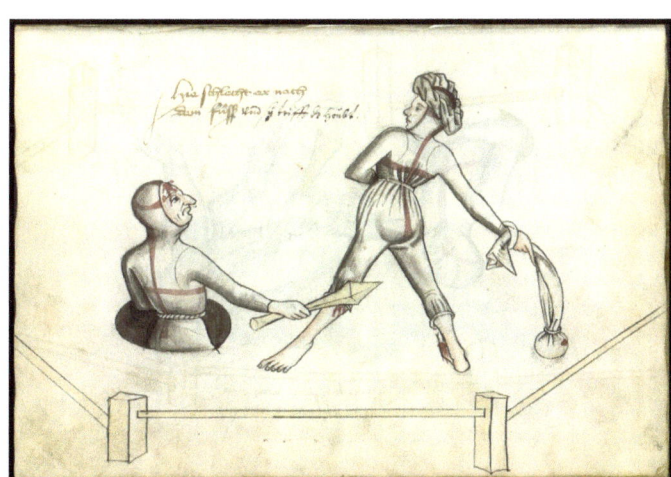

A man fights a woman in a judicial duel in this Talhoffer depiction. Wooden barriers contain the fight. The man is in a hole with a wooden club while the woman is armed with a cloth and a stone inside of it.[35]

This idea of fairness in the judicial duel meant that it was not the choice of weapon or even the skill of the duelists that mattered, but rather that God favored the winner. The best way to give God an even playing field to work with was to make the odds as even as possible. One easy way to seek out a fair result was to allow women, the elderly or the disabled the right to choose a champion to fight

---

33   Alfred Hutton, The Sword and the Centuries, (Staffordshire: Wren's Park Publishing, 2003 org. 1901), 19-20.
34   Barbara Holland, Gentlemen's Blood, (London: Bloomsbury Publishing, 2004), 10.
35   Talhoffer Image courtesy of the Royal Library of Copenhagen

in their stead. The end desire was to make things even and all things being even, God would sort out the rest.

The nobility could also ask for a champion, but the social stigma was intense. When a Norman noble elected to have his brother fight a duel in his stead, the brother won, but so shamed was the elder that he hung himself.[36]

Some clergymen were also permitted to duel, which may explain why the earliest treatise, *MS I.33* depicts fighting monks. In the 12th century a man named Engelardus quarreled with the monks of a local monastery over who owned a particular spot of land and the mills upon it. An abbot recounted the event and how a day-long judicial duel with sticks and shields took place.

> The quarrel concerning this matter dragged out to the point that lord Geoffrey of Mayenne, bishop of Angers, came to inspect the place in question. And, when he was unable to peacefully impose an end to the contentious quarrel, he determined that a judicial battle ought to be fought concerning this matter between Engelardus and the monks at the villa which is called Vi, doing so under his judgment.
>
> In which place, after neither the bishop nor the great lords who had gathered there were able to bring concord, they [the bishop and lords] observed, against their will, the two champions taking an oath on the sacrament and deciding with shields and staves for most of the day. And just as it is written that God opposes the prideful, so he weakened the champion of Engelardus, so that the enemies of the holy martyrs Sergius and Bacchus were utterly terrified; where these enemies had previously not wanted to make peace [with the monks], now they themselves were the ones who suggested it. They offered to the monks as a means of concord the entire tithe of the mills and the fish caught there, as well as four deniers in rent from every mill that either existed there now or would exist there in the future.[37]

The duel took all day and no one was killed. There was also much deliberation before, during and after. This in itself was not unusual, and an Italian chronicler noted that most judicial duels were entered upon in all seriousness but ended at the last moment in a compromise.[38] The same would be true for the private duels that followed the judicial. A first glance at the sources may suggest otherwise, but it must be remembered that a historian might comment on an actual duel but probably not on an almost-duel. Contemporaries often noted how uncommon duels were, or how potential duelists achieved peace before drawing blood.

Even dogs, supposedly, could demand a judicial duel. A surviving letter from Julius Caesar Scaliger from the 16th century claimed that in 1371 Charles V of France allowed a dog to have a trial by combat with the suspected murderer of its master. The dog, chosen by God, won and justice was served with the prompt hanging of the murderer.[39] The story is likely fabricated, or a retold legend, but indicates that judicial duels could involve unlikely participants.

---

36 E. Searle, Merchet in Medieval England, Past and Present, (1979), 34.
37 Yves Chauvin, Memoire dactylographie soutenu devant la Faculte des Lettres de Caen (1969), 285- 288.
38 R. C. Caenegem, Legal History: A European Perspective, (London: Bloomsbury Academic, 2004), 90.
39 George Neilson, Trial by Combat, (Glasgow: W. Hodge and co, 1891), 16.

The dog, Dragon, supposedly forced Macaire to confess to the crime of murder, for which he was hanged.[40] The scene has the hallmarks of a judicial duel, including a barrier to contain the fight and a lord observing it as a judge might any trial.

These duels were called judicial because a crime of some sort had to be presented and the parties separated into the accuser and the defendant. The two even had their own lawyers and the duel needed the approval of a religious authority, lord or king. The trial itself was that of combat, with God singling out the winner. Whoever won was the innocent party.

Sixteenth century Frenchman Duke Maximilien de Sully sarcastically noted that when it came to duels, "Heaven always gave victory to the right cause."[41] Two centuries later, historian Henry Charles Lea echoed the statement by saying, "There is a natural tendency in the human mind to cast the burden of its doubts upon a higher power."[42]

Not all judicial duels were to the death, nor did extreme punishment always result after one of the duelists capitulated. A land dispute could be simply considered settled in a judicial duel in which there was a winner, but no one died.

40   Duel with a Dog Public Domain Art.
41   Mika LaVaque-Manty, "Dueling for Equality: Masculine Honor and the Modern Politics of Dignity", University of Michigan, (2006): accessed May 18, 2016, http://www-personal.umich.edu/~mmanty/research/Dueling.PT.pdf
42   Henry Charles Lea, Wager of Battle, In Superstition and Force: Torture, Ordeal, and Trial by Combat in Medieval Law, 95. 3rd ed, (Philadelphia: Bodleian Library, 1878), 74.

Judicial duels, like this one, could lead to death. In this Talhoffer depiction, the duelists do not have matched weapons. This was likely by agreement, or some legal convention.[43]

The monks of St. Martin and Fontaines demanded a judicial duel over ownership of a swamp. Both sides picked a champion and each champion swore that the land belonged to their respective party in the presence of a local count. The practice of compurgation would not work, since both champions made an oath, and that oath was accepted by their mutually comparable supporters. The count allowed the duel to take place, and the champion of the monks of Fontaines defeated, but did not kill, the champion of the monks of St. Martin. The losing side left in tears, denied their swamp, but otherwise unharmed.[44]

James I, King of Scotland and England, noted that if a judicial duel was over a small legal matter or honor, only the weapons and armor of the loser were at stake.[45]

Phillip IV of France decreed that the loser of a judicial duel have his arms and armor torn from his body and scattered about the lists.[46]

Such a duel took place in France in 1549. Claude d'Aguerre and Jacques de Fontaine entered a dispute in which a lie was given and blows delivered. Each on their own was sufficient cause of a duel, and King Henri II granted it. The lists, an area to contain the fight, were created, stands for spectators erected and the two met to settle the matter of the lie. Here, the difference between a judicial and private duel blend as was often the case in the 16th century. Technically, the duel was not judicial, because no courts were involved and no legal matter had to be solved. In many ways the duel had the hallmarks of a private duel, in which honor was at stake. Yet, the king approved the duel, it was conducted in public and it was regulated in the same manner as a judicial duel.

The two fought wearing armor and using longswords. D'Aguerre attempted to drive his opponent past the barrier. Had he succeeded, he would have won the duel then and there. Fontaine avoided

---

43   Image courtesy the Royal Library of Copenhagen
44   Paul Marchegay, "Duel judiciaire entre des communautes religieuses, 1098," Bibliotheque de l'Ecole des Chartes, 1 (1839-1840): 552-564.
45   V.G Kiernan, The Duel, (Oxford: Oxford University Press, 1988), 35.
46   F. Kottenkamp, The History of Chivalry and Armor, (Mineloa: Dover Publications, 2007 org. 1857), 110.

being pushed out of the lists and countered by cutting D'Aguerre in the thigh. D'Aguerre abandoned his sword and wrestled Fontaine to the ground.

Unexpectedly, the stands for the spectators collapsed and in the confusion D'Aguerre was prompted by his friends to use the sand at his feet. Speaking to the duelists was forbidden, but the Master of the Lists and judges were distracted by the wailing and cries of the spectators. D'Aguerre scooped sand into his hands and nearly suffocated Fontaine.

Fontaine was compelled to confess and D'Aguerre was declared the winner. Though the fight could have ended in death, instead, the confession was enough. Fontaine left the lists without his weapons or armor while D'Aguerre was paraded around as the victor.[47]

Italian customs in the 16th century were similar, with the victor of the duel having the right to the loser's arms and armor. In 1512 in Ferrara, two captains, Azevado and Saint-Croix, entered into a dispute and were granted a duel. As in the case of Fontaine and D'Aguerre in France, the duel was not technically a judicial one, but had all the trappings of a judicial duel none the less. Bayard, a famous knight, acted as a judge, while the Duchess Lucrezia Borgia oversaw the combat. After both parties were searched for hidden armor and magic charms they were allowed to fight. The duel was fought in the Borgia palace courtyard and resulted in Saint-Croix being struck in the thigh so deeply that he collapsed. Azevado beseeched his opponent to surrender, which Saint-Croix reluctantly did. The two were separated and Azevado went to a victor's feast and Saint-Croix to the doctor. When Azevado asked for Saint-Croix's weapons as a prize, the defeated captain refused. Azevado insisted that Saint-Croix's thigh be stitched up and the duel resumed. Wisely, Saint-Croix demurred and had his arms handed over.[48]

Other punishments for the vanquished, assuming they didn't die during the duel, varied. A perjurer could have his hand cut off or be hanged. If a champion was fighting, and lost, he could be executed, but his employer would merely be fined. If the case was serious and the champion lost, he would be hanged, along with his employer and any witnesses he produced. If a woman were involved, she could be burned.[49] Region and time affected the punishments. In its earliest history, the judicial duel had savage repercussions such as being buried alive. However, as the judicial duel was further codified fines were more common than mutilation or death.[50]

The Assizes of Jerusalem from the 13th century detail medieval law concerning a judicial duel. Reasons for a duel include land disputes and horse-trading in bad faith, as well as crimes, such as murder, treason and perjury. When making a challenge, the accuser handed a glove to the presiding judge, or judges, who then determined if the duel would proceed or not. From this came a later tradition of tossing a gauntlet and later still in the 16th century, having a glove delivered to an opponent and in the 19th century, slapping an opponent with a glove.[51]

In court, a judge could be challenged to a duel if the defendant claimed a false judgment. The word

---

47 Alfred Hutton, The Sword and the Centuries, (Staffordshire: Wren's Park Publishing, 2003 org. 1901), 33-34. Hutton, who gleefully compiles narratives out of historical accounts, is dubious over the exact details of this particular duel.

48 Frederick R. Bryson, The Sixteenth-Century Italian Duel, (Chicago: University of Chicago Press, 1938), 180.

49 F. Kottenkamp, The History of Chivalry and Armor, (Mineloa: Dover Publications, 2007 org. 1857), 109-110.

50 Frederick R. Bryson, The Sixteenth-Century Italian Duel, (Chicago: University of Chicago Press, 1938), XV.

51 F. Kottenkamp, The History of Chivalry and Armor, (Mineloa: Dover Publications, 2007 org. 1857), 39.

"challenge" itself derives from the Latin word *calumnia*, or false accusation. Nobles tried by their peers often faced a group of three or more judges who delivered unanimous verdicts.[52] The judges noted it was far too tempting for an unhappy defendant to challenge one man to a duel than three or more at once.

Class distinctions were developed early on. While fairness was important, it did not fully trump society. Nobles could challenge one another to combat, but any cross between the classes led to mismatched equipment. In the laws of St. Louis, if a knight was challenged by a commoner, he would fight the commoner while mounted, giving him an advantage. If a knight challenged a commoner, then both would fight on foot. Other French customs included the use of clubs in potentially mortal combat between nobles, or judicial duels between commoners.[53]

In 1360, the regulations of Gelnhausen were numerous and directed at the commoners rather than noble class. Only citizens from the city could ask for a judicial duel, though they could challenge outsiders. The aggrieved party would stand before the judges and bang a mace against a shield and proclaim his right to a judicial duel. This was declared as an ancient right that descended from the Franks. The judges would attempt to reconcile the two parties, but failing that, the duelists were granted assistants if they so chose and directed to fight in a circle drawn in the earth. Neither was permitted to wear armor of any kind and fought with mace and shield alone. A great deal of ceremony took place and it would take days for a duel to be agreed to and fought, giving both parties plenty of time to reconsider.[54]

Rules and regulations for a judicial duel were agreed upon beforehand and could include numerous variables. Some included, who had the right to strike first and which weapons and armor were to be used. Other factors to be determined were what to do if a weapon were lost or broken, what happened if someone stepped back from the fight once it started, what happened if the audience interfered, how long should the duel proceed and should breaks be allowed?[55] All of these were up for negotiation and varied by class and the customs of the region.

In certain cases, the duelists wore different equipment. A knight accused of murder would fight a judicial duel without armor, but with a large shield covered in spikes and a sword. Judicial dueling shields covered in spikes remained popular, but knights and nobles were also permitted to wear their entire suit of armor and were given spears, swords and daggers to use.[56] If the duel was not to the death, the armor largely protected the combatants from lasting harm.

Fiore de Liberi, a master of arms, wrote in the early 15th century in his *Flower of Battle*, that fighting in armor was far safer because with armor a person could miss a cover and survive, while, unarmored, a single missed cover could result in death.[57] His students were noted for the duels that they fought. They fought while wearing armor and so were not killed—and neither were their opponents.

---

52   V.G Kiernan, The Duel, (Oxford: Oxford University Press, 1988), 33.
53   Catherine Emerson, Olivier de La Marche and the Rhetoric of the Fifteenth-century Historiography, (Woodbridge: Boydell Press, 2004), 204-205.
54   Jens P. Kleinau, "1360 the Law of Judicial Duels in the City of Gelnhausen", accessed May 30, 2016, https://talhoffer.wordpress.com/2013/06/13/1360-the-law-of-judical-duels-in-the-city-of-gelnhausen/
55   Jens P. Kleinau, "What do you do if you are called for the judicial duel with mace and shield", accessed May 30, 2016 https://talhoffer.wordpress.com/2015/04/16/what-to-do-if-you-are-for-the-judicial-duel-with-mace-and-shield/
56   F. Kottenkamp, The History of Chivalry and Armor, (Mineloa: Dover Publications, 2007 org. 1857), 110.
57   "Wiktenauer, "Fiore de'i Liberi", last modified August 16, 2016, accessed May 26, 2016, http://wiktenauer.com/wiki/Fiore_de'i_Liberi

Randy Reyes and Christopher Nelson of the Phoenix Society of Historical Swordsmanship demonstrate that every part of the sword could be used in battle.

One of Fiore's students, Galeazzo da Mantova, engaged in duel with the Frenchman Boucicaut in 1395 in Padua[58]. An insult had been shared by them over the valor of Italians and the duel was a mix of private, due the nature of honor, and judicial in that it was sanctioned by an authority. Over twelve-thousand people attended the duel, the details of which were well-documented.

At first, attempts were made to prevent the duel from happening, a custom that would continue throughout the history of both judicial and private dueling.

> …the Lord of Padua and the Lord of Mantua tried to see to it that the combatants would reconcile, but to no avail. Those attempting this with Boucicaut and with Galeazzo went now to one, now to the other combatant for two hours without affecting anything—measuring spears, axes and other armament. Upon seeing that no agreement could be reached, Mr. Boucicaut decided not to wait any longer, had his horse brought to him and mounted it, wearing his helmet, carrying his target before his chest and a spear in his hand. He began pacing around the field, waiting for Galeazzo to also mount his horse. Galeazzo took his horse by the reins and waited for the gauntlet of combat to be thrown.
>
> Galeazzo took his horse by the reins and waited for the gauntlet of combat to be thrown. Seeing that Galeazzo would not get on his horse, however,

---

58   Boucicaut led a colorful life that included numerous duels, jousts and war-time activities leading to his capture during a crusade and second capture by the English during the 100 Years War. He died in England, still a prisoner. Galeazzo da Mantoa was a *condottieri* and lived a life of war and intrigue, eventually becoming commander of Venice's armies. He was killed by a crossbow bolt to the eye during a siege, a month after dueling his rival Boucicaut a second time.

> Boucicaut dismounted, headed for his chair and had his spurs removed (it had been agreed that if one of them were to go to his chair, the other should not give himself any trouble). His spurs removed, Mr. Boucicaut grabbed his spear and boldly proceeded against Mr. Galeazzo, thinking that the gauntlet had already been thrown.

The tossing of the gauntlet remained a mainstay in dueling culture up until the 17th century when a glove might be sent to an opponent.

> Now, Mr. Michael of Rabara did throw the gauntlet of combat. When they saw this, Mr. Galeazzo and Mr. Boucicaut boldly went against one another on foot with spears. Mr. Galeazzo had his helmet visor raised, and as he saw that Boucicaut was coming towards him also in that same condition, spear-in-hand[59] he hit Boucicaut's aventail in such a way that the latter recoiled by three steps. Mr. Boucicaut threw away his spear and put his hands on Galeazzo's, broke it and reached for his axe which was nearby.
>
> He brandished it with both hands and headed for Galeazzo, but the Lord of Mantua, along with the Lord's regulars, ran towards him and grabbed him by the waist saying: "No more! You have already done much, now do you not want to honor what you have promised and sworn on the missal—to do the wishes of the Lord of Padua and me?"
>
> On the other side, the Lord of Padua with his regulars had gone to Mr. Galeazzo and after grabbing him in the same way and saying the same words that were said to Mr. Boucicaut, he eventually reconciled them after much talking.
>
> He then led them to the middle of the field and removed their helmets, and they hugged and kissed with the utmost cheerfulness.[60]

Having shown up and fought, though neither had been seriously wounded, the duel was over and honor had been satisfied for both parties. The kiss as a means of ending the conflict was at the time an Italian tradition and used to settle family vendettas and worked equally well to end a dispute between quarrelling knights.[61] The quarrel was not quite over though, and the two would meet again in 1406, where Fiore's student proved victorious.

Private disputes over honor rather than legal issues, like that of Galeazzo and Boucicaut, were treated similarly to judicial duels until the end of the 16th century. These sanctioned duels were most common among the knightly class.

Georg of Rosenberg of Schüpf and Boxberg was a robber-knight of some great infamy who had a quarrel with Simon von Stetten. They exchanged letters, as would remain a custom in dueling, and agreed battle would settle their differences. They claimed the knightly right to fight over matters of honor known as *Ritterrecht*. This was granted by a presiding lord, the Margrave Albrecht Achilles, in 1478. The Margrave was not entirely pleased to allow this duel of honor for the same reasons judicial dueling irked the authorities- they could deprive the lord of a useful servant and supplanted their authority.

---

59   The wording, *con la sua lanza in mano* suggests that the blow was delivered without letting the spear run through the forward hand.
60   Account provided graciously by Greg Mele and translated by Tom Leoni.
61   Peter Spierenburg, A History of Murder, (Cambridge: Polity Press, 2008), 43.

A recreation from the Paris version of Fiore's treatise. Fiore's techniques were for fighting in, or outside of armor, in the barriers for a duel, or for the purposes of self-defense. The image shows the use of the poleaxe. Fiore was Galeazzo's teacher.[62]

Georg and Simon agreed beforehand that the duel was not to the death, but rather until one of them called out for mercy. They arrived and stayed in different rooms while their armor was inspected, weapons were chosen and terms of combat settled upon. Meanwhile, the Margrave tried, to no avail, to settle the matter peacefully.

The day of the duel, the Margrave warned the spectators to keep quiet and to interfere in any way would result in their execution. Georg and Simon arrived, each with a second, another custom that would carry on through the ages, and entered the barriers. The duel was a matter of honor and so each proclaimed his cause to the audience.

Simon said,

> You beloved people, the reason I will fight Georg of Rosenberg today is genuine by his huge arrogance and haughtiness. I beg you to pray to the almighty God for me because my case is righteous and true.

While Georg said,

---

[62] Recreation by Ashton Warren.

> You, Graves, Free Men, Knights, Squires and beloved friends! As Simon of Stetten speaks I should fight him today because of my arrogance and haughtiness, this is not true. I tell you what this fight is about. He had captured my friend and did not respect his honor; therefore I challenged him for the honor of my friend in front of my gracious master the margrave and his council. In front of my gracious master the count palatine and his council I have received the honor and the right to do so. Therefore I beg you for the justice of the Lord to pray at the Almighty for me in my misery.

Simon refuted Georg's statement and both prayed that God would see them as the victor. The two fought within the barriers on horseback. After attempting to harm one another with lances, then swords, the fight was taken to the ground. The knights wrestled until Georg was able to throw Simon to the ground. Still standing, Georg put his sword to Simon's throat, underneath his armor and demand he surrender.

Simon called out to the Mother Mary for help, at which point the Margrave considered the fight over. He ordered the men separated. Simon was carted off to recover, while Georg fell to one knee and thanked God for his victory.[63]

In the earliest history of the legal duel, fighting occurred in a specified area removed from society. As the duel became more organized and ritualized, the venue changed dramatically. In the medieval era, the actual place where a judicial duel was fought was very much geared toward it being a spectator sport, including wooden barriers, or rope, to keep the combatants in view and the crowds out of harm's way. The barriers also could end a duel. In Italy, if a man was driven back and touched the barrier, the duel could be ended. If a man were thrown over the barrier, then assuredly so![64]

Meanwhile, elevated stands were provided for the spectators of note to watch the drama unfolding below. In the case of the duel between Galeazzo and Boucicaut, the stands had several sections and accommodated a huge throng of people. In the case of Georg and Simon, their peers avidly watched, while the Margrave likely towered above the barriers in his own box.

While judicial duels did not always end mortally, and armor helped protect the combatants, at times, only death would satisfy the parties involved.

Such an instance occurred in 1127 when a band of conspirators were tried and executed for the murder of Charles the Count of Flanders. A strong and powerful knight, Guy of Steenvoorde, was married to the niece of one of the conspirators and so, another knight, Herman the Iron, accused him of being involved in the conspiracy as well. Guy called this a lie, Herman said it was truth, and a judicial duel was arranged. Galbert of Bruges relayed an account of the bloody engagement in a spectacular, and perhaps overly embellished, fashion.

> …both fought bitterly. But Guy knocked his adversary from his horse and kept him down easily with his lance as he was struggling to get up. Then his opponent, running nearer, ran Guy's horse through with his sword, disemboweling it.
>
> Sliding from the horse, his sword drawn, Guy attacked his adversary. A

---

63   Jens P. Kleinau, "1478 a Knightly Duel", accessed May 30, 2016, https://talhoffer.wordpress.com/2011/12/20/1478-a-knightly-duel/

64   George H. Powell, Dueling Stories of the 16th Century: From the French of Brantome, (London: 1904), 87.

> continuous and bitter encounter followed with exchanges of sword blows, until, worn out by the weight and burden of their arms, they threw away their shields and hastened to win the fight with their strength in wrestling.
>
> Iron Herman fell prostrate to the ground, and Guy threw himself on top of him, pounding the knight's mouth and eyes with his iron gauntlets. But just as one reads of Antheus, the prostrate man gathered strength bit by bit from the coolness of the ground and slyly made Guy think he was certain of victory while he rested.
>
> Meanwhile, having raised his hand very smoothly to the lower edges of the mail coat, where Guy was unprotected, and grabbed him by the testicles, he collected his strength for a single effort and threw him from him, breaking open all the lower parts of his body by this grabbing throw so that the prostrate Guy grew weak and cried out that he was defeated and was going to die.[65]

Guy's loss was enough to condemn him, and he was taken from the field and hanged as a murderer. From Herman's perspective, the right to do battle had brought a murderer to justice, because God willed it so.

In 1386 a French knight, Jean de Carrouges, accused a squire, Jacques Le Gris, of raping his wife. This was a serious offense for all parties involved. Rape, of course, was an outrage, but the accusation of rape, if false, was a crime punishable by death.

The concept of honor was another matter at stake. Carrouges' wife had been raped, and this was public knowledge. If Carrouges did nothing to avenge the slight, he would be forever saddled with the shame of it. Furthermore, Le Gris was a rival to Carrouges, which was all the more reason to remove him. Carrouges sought, not a duel of honor, but a judicial duel- potentially to the death. By the late 14th century, judicial duels were rare in France, and Le Gris was found innocent of all charges by the local lord.[66]

Determined, Carrouges appealed directly to the King of France, Charles VI, and was granted permission for a duel after a year of legal deliberations. Unlike duels in England where only weapons and armor might be forfeit, the judicial duel between Carrouges and Le Gris had much higher stakes.

If Carrouges won, then his honor and that of his wife would be restored. If he lost, then he would be dead, but his wife would also follow him to the hereafter, being executed for her perjury against the innocent Le Gris.

Several accounts cover the duel, though in no great detail. History can be a very interpretive field, and in 2004 Eric Jager released the book *The Last Duel*, which lavishly described the exciting events leading up to the duel, and a blow by blow account of the duel itself. Although it was entertaining reading, Ariella Elema determined that Jager's work was as much the author's imagination as it was source material when it came to the duel itself. Examining the actual sparse accounts, Elema paints a far more sober, less exciting, but truthful account of the duel between Le Gris and his accuser, Jean Carrouges.

---

65   Jeff Rider, "The Art of History". God's Scribe: The Historiographical Art of Galbert of Bruges. (Washington: Catholic University of America Press, 2001), 106.

66   Private duels conducted in a similar manner to judicial endured in France until the Jarnac and Châtaigneraye duel of 1547.

Michel Pintoin, a monk and an official historian of King Charles VI, possibly witnessed the duel. Charles VI certainly did, and from there Pintoin could have easily acquired the details. His account is as follows:

> Therefore, with a ring of innumerable crowds standing by, and also the king and princes ranged about according to custom, with the contested lawsuit before them, and both men having entered the agreed place for the upcoming battle, next to the walls of Saint-Martin-des-Champs, they were about to test a questionable martyr.
>
> For as soon as the marshal gave the signal for mutual attack, the two men abandoned their horses and, with threatening swords lowered, advanced in slow steps and engaged one another bravely and boldly. In this first attack, the other man (Le Gris) pierced Lord Jean's thigh with his sword. This blow would have served him well if he had pressed it into the lord's wound; but, having drawn it out right away, blood arose, a spectacle for the crowd.
>
> Although Jean was wounded, it increased his courage rather than his confusion. At this point, a great horror stifled the audience. With hope favoring neither one man nor the other, voices and spirits were muffled.
>
> Then Jean, marshaling his soul into his strength, stepped in closer and exclaimed "Our quarrel is judged this day!" With his left hand, he seized the peak of Jacques' helmet and drew the man to himself. Stepping back a little, he threw him alone to the ground, prostrate and weighed down by heavy armor. Having done that, he drew his sword and killed his enemy with great difficulty, because he was encased in armor.
>
> Even though the vanquished man had not renounced his claim when the victor threw him down and commanded him many times to admit the truth, it was adjudged that he [Le Gris] be dragged to the gibbet, as was the custom for duels.[67]

The other accounts are less detailed, or were written many years after the actual duel. Needless to say, Carrouges killed Le Gris, and it was the last official judicial duel in France. Duels over matter of honor continued however, and had many of the trappings of judicial dueling.

Dueling culture in Europe was by no means monolithic. The customs of England, Italy, the Holy Roman Empire, France, Spain and Eastern Europe were different, and the temperament of the monarch could also affect the attitudes toward dueling.

In urban areas, the middle class sought to mimic their betters and demand equal treatment in a duel- or do away with judicial dueling altogether.

In places such as Spain, England and the Holy Roman Empire, it was possible to enter the ranks of the nobility and acquire their privileges, including dueling rights. In medieval France, the nobility even at the lowest knightly level were as closed off as much as possible, to the point that French knights had to prove they had no common blood and if a knight married a commoner, his spurs were to be tossed on a dung heap.[68] By the 16th century the French nobility was not as closed off,

---

67   Ariella Elema, "What Really Happened at the Last Duel," HROARR, last modified March 4 2016, accessed May 27, 2016, http://hroarr.com/what-really-happened-at-the-last-duel-part1/
68   F. Kottenkamp, The History of Chivalry and Armor, (Mineloa: Dover Publications, 2007 org. 1857), 99.

but those who were born to title looked down upon those who earned it in some other fashion. No matter how title was earned, the right to duel was seen as part of class expectations.

The various nobles of Italy reigned in judicial dueling in 938 at the Diet of Verona by stating they controlled dueling laws trumping any local customs. In the following century they required the local lord's permission for there to be a duel of any sort. The cities took this a step further in Italy, and starting with Genoa in 1056, banned the practice of judicial dueling entirely.[69] The middle class who ran the cities, such as Genoa and Florence, were quick to discover that judicial dueling favored the noble classes and martial men far too much for their liking.

King Henry II of England in 1179 tried to limit judicial dueling by making trial by jury before royal judges a right, giving nobles a means of avoiding a trial by battle.[70] This was known as the Assize of Windsor and was the first step of many to make the duel, at least in England, harder to arrange.

In the Holy Roman Empire the middle class members of society abolished or weakened judicial dueling in the towns and cities. Certain cities decreed only their citizens could issue a challenge, thus protecting them from the nobility. Burghers were made exempt in some townships, while in other places the judicial duel still existed, but, as in England, there were other legal recourses a person could take.[71]

Emperor Frederick II of the Holy Roman Empire tried to limit judicial dueling in 1231. No longer could the duel be demanded for any crime, rather, only for treason or murder done in secret. His attempts were not entirely successful as the Holy Roman Empire had differing laws within it, whereby some regions within the empire followed the Emperor's lead and others continued to look to ancient Salic or Lombard law when it came to judicial dueling.[72]

King Louis IX of France, a deeply religious king and the last to go on crusade, replaced the judicial duel with torture. This was called a trial by ordeal, or to be put to the question, or to be judged by investigation. Two generations later, Philip IV was forced to bring the judicial duel back in 1306. His nobles were quite displeased with the thought of torture as a method to try them. One proclamation by the nobles made their case clear to all. [73]

> Gentlemen of France, you are amazed
>
> I say to all who are born of fief (noble)
>
> As God is my witness, you are free no more
>
> You are relieved of your freedom
>
> As you are judged by investigation (torture).[74]

Not wanting to cede too much royal authority, Philip IV passed edicts that limited the conduct of judicial duels, not only of the participants, but also the spectators. Speaking, or even spitting, could be punishable by death.[75]

---

69   Frederick R. Bryson, The Sixteenth-Century Italian Duel, (Chicago: University of Chicago Press, 1938), XVII.
70   Stephen Banks, Duels and Duelling, (London: Shire Publications, 2012), 6.
71   R. C. Caenegem, Legal History: A European Perspective, (London: Bloomsbury Academic, 2004), 89.
72   Frederick R. Bryson, The Sixteenth-Century Italian Duel, (Chicago: University of Chicago Press, 1938), XIX.
73   R. C. Caenegem, Legal History: A European Perspective, (London: Bloomsbury Academic, 2004), 89.
74   Translated by Maxime Chouinard with aside by author.
75   F. Kottenkamp, The History of Chivalry and Armor, (Mineloa: Dover Publications, 2007 org. 1857), 39.

In Spain the nobility favored the judicial duel, but the monarchs saw it as an infringement on their authority and sought to abolish it.[76]

Overall, from the 14th century onwards, the judicial duel steadily lost favor, even as *fechtbuchs* and other treatises were produced describing how to best fight in one. State and Church alike voiced stronger, though not uniform, condemnation towards dueling.

For the state, it was a matter of manpower and authority. Judicial dueling, or sanctioned duels, could result in the death of a noble. Such a servant to the state was far better alive, fighting in wars, managing land and paying taxes, than dead at the feet of an angry rival. Kings and lords showed greater reluctance to support judicial trials by combat during the medieval era. Royal authority was weakened by judicial dueling. What point was there to courts, laws and edicts if they could be ignored with a demand for battle? For commoners, the argument was similar. If the law could be brushed aside through combat, and that combat favored the nobility, then what good was the law?

In the 15th century, European monarchs and powerful lords largely forbid judicial dueling, though the amount of dueling *fechtbuchs* from the same time period gives a clue that what the Holy Roman Emperor or King of France wanted wasn't necessarily what happened. In his book *The Duel in European History*, V.G Kiernan makes a convincing argument that the nobles clung to the judicial and later private duel as a means of exerting themselves over their monarch.

The nobility were fighting a losing battle. In Western Europe, starting with the towns and cities and stretching out to the countryside, the judicial duel was abolished by the 16th century. In Eastern Europe, where records are sparse, legal dueling receded or grew. In Hungary, King Mathias replaced the judicial duel with a regular trial in 1486, while in Poland legal dueling of a sorts remained, whereby whole families could legally declare war on one another or even the king![77] Meanwhile in Russia, judicial dueling was actually expanded on in the 16th century, where nearly everywhere else it was extinguished.[78]

Gunpowder further eroded the interest in judicial dueling. Before, the nobles and knightly classes were dominant in warfare. The earliest fencing treatises, such as that of Fiore and those of the early Liechtenauer tradition, were directed at these classes. For them, the arts were viable as a means of judicial dueling, self-defense and warfare. However, as the use of gunpowder increased, the traditional fighting classes became less important. Society lost interest in these older arts as the armored knight made way for the pike, cannons and shot. This state of affairs was much lamented by Paulus Hector Mair, a compiler of fencing techniques, and Joachim Meyer a fencing master in the mid-16th century. Each blamed gunpowder for the falling interest in the older fencing traditions.[79]

Jacques Lalaing, a notable knight from the mid-15th century, was undefeated in his many duels and Passage of Arms, or *pas d'armes*. However, he was killed by a cannonball in 1453.[80] Pierre Terrail, seigneur de Bayard, was equally famous, participating in dozens of battles. The penultimate knight,

---

76   R. C. Caenegem, Legal History: A European Perspective, (London: Bloomsbury Academic, 2004), 90.
77   Ibid 92.
78   V.G Kiernan, The Duel, (Oxford: Oxford University Press, 1988), 91.
79   Joachim Meyer, trans. Jeffery L. Forgeng, The Art of Combat, (London: Frontline Books, 2015), 37.
80   Robert Douglas Smith, The Artillery of the Dukes of Burgundy, 1393-1477, (Rochester: Boydell Press, 2005), 131.

he was mortally wounded by an arquebus, a type of hand-held gun, in 1524.[81]

With the very best of knightly arms being killed by gunpowder weapons, it is easy to see why interest in knightly arts declined during the 16th century.

The Catholic Church was part of the sanctioning process of judicial dueling at first. In 1155, in Northern France, an abbot took a local lord to court for the right to preside over judicial dueling. The Norman lords sided with the abbot, giving him the right to hold such courts.[82] Meanwhile, monks fought in, or picked champions for, judicial duels over land ownership.

However, by the 13th century, the Catholic Church's position had reversed. The Church became morally opposed to judicial dueling. With a few exceptions, the Church was quite clear that judicial duels were murder and that God favored neither party, but the Devil approved of both. Lacking a means of enforcement, the Church leaned on its own members, the monarchs and the lords to clamp down on dueling. Pope Innocent III brought up the matter and in the 4th Lateran Council of 1215, which stated:

> No cleric may decree or pronounce a sentence involving the shedding of blood, or carry out a punishment involving the same, or be present when such punishment is carried out... A cleric may not write or dictate letters which require punishments involving the shedding of blood, in the courts of princes this responsibility should be entrusted to laymen and not to clerics.

The decree further went on to remind its readers that all prior condemnations of dueling and trial by combat remained firmly in effect.

Church condemnation of dueling only intensified during the Catholic Counter-Reformation. At the Council of Trent in 1563, the practice of dueling was deemed an offense serious enough to bring about excommunication—not just to the duelists, but to all parties involved. The decree singled out judicial as well as private duels and those who encouraged, or in any way aided, the practice of dueling:

> Dueling is Punished with the Severest Penalties
>
> The abominable practice of dueling, introduced by the contrivance of the devil, that by the cruel death of the body he may bring about also the destruction of the soul, should be utterly eradicated from the Christian world. Emperor, kings, dukes, princes, marquises, counts, and temporal rulers by whatever other name known, who shall within their territories grant a place for dueling between Christians, shall be excommunicated and shall be understood to be deprived of the jurisdiction and dominion obtained from the Church over any city, castle or locality in which or at which they have permitted the duel to take place, and if they are fiefs they shall forthwith revert to their direct rulers. Those who entered the combat as well as those who are called their seconds shall incur the penalty of excommunication, the confiscation of all their property, and perpetual infamy, and are in conformity with the sacred canons to be punished as homicides, and if they are killed in the combat they shall be forever deprived of Christian burial. Those also who give advice in the matter

---

81   Hugh Thomas, The Golden Empire: Spain, Charles V, and the Creation of America, (New York: Random House, 2011), 584.
82   Paris, Bibliotheque Nationale, MS. lat. 5430A, 15.

> of a duel, whether in questions of right or of fact, or in any other way whatever persuade anyone thereto, as also those who are present, shall be bound by the fetters of excommunication and everlasting malediction; any privilege whatsoever or evil custom, even though immemorial, notwithstanding.[83]

Catholic doctrine regarding the duel, both judicial and later private and even in the case of a 'friendly' tournament, remained largely the same in its hostility. Duelists in the 16th century were to be denied Christian burials and the Spanish theologian Juan Ginés de Sepúlveda advised mortally wounded duelists to seek absolution from a priest and failing that, vehemently apologize to God. Although the duelist would not be buried in a Christian graveyard, he would at least have his soul saved.[84]

By the late 15th century, judicial dueling had all but vanished from Western Europe. It was no longer tolerated by the Catholic Church, and the state had come to the understanding that judicial dueling undermined the ruler by empowering the nobility the right to violently challenge not only one another, but also the state's legal system.

Throughout Europe, a variety of laws were passed to make judicial dueling difficult as early as the 10th century and accelerating into the 15th century. In France, laws made the process of being granted a judicial duel arduous. In Swabian law, a judge or jury could have their verdict appealed by battle, but only in the presence of the monarch himself. Throughout the Holy Roman Empire, the judicial duel was curtailed. Brothers couldn't fight, no fight could take place if enough evidence existed, no fight could happen if the men were of a different rank and so forth. Finally, laws enabled the courts, nobles and the sovereign to simply say "no" to a request for a judicial duel.[85]

The matter is not quite so clear, though. While officially the last judicial duel in France was between Le Gris and Carrouges in 1386, the duel between Jarnac and Châtaigneraye in 1547 took place publicly in front of the King of France, Henri II and various lords. While this was a duel between nobles over a matter of honor, it included barriers, an audience, and a presiding lord making it all but judicial in name.

In Italy, the judicial duel had largely vanished as early as the 13th century, but the sanctioned private duel, with all its judicial appearances, remained into the 16th century.[86] The Council of Trent in 1545 did much to make clear, again, the danger to a duelist's soul and ended all sanctioned dueling in Italy, but the unofficial private duel remained.[87]

In England, the last judicial duel was in 1446 when a servant accused his master of treason and cowardice and legally defeated him the following year.[88]

In Scotland, a judicial duel took place in 1530 between Sir Robert Charteris the 8th Laird and chief of Clan Charteris and Sir James Douglas of Drumlanrig. It was one of the last of its kind, fought in the barriers under the watchful gaze of King James V, whose son would go on to denounce dueling

---

83   "Council of Trent," American Catholic Truth Society, accessed May 18, 2016, http://www.american-catholictruthsociety.com/docs/TRENT/trent25.htm
84   Frederick R. Bryson, The Sixteenth-Century Italian Duel, (Chicago: University of Chicago Press, 1938), 116.
85   Henry Charles Lea, Wager of Battle, In Superstition and Force: Torture, Ordeal, and Trial by Combat in Medieval Law, 95. 3rd ed, (Philadelphia: Bodleian Library, 1878), 95-97.
86   Frederick R. Bryson, The Sixteenth-Century Italian Duel, (Chicago: University of Chicago Press, 1938), XVII.
87   **Ibid 131.**
88   George Neilson, Trial by Combat, (Glasgow: W. Hodge and co, 1891), 201.

throughout his reign. The duel was so violent that Charteris' sword broke and the king had to send his men in to break up the combatants.[89]

In England in 1571 a judicial duel between champions was arranged. Gauntlets were traded and paraded about, judges summoned, lists prepared and a crowd assembled. However, when the defendant didn't show up, the whole thing was called off.[90]

In 1818, the judicial duel was briefly revived in *Ashford v Thornton* when the accused, Thornton, demanded a wager of battle, the English name for a trial by combat. Parliament had never repealed trial by combat, and in a testament to the British love of the written law, a judge reluctantly granted Thornton his legal privilege. The judicial duel never took place, and the wager of battle was officially repealed in 1819 before anyone else decided to mimic Thornton.

Though judicial dueling steadily vanished during the late medieval era and the Renaissance, it gave way to the far more ubiquitous private duel and lingered as a form of entertainment and martial prowess in tournaments.

Early private duels of the 16th century continued on with much of the ceremony of the judicial duels they replaced, including the use of a glove to demand a fight and the selection of an area with a barrier around it to do battle in.

Georgios Anamourloglou of the Academy of Historical European Martial Arts 'Leontes' in Byzantine attire of the 15th century. Efforts to reconstruct Historical European Martial Arts is ongoing and Byzantine swordsmanship has just recently been explored.

---

89   Herbert Maxwell, A History of the House of Douglas, (London: Freemantle and Company, 1902) Chapter V.
90   George Neilson, Trial by Combat, (Glasgow: W. Hodge and co, 1891), 158.

Kyle Griswold of the Phoenix Society of Historical Swordsmanship with the sword and buckler, a combination that was popular in dueling as well as self-defense in the 14th, 15th, and 16th centuries.

The Private Duel

Le Duel après le bal masque by Thomas Couture 1857. Seconds discuss weaponry with the two combatants who are in costume for a masquerade ball.[91]

Where and when the judicial duel ended and the private duel began is murky at best. A duel overseen by a court was judicial, and this court could be presided over by a powerful lord or king. Then again, numerous duels took place that were in front of such august persons and yet were not officially legal affairs, but rather matters of honor between nobles. Though cross-over did exist, nations steadily abolished the judicial duel, and the private duel filled the vacancy in the 16th century. At first, these duels appeared to be in many ways judicial, but after they too were abolished, dueling was driven underground.

In a judicial duel, a serious crime was leveled from one party to another through legal channels. This was not a slap in the face with a silk glove and a demand for swords at dawn, but, rather, a complicated process that involved lawyers, judges and even the king. By the late medieval era, the judicial duel had to be agreed upon by nearly every party and included such legal wrangling as electing a champion to fight in one's stead, setting a time and place and agreeing upon how the fighting would take place. Local laws and customs varied, and thus judicial duels were as

---

91   Le Duel après le bal masque Thomas Couture 1857. Wallace Collection. Public Domain Art.

complicated as one might expect legal proceedings to be. Furthermore, judicial duels determined guilt or innocence, while in a private duel, guilt and innocence was not as important as honor.

The private duel was a matter of honor and not a matter of law. The concept of honor is even more difficult to understand than the often convoluted legal matters of a judicial duel. Honor was not clearly defined in Europe. What is honor? It is a question that could fill a book and a question that puzzled philosophers.

Antonio Possevino, a 16th century Jesuit humanist tried, as many others would, to explain the private duel in relation to honor. He stated that there were duels of hatred, but they could be settled without the loss of life. There were duels of glory and righteousness, but they were akin to judicial duels. The private duel was a matter of honor. The duel was not about gaining honor but keeping it.[92]

For brevity's sake, the best way to envision honor is a person's self-worth. If it were in any way impinged privately, and doubly so if publicly, one's honor was tarnished and satisfaction of some sort was needed. The honor had to be, as Possevino put it, regained, or as was often said, defended. An apology might do, but some insults demanded blood, or at least the threat of it.

Salvator Fabris discusses dueling in his early 17th century treatise on fencing, *Lo Schermo, overo Scienza d'Arm*. When straying into topics outside the rapier, he excuses himself for being brief, but reminds the reader that his treatise is about violence that arises from conversation—meaning an insult.

> I have also decided against speaking of the spadone[93] (and many other weapons), since doing so would have required many more words and I wish to keep this book reasonably brief.
>
> Furthermore, weapons of that sort are neither really used among gentlemen nor in occasional encounters; they are more suitable in military campaigns and on the ramparts (a field very far from our intended subject).
>
> I have only treated of gentlemanly arms and of situations that arise from noblemen's conversations.[94]

Honor supplanted the law to the point that even monarchs were at odds with themselves, for they too well-understood the concept of defending one's honor.

Who could claim the right to defend their honor was another matter as well. Nobles continued to claim the privilege, but the lesser nobility, courtiers, the urban middle class and eventually just about anyone might claim the title of gentleman and demand satisfaction for an insult.

In England and Scotland, King James I outlawed dueling, and between 1602 and 1629 over two hundred gentlemen were tried in the Star Chamber for dueling. Yet, repeatedly, James personally intervened and pardoned duelists for their crimes. Examples of his contradictions abound. James passed laws outlawing writing about duels in 1614. The decree was published by the Earl of Northampton and entitled *A publication of his majesty's edict and severe censure against private combat and combatants*. That same year, Edward Sackville killed a Scottish lord in a duel, and James not only pardoned Sackville, he later promoted him to the rank of Earl.[95]

---

92 Frederick R. Bryson, The Sixteenth-Century Italian Duel, (Chicago: University of Chicago Press, 1938), XXIII.
93 A large two handed sword.
94 Salvator Fabris, trans. Tom Leoni, The Art of Dueling: Salvatore Fabris' Fencing Treatise of 1606, (Highland Village: Chivalry Bookshelf, 2005), 263.
95 Stephen Banks, Duels and Duelling, (London: Shire Publications, 2012), 18-21.

In France, a generation prior, King Henri II presided over the last legal duel. Technically, the matter was not judicial, but rather a private matter in which the king granted the aggrieved parties the right to settle their differences in public.

Two French nobles, Jarnac and Châtaigneraye came to a severe dispute. Châtaigneraye told King Francis I that Jarnac's rich lifestyle was because he was sleeping with his father's second wife. Francis tried to play the affair off, but Jarnac insisted on a duel, calling Châtaigneraye a liar. Châtaigneraye was eager to fight and demanded a public duel. Francis I refused this; alas, he died that year.

Henri II allowed the duel to proceed. Here, what is a judicial duel and what is a private duel blends. There were no judges involved, nor court case, but rather an insult, an accusation of a lie and a demand of satisfaction by blood—all hallmarks of a private duel. However, King Henri II granted the duel, giving it a judicial flavor.

The story of the duel is as famous as it is dubious and was compiled by less than reliable sources, but they are the only sources available and entertaining as any good history should be.[96]

The two had thirty days to prepare, as was standard in private dueling codes set down by Italians. Châtaigneraye was already an accomplished swordsman and wrestler and did little to prepare, while Jarnac went to an Italian captain by the name of Caizo and taught him techniques that Alfred Hutton claims were derived from Achille Morozzo, whose *Opera Nova* was published in 1536. Several Italian techniques described a means of cutting the leg. In the 17th century, such attacks were described by Capoferro and Nicoletto Giganti. One gets the sense that, knowing little of swordplay, Caizo taught Jarnac one trick over and over for 30 days.

On the day of the duel, everything was prepared as if it were judicial. The lists were set up, stands erected and referees put into place. The duel was to be witnessed by the leading nobles and the king himself, while thousands of spectators flocked to Paris to witness it.

The two opponents were armored, but not head to toe. Jarnac had been officially challenged, and so he had the right to choose what weapons and armor they would wear. He selected a helmet, breastplate and gauntlets for each, as well as a curious bit of armor for the left arm that allowed the support of a small shield but locked the arm in place, preventing any wrestling. This bit of craft was supposedly suggested by Jarnac's teacher Caizo, who also went about placing bets on his student's victory. Châtaigneraye was not concerned and assured the king that a great banquet in honor of his victory was but a moment away.

After Châtaigneraye agreed to the unusual armor, the two took to the *champ clos*, which was the area within the barriers. With sword and shield, the two commenced the fight.

After some initial sparring, Jarnac feinted a blow towards Châtaigneraye's head. The able swordsman lifted his shield and for a moment was blinded.

Jarnac changed the direction of his blow and struck the back of Châtaigneraye's leg using the false edge of his sword—at first lightly, but then again with more force, causing the man to drop.

---

96   Pierre de Bourdeille (Brantome) wrote about the duel in the 16th century and Vulson de la Colombière wrote about the duel in the 17th century. Pierre was a collector of gossip and Colombière's sources are unknown.

Unable to rise, Châtaigneraye was dumbfounded. Jarnac, who perhaps had no idea what to do after performing the one trick he knew, approached the king and asked that the fight be ended, he declared the winner and Châtaigneraye given over to the king's mercy.

The king did not reply at first, giving Châtaigneraye a chance to rise, which he was unable to do. Not wanting one of his favorites to die, Henri II conceded that Jarnac was the victor and planned to give mercy to Châtaigneraye. The noble would have none of it. Bandages were given for his wounded leg, but he tore them off and chose to bleed to death.

Henri II was much disturbed by the death, feeling, rightly, responsible for it by allowing the duel to take place.

The crowds were overjoyed, however, stormed the area and devoured the feast that was supposed to be in honor of Jarnac's death.[97] Into fencing lore came the *Coup de Jarnac*, which was a derogatory term for any cut launched at the leg.

The death of Châtaigneraye led the king to outlaw dueling entirely. Most of Europe had already done so, or soon followed suit.

This did not stop dueling, but drove it underground. No longer would it take place in front of a king, or respected lords. Instead, it would take place at dawn in remote areas and sometimes even in foreign countries. The private duel was born.

Where exactly the private duel started is debatable, but one contemporary source, Brantome, placed its origins in Naples, where men fought *a la mazza*, which was a free-fight, meaning outside the gaze of the law, but not without customs.[98]

The fight, *a la mazza*, was further defined as other forms of dueling were curbed or abolished. This brought about written rules. These rules for dueling were set down by Italians in such works as Girolamo Muzio's *Il duello*, published in Venice in 1550 and Castiglione's *Libro de Cortegiano* published in 1528 and adopted, more or less, across Western Europe and haphazardly followed in Eastern Europe.[99] Other national versions of the dueling code were introduced, mimicking the Italians, including an English version, *The Court of Ciulle Courtesie,* in 1577. There was also an Irish code, as well as a 19th century Polish version.[100] The rules went beyond just when it was proper to fight, but also delved into how a gentleman was expected to behave.

Castiglione in his *Libro de Cortegiano* suggested a gentleman be supple of body and that he understand that in war, brute strength might prevail, but in a duel, agility and subtlety were an advantage. He wrote:

> …Men thus huge of body are also unfit for every exercise of agility, which thing I should much wish in the Courtier. And so I would have him well built and shapely of limb, and would have him show strength and lightness and suppleness, and know all bodily exercises that befit a man of war: whereof I

---

97   Alfred Hutton, The Sword and the Centuries, (Staffordshire: Wren's Park Publishing, 2003 org. 1901), 48-52.
98   George H. Powell, Dueling Stories of the 16th Century: From the French of Brantome, (London: 1904), 134.
99   V.G Kiernan, The Duel, (Oxford: Oxford University Press, 1988), 48.
100   Stephen Banks, Duels and Duelling, (London: Shire Publications, 2012), 16.

think the first should be to handle every sort of weapon well on foot and on horse, to understand the advantages of each, and especially to be familiar with those weapons that are ordinarily used among gentlemen; for besides the use of them in war, where such subtlety in contrivance is perhaps not needful, there frequently arise differences between one gentleman and another, which afterwards result in duels often fought with such weapons as happen at the moment to be within reach...[101]

He further suggested that men know how to wrestle and be ready to take any advantage in a fight. More than a few duels at some point turned into wrestling.

Jay Simpson and Christopher Nelson of the Phoenix Society of Historical Swordsmanship demonstrate a wrestling technique from Fiore de Liberi.

An example of wrestling in the duel comes from the 16th century. Ursino and Maigrin argued while at a gaming table. As was custom, they exchanged challenges and met to fight, but after only a few strokes of the sword, the two wrestled, losing control of their weapons in the process. Maigrin gained the upper hand, but lacking a weapon, grabbed a nearby thorn from a bush and threatened to gouge out Ursino's eyes if he did not yield.[102]

> The delight of playing with varied and diverse players makes a man cunning, perceptive, and nimble of hand...
>
> - Antonio Manciolino

---

101 https://archive.org/stream/bookofcourtier00castuoft/bookofcourtier00castuoft_djvu.txt may 23 2016
102 George H. Powell, Dueling Stories of the 16th Century: From the French of Brantome, (London: 1904), 134.

Shane Gibson and John Patterson of the Phoenix Society of Historical Swordsmanship demonstrate the use of the off hand and the saber.

To supply the techniques needed to survive a duel, fencing masters hovered like crows at a gallows. They had already existed, but in the early 15th century, they were men like the Italian weapons master Fiore de Liberi, who were hired directly by wealthy patrons. As the duel was driven underground, fencing masters began to ply their trade differently to a larger audience, promising a perfect science in the art of defense, but the private duel loomed ever larger as the motive.

Achilles Marozzo, a fencing master from the 16th century, informs his readers that his book can be used in war and self-defense, but then explains how to properly issue a challenge to a duel. Manciolino, a contemporary, complained how masters were selling their art, bit by bit, as if the techniques were whores. It was clear that in their time the art was marketable to a much larger audience than it had been before.

While Nicolaes Petter was already dead at the time his work on wrestling was published in 1674, in the introduction his successor gives readers directions on how to contact him so that they can, for a reasonable fee, learn the art of wrestling.

Jéann Daniel L'Ange in his fencing treatises tells his readers of many secrets and tricks he did not include in his work and suggests readers come to learn from him in person- for a price of course. He tips his hand as to the purpose of his treatise by giving advice on how best to pick a place for a duel.[103]

---

103   Reinier van Noort, Lessons on the Thrust, (Glasgow: Fallen rock Publishing, 2014), 149.

By the 17th century, while some treatises claimed they were for self-defense, masters like Fabris were quite blunt in proclaiming the private duel as the purpose behind their work and that the battlefield was a long way off from what they were writing about.

Italian masters went abroad teaching their art, some having books printed to reveal some, though not all of their techniques. The 17th century in particular is laden with printed books concerning fencing from Italian masters such as Fabris, Giganti, Capoferro, Alfieri and Marcelli, as well as works by non-Italians who, none the less, adopted the Italian methods, such as Jéann Daniel L'Ange.

Historian Alfred Hutton noted that an 18th century fencing master could be spotted because he wore an eye patch and had missing teeth. French fencing instructor Augustine Grisier in the 19th century said of prior fencing masters,

> (They were) iron bangers, illiterate, uncultured, gruff, impatient, and hasty, dominating taverns and unsavory places, quarrelsome savages, calculated to flee away from well-educated men and elegant manners.[104]

While some fencing masters were treated as illustrious men and their teaching was coveted by high society, the vast majority wandered Europe selling their services drawn in particular to urban areas where larger populations could support their trade. They would have had reputations similar to gypsies, Jews and merchants, all of which were accused of being vagabonds that were somehow cheats because they offered a service rather than a physical product or labor. A 16th century fencing master, Manciolino, likened them to pimps.

Roaming masters at times even relied on charity, wandering into a town and asking to set up a school and if refused, asking for some money to help them on their way. Masters even cited their poverty as a reason to set up a school, not the actual usefulness of their trade![105]

To the fencing guilds, the wandering masters were a threat, to the state, they were men selling death, and to the masters who wrote, they were those that cheapened the art by selling it, one technique at a time. To the citizens of the various towns and cities, they could be a nuisance.

Conrad, a German fencing master, hung a black sword up at the town hall of Rothenberg and offered up his services to the populace. Another master from Württemberg arrived and declared Conrad a false-teacher. The town mayor decided to let them fight it out. Within a ring of rope they faced off with longswords with broken points to prevent thrusting. Conrad swung for his rival's head and missed, striking him in the hand. This was considered a dishonorable strike and the duel was ended.

Afterwards, the mayor and town councilors decided on a sensible solution. They kicked both men out of town.[106]

Fencing, even in practice, was hardly safe and could lead to unexpected consequences. A Scotsman killed his fencing instructor for blinding him. At his murder trial, he believed he should be let go

---

104   Patrick T. Morgan, "Escrime Classique," accessed May 30, 2016, https://foiled4once.files.wordpress.com/2013/09/montreal-presentation.pdf
105   B. Anne Tlusty, The Martial Ethic in Early Modern Germany: Civic Duty and the Right of Arms, (New York: Palgrave Macmillan, 2011), 216.
106   Jens P. Kleinau, "1444 Two Fencing Masters in Rothenberg", accessed May 30, 2016, https://talhoffer.wordpress.com/2012/12/03/1444-two-fencing-masters-in-rothenburg/

because his instructor promised not to hit him in the face.[107]

Other institutions to learn fencing existed, some of them quite ancient. Catholic monks may not seem like violent individuals, but they engaged in judicial dueling when it was allowed and authored the first European fencing treatise, *MS I.33*. Jesuits, in the era of the Counter-Reformation taught fencing as a useful skill from Paris to Krakow using sticks.[108] Furthermore, universities, which were formed by the Church, employed fencing masters.

Charters for guilds were approved to safeguard the teaching of fencing and make a profit at it. For the state, it made sense to regulate fencing as means of training the population for war. These guilds included the *Marxbrüder*, and the *Federfechter* in the Holy Roman Empire. In England, Henry VIII granted a guild a charter by the name of the Company of Masters of the Science of Defense of London.[109] In the Low Countries, urban areas armed their various guilds, which in turn, produced guilds specific to fencing, such as the Guild of Saint Michael, Saint Adrian and Saint Lambert, with each being connected to a particular city.[110] Officially, the guilds were given the right to be the only ones able to teach fencing within a certain area, usually city-limits and they were the only ones who could grant the title of master.

These guilds appeared in the 15th, 16th and early 17th century and faced increasing criticism and challenges. The fencing guilds in particular may not have been highly valued because their purpose was in question. Why train men to fight with swords when guns were of more use? As state armies replaced city militias and as policing methods improved, why train the populace to fight? As the age of the knight faded, who was left to teach? Meyer and Mair, in their 16th century works on arms, both lament the lack of interest in fencing in their introductions and both blame gunpowder. Yet, the prevailing view in the 16th century was that swordsmanship in particular was largely archaic.[111]

Fencing, as a skill to be learned from a guild or school, was in the 16th century on par with such common activities as dancing and acting. At the funeral procession of Charles V in Bruges in 1559, the Saint Michael's fencing guild was given a position of less importance than those of other guilds. German fencing masters may have called their art noble and knightly in the 16th century, but it was the middle class that took interest in it. Not until the 17th century was fencing a skill seen vital to a gentleman, and not for purpose of military pursuits, but rather for private dueling.[112]

> Also, I should tell you that I always taught this art secretly....
> — Fiore de Liberi

---

107   Hugh Chisholm, Encyclopedia Britannica: A Dictionary of Arts and Sciences, Volume 9 (Cambridge: Cambridge University Press, 1910), 667.

108   Jędrzej Kitowicz, "On Customs and Traditions in the Reign of Augustus III", trans. Daria Izdebska, (Author given personal copy).

109   Jay P. Anglin, "The Schools of Defense in Elizabethan London," Renaissance Quarterly, Volume XXXVII, Number 3, Autumn 1984, 395-396.

110   Bert Gevart, Reinier van Noort, Evolution of Martial Tradition in the Low Countries: Fencing Guilds and Treatises, (Boston: Brill, 2016), 380-382.

111   B. Anne Tlusty, The Martial Ethic in Early Modern Germany: Civic Duty and the Right of Arms, (New York: Palgrave Macmillan, 2011), 215.

112   Bert Gevart, Reinier van Noort, Evolution of Martial Tradition in the Low Countries: Fencing Guilds and Treatises, (Boston: Brill, 2016), 382.

Randy Reyes of the Phoenix Society of Historical Swordsmanship demonstrates a guard from Fabris, an Italian master who traveled far from home and was quite successful.

Like all guilds, the fencing guilds faced competition from roaming masters who worked outside the approved charters. In England, it was imported Italians in the late 16th century that threatened the established fencing guild, in the Holy Roman Empire the *Marxbrüder* officially recognized Free-Fencers or *Freifechters*, from which sprung a rival guild the *Federfechter*. In the Low Countries, the fencing guilds were eventually abolished as unnecessary, or they declined, or they directed their energies toward sport fencing to stay relevant.

In Spain the monarchy managed the teaching of fencing. In Spain, Carranza and his student Pacheco were so successful, that they created a near-monopoly on Spanish fencing with the *Destreza* school of fencing starting in the late 16th century and lasting into the 18th. In his, opinionated but in-depth history of fencing, Egerton Castle noted that masters in Spain spent more time defending their principles, already set down, than incorporating and modifying ideas as had happened with the Germans and French when they took hold of Italian notions.[113]

In France, the monarchs had fencing schools, but there were many that took on the official-sounding name *Académie* and had no royal charter at all. The *Académie d'Armes* was the royal school and increasingly gained favor, earning praise and titles from Charles IX, Henri III, Henri IV, and Louis XIII. Finally, the school was granted a monopoly on fencing by King Louis XIV, as was his pattern.[114]

From these schools and guilds in the late 16th century and into the 18th century came fencing that was directed at self-defense—gentlemanly dueling—but also the sport of fencing. Fencing as a form of sport existed in the form of the *Fechtschule* in the Holy Roman Empire and the *Assaulto* in Italy in the 16th century and prior with tournaments. In the Low Countries in the 17th century, fencing competitions were held, one in which Thibault won first place and acclaim for his Spanish-influenced method of fencing. In England, country fairs had sporting matches using the singlestick. Poland had similar phenomena as seen in Almonte's painting of a Polish diet that depicts teens, under the eye of adults, sparring with sticks in a game called *palcaty*.

Rules and weapons varied in sport fencing. In the 16th century *Fechtschule*, the longsword was used and certain targets were off limits, such as the hands, while thrusts were not allowed. Breaking of a sword was punishable with a fine, as was seriously injuring an opponent.[115] In the Franco-Belgian rules the longsword could not be used one-handed and thrusts were disallowed as was grappling. With the rapier, a thrust to the face was not allowed, nor to the sword arm and parrying with the off-hand was discouraged.[116] In 1531 Manciolino describes the use of sword and buckler in the *Assaulto* and points are scored with preference given to the riposte opposed to an initial strike. More points are awarded for a strike to the head or foot, because the foot is difficult to strike, while hits to the hand in a friendly bout were not counted.[117] English single-stick fencing was won by drawing blood from the opponent's head, but only cuts were allowed and at times the left arm was restrained to prevent its' use.[118] In Poland, *Palcaty* had rules in which a group of youths fought with sticks, aiming likely for the head and hands with the winner attaining rank and certain privileges in the game.[119]

Sport was not the primary aim of the treatises, but did take on a larger role by the mid 16th century. As already noted, Manciolino and Meyer from the 16th century had sporting aspects to their works and Philibert de la Touche, a 17th century French fencing master, depicts rounded safety tips on the ends of the opponents' swords.

---

113 Egerton Castle Schools and Masters of Fencing, (London: George Bell and Sons, 1885),145-146.
114 Ibid 145-146. Louis XIV liked to organize all things under monopolies, from music to dance to fencing.
115 "A Fechtschule in 16th Century Germany" accessed September 22, 2016, https://fechtschule.wordpress.com/2010/03/13/fechtschule-secret-history/
116 Matthew Galas, "Historical-Rule Sets", accessed October 1, 2016, http://hemaforums.com/viewtopic.php?t=664
117 Antonio Manciolnio, trans. Tom Leoni, The Complete Renaissance Swordsman, (Wheaton: Freelance Academy Press, 2010), 77-78.
118 Alfred Hutton, The Sword and the Centuries, (Staffordshire: Wren's Park Publishing, 2003 org. 1901), 348.
119 Jędrzej Kitowicz, "On Customs and Traditions in the Reign of Augustus III", trans. Daria Izdebska, (Author given personal copy).

Detail of Almonte's painting of a Polish Diet. The youth are engaged in Palcaty, a stick-fencing game.[120]

Richard Marsden and John Patterson of the Phoenix Society of Historical Swordsmanship fencing with Palcaty.

120 Martino Almonte Public Domain Art.

An 18th century fencing school in Altdorf.[121]

Once a man knew how to fence, wherever he happened to learn the art, it was not enough. The private duel of the 16th century involved rules and customs that the fighters were, theoretically, to follow.

James Harvey Grant and John Patterson of the Phoenix Society of Historical Swordsmanship fence with small swords. The small sword was popular in the 18th century.

---

121 https://commons.wikimedia.org/wiki/File:Dendrono_-_Der_fechtende_Student.jpg Public Domain Art.

Adam Barrett and Kyle Griswold of the Phoenix Society of Historical Swordsmanship demonstrate a technique found in numerous treatises called slipping the leg. As the opponent goes low, the fencer withdraws his leg and strikes toward the opponent's head.

In a proper private duel, the first rule was that when an insult occurred, the parties should not draw swords then and there. The insulted party could toss a glove or deliver it in mimicry of a judicial duel. The insulted party could also have a discussion and ask to immediately go somewhere private. More often, intermediaries handled the issuing of a challenge via letters. Originally, gloves were traded or tossed as had been done when dueling was legal, but letters quickly became more fashionable. There were three primary means of issuing challenges in the 16th century. A *rogito* was an official document with signed witnesses that was notarized, and due to the illegal nature of the duel, rarely used. A *manifesto* was the same, but minus the notary, so it was rather popular. A *cartello* was when the duelists used seconds to exchange personal letters.[122] All three had their own complicated sets of protocol.

A proper duel involved seconds who were friends of the two potential duelists. The seconds sent letters back and forth between the participants. These seconds were generally trying to diffuse the situation and seeing if time and distance could bring peace between the aggrieved parties. Failing that, terms were worked out, including which matched weapons were to be used and where the duel would occur. Duels took place usually at sunrise before anyone was awake and usually somewhere remote. Given the illegality of the duel, neither is a great surprise.

---

122   Frederick R. Bryson, The Sixteenth-Century Italian Duel, (Chicago: University of Chicago Press, 1938), 7.

Before Sackville dueled Lord Bruce in a meadow outside Antwerp in 1614, the two used seconds to exchange semi-cordial letters, *cartelli*, back and forth to determine when and where they would fight and with what weapons.

Lord Bruce wrote to Sackville,

> …Now be that noble gentleman my love once spoke you, and come and do him right that could recite the trials you owe your birth and country, were I not confident your honor gives you the same courage to do me right, that it did to do me wrong.
>
> Be master of your weapons and time; the place wheresoever, I will wait upon you. By doing this you shall shorten revenge and clear the idle opinion the world hath of both our worths.

Lord Bruce's letter was a typical challenge and invoked all the elements needed for a private duel. The crime in question was not explicitly spelled out, which was proper. Lord Bruce complimented Sackville's class, birthplace and sense of honor in a backhanded manner that would force Sackville to either accept the duel or give up on his right to being an honorable English gentleman. That simply would not do.

> Sackville in turn wrote to Lord Bruce's second, asking him to convey the following,
>
> As it shall always be far from me to seek a quarrel, so will I always ready to meet with any that desire to make a trial of my valor by so fair a course as you require; a witness of whereof yourself shall be, who within a month shall receive a strict account of time, place and weapon, where you shall find me ready disposed to give you honorable satisfaction, by him that shall conduct him thither. In the mean time, be as secret of the appointment as it seems you are desirous of it.

Sackville's reply hits all the staples of a proper duel, indicating seconds were to be used and that within thirty days he would be ready to fight. Furthermore, he asked that the affair be kept private, likely out of fear of James I, which is also why the duel was eventually fought on the continent rather than in England or Scotland. Lord Bruce agreed and the negotiations were on.

After the seconds delivered another round of letters, Lord Bruce sent a final missive to Sackville.

> I have received your letter by your man and acknowledge you have dealt nobly with me; and now I come with all possible haste to meet you.

They met in a meadow in ankle deep water outside of Antwerp in the Netherlands. There, final deliberations were had, again through seconds, and Sackville as the challenged party rejected the sword Lord Bruce brought. Though the sword was of the right length, it was twice as broad as Sackville's. After they agreed to matching rapiers, Sackville in his account claimed he made a final attempt to avert the duel but that Lord Bruce said to him, "A little of my blood would not serve."

Their letters don't reveal the original cause of the duel. A 19th century writer claimed, somewhat dubiously, that it was over the two coming to blows while in the presence of a lady. The duel was, in the end, a private affair, and Sackville and Lord Bruce were not unusual in never clearly stating in writing what exactly brought them into conflict.

Standing in ankle deep water, Sackville and Lord Bruce had matching rapiers and were stripped down to their shirts. This was a common practice in case someone had thought to be clever and wear armor underneath their clothing.[123] They closed upon one another under the nervous gaze of their seconds. Sackville recounted the duel in full.

> I made a thrust at my enemy, but was short; and, in drawing back my arm, I received a great wound thereon, which I interpreted as a reward for my short shooting; but in my revenge I pressed into him, though I then missed him also, and received a wound in my right pap, which passed level through my body, and almost to my back.
>
> And there we wrestled for the two greatest and dearest prizes we could ever expect trial for, honor and life. In which struggling, my hand, having but an ordinary glove upon it, lost one of her servants, though the meanest. But at last breathless, yet keeping our hold, there passed on both sides propositions of quitting each other's swords. But when amity was dead confidence could not live, and who should quit first was the question, which on neither part either would perform; and re-striving again afresh, with a kick and a wrench, I freed my long captive weapon, which, incontinently levying at his throat, being master still of his, I demanded if he would ask his life, or yield his sword, both which, though in that imminent danger, he bravely denied to do.
>
> Myself being wounded, and feeling loss of blood, having three conduits running on me, which began to make me faint, and he courageously persisting not to accede to either of my propositions, through remembrance of his former bloody desire, and feeling of my present estate, I struck at his heart, but, with his avoiding, missed my aim, yet passed through the body, and, drawing out my sword, re passed it again through another place, when he cried:
>
> "Oh! I am slain!" seconding his speech with all the force he had to cast me.
>
> But being too weak, after I had defended his assault, I easily became master of him, laying him on his back. When being upon him, I re-demanded if he would request his life; but it seemed he prized it not at so dear a rate to be beholden for it, bravely replying, "He scorned it."
>
> Which answer of his was so noble and worthy, as I protest I could not find in my heart to offer him any more violence, only keeping him down until at length his surgeon, afar off, cried, " He would immediately die if his wounds were not stopped."
>
> Whereupon I asked him if he desired his surgeon should come, which he accepted of; and so, being drawn away, I never offered to take his sword, accounting it inhuman to rob a dead man, for so I held him to be. This thus ended; I retired to my surgeon, in whose arms, after I had remained awhile, for, want of blood I lost my sight, and withal, as I then thought, my life also.
>
> But strong water and his diligence quickly recovered me; when I escaped a great danger; for my Lord's surgeon, when nobody dreamt of it, came full at me with his Lord's sword, and had not mine with my sword interposed himself, I had been slain by those base hands; although my Lord Bruce, weltering in his blood, and past all expectation of life, conformable to all his former carriage, which was undoubtedly noble, cried out, "Rascal, hold thy hand!"[124]

---

123   V.G Kiernan, The Duel, (Oxford: Oxford University Press, 1988), 47.
124   Benjamin Cummings, The Field of Honor, (London: Forgotten Books, org. 1884), 183-184.

Another reason for bringing a second is thus revealed; he was good insurance against the other second stepping into the fight! [125]

What to do about seconds during a duel and their exact role changed over time. Seconds acted as intermediaries and would act to safeguard a duel to ensure it was not an ambush. Seconds had been introduced in the judicial duel and legal private duel prior, where they would ensure fairness on the field of battle. That role did not change. Ideally, they tried to prevent a duel, or at worst, encourage it to end the moment first blood was drawn. However, on more than one occasion the seconds joined in the fray, fighting one another.

Some of these duels could transcend into what might even be considered a skirmish, though one that had loose rules.

During the reign of Henri III of France in 1578, two French gentlemen, Jacques de Caylus and Antrauget came to a disagreement over a woman; this was a common enough reason to have a duel. However, there was more to it. First, the woman may have been the Queen of France. Second, Caylus and his companions were close with King Henri III and accused of being effeminate and perverse.[126] They were given the derogatory title of Mignons, or Dainties. Third, Antrauget represented a faction opposed to Henry III, favoring the Duke of Guise. In short, they had many reasons to fight.

The Mignons and their opponents decided their fight would be an homage to a play from antiquity in which two sets of triplets fought one another.

They arrived at a quiet spot at 3 a.m., each bringing two companions. Mild formalities were followed, though not strictly, and the duelists and their seconds and thirds all fought.

Caylus was mortally wounded and had enough time to complain about the affair. Antrauget had brought a rapier and dagger while Caylus had left his dagger at home.

"You have a dagger, I have not!" Caylus said.

"The more fool you to have left it behind, we are here to fight…" replied Antrauget.

Caylus did his best, using his hand to parry as needed, but it was cut to pieces. He suffered nineteen wounds, both from cuts and thrusts, and lived long enough to claim the duel was a bit unfair.

Meanwhile, of the four seconds, all but one died in the duel, or soon after. Liverot was heavily wounded in the head, but survived, only to get involved in yet another duel. Liverot was run through in a duel over a woman by the Marquis de Malleraye, who in turn was murdered on the spot by Liverot's servant![127]

The whole affair was condemned for being not very French and very much Italian, in which men sought private repose and murdered one another. There was nothing to be done about it, though, and the private duel remained as popular in France as ever.

---

125 Lorenzo Sabine, Notes on Duels and Dueling, (Whitefish: Kessinger Publishing, 2010 org. 1856), 75-78.
126 William Henry Ireland, Memoirs of Henry the Great: And of the Court of France During His Reign, (Lexington: Ulan Press, 2012, org. 1923), 264-265.
127 George H. Powell, Dueling Stories of the 16th Century: From the French of Brantome, (London: 1904), 98-107.

Seconds did not always get involved in a duel, and more often than not they prevented them. Abraham Bosquette proudly stated he had been the second for 25 duels and in all of them neither honor nor life was ever lost.[128]

In the 16th century, Cellini recounted an example of a called-off duel, likely in part because of who he chose to be his second.

> Next day he (Cellini's opponent) sent round a challenge which I was only too glad to accept, saying that the business was something I could polish off far quicker than any of my ordinary work. I immediately went to confer with a fine old fellow called Bevilacqua, who had a reputation of having been the finest swordsman in Italy. He had fought more than twenty duels in his time, and come out of them all with honor. This upright man was a great friend of mine, he knew me as a goldsmith and besides that he had acted as a go-between in some violent quarrels I had.
>
> He took on the job of second and we went along, armed, to the place that had been agreed on. In fact no blood was shed, because my opponent withdrew. I came out of the affair with honor.[129]

Even fencing treatises gave advice on how to prevent a duel. Giovanni Battista Gaiani in 1619 wrote dialogues between a master and a student in a fashion reminiscent of ancient Greek philosophers. In one such dialogue the topic of ending a fight or duel is brought up in which the master believes a man's status can do much to bring peace.

> Master: Please, ask me whatever you wish, you always have every liberty with me.
>
> Student: That is all thanks to your grace. But since it pleases you, please explain to me the method and approach you must take to divide two people in combat, so that they cannot injure one another, while the person who separates them remains safe and secure.
>
> At times I have seen someone attempt to separate, and not only were they unable to do anything, but they were badly wounded by those they tried to divide. Therefore I would like some method for such occasions, to accomplish it without danger. It seems a failing for a man of honor who wears a sword, while a combat takes place, not to seek to mitigate the harm as much as possible. I would not wish to commit such a failing, nor run into danger, as I said.
>
> Master: This is truly a most noble question, both of a good Christian and of an honorable solider. As you said it is certainly a failing to have a sword but not to mitigate the harm than can arise in such instances. In my view, when you encounter men in combat and do not struggle to divide them as best you can, you commit a grave slight against yourself. You show yourself either as a coward, or without pity.

---

128 Stephen Banks, Duels and Duelling, (London: Shire Publications, 2012), 48.
129 Jean Chandler, A comparative analysis of literary depictions of social violence in two important 16th Century autobiographies, from the perspective of the fencing manuals of the Renaissance. Acta Periodica Duellatorum. Volume 2015, Issue 1, 101–137.

> However this must be approached with judgment and impartially, both to keep yourself safe, and to avoid creating an opening for one of them to wound their opponent.
>
> To briefly summarize, I will say that to separate a combat in earnest, that is, where both parties wish to fight, one man will never be sufficient to separate them. Yet one man can definitely be more than sufficient to separate them.
>
> I assure you that if you happen upon a combat with swords, and having one of your own you draw it and try to divide them, you will achieve nothing except to put yourself in danger, if they are intent to fight in earnest. So I say again that a simple and ordinary man, no matter how accomplished, will achieve little or nothing.
>
> Student: What do you mean then, when you contradicted yourself, saying that one man was sufficient to divide them?
>
> Master: I will continue to explain. I said that one man would never separate them, but I added a simple and ordinary man. However if a foremost gentleman, of authority, encounters this combat, he can easily divide them even with a sword alone. This depends on the quality of his personage, which both parties respect, therefore a man alone is sufficient to separate them.[130]

In the 18th century, Rousseau echoed the belief of Gaiani that a duel was best deterred, not by the duelists, but by men society respected.

If the duel could not be called off, seconds also ensured that a duel remained fair. Brantome, who documented duels in the 16th century, gave a case of a man who, under his shirt, wore mail painted to look exactly like flesh. His ruse was so well-played that the seconds did not notice it until after the fight. Though the duelist wore armor, he was killed when, after he tried to cut, his opponent parried and ran him through.[131]

A final requirement of the duel was that it be fought bravely, which meant not showing signs of weakness or backing up. For all the fencing treaties that were written in the 16th, 17th and 18th centuries which taught how to fence safely, there may be a cultural reason why men in duels did not dally and fence with caution, but went straight to it and on more than one occasion killed one another.

Sometimes, the prior agreements for the duel nearly ensured death or a serious wound. For example, a duel might be arranged to the first of three hits. However, hits to the hand were considered dishonorable, as were hits to the feet, and strikes to the arm were not nearly as noble as strikes to the body, but best of all, were strikes to the face or a thrust through the body, which in a sense was two hits since the blade had to enter and exit. Because of these obligations, a duelist might stab the hand of his opponent and end the duel but lose honor. By the mid 16th century if two duelists did come to blows, it was generally agreed that each intended to kill the other.[132]

---

130 Piermarco Terminello, "Hema Tome", accessed September 20, 2016, http://pterminiello.tumblr.com/post/106061253345/notes-on-preparing-for-a-judicial-duel-from-altoni

131 George H. Powell, Dueling Stories of the 16th Century: From the French of Brantome, (London: 1904), 111-112.

132 Frederick R. Bryson, The Sixteenth-Century Italian Duel, (Chicago: University of Chicago Press, 1938), 73.

Seconds, who up until the last moment were to try and discourage the duel, were expected to change their behavior once battle commenced and extort their principle to fight and if needs be die. To recant or back down after blades had crossed before being wounded was considered shameful.[133] However, once it appeared honor had been satisfied, the seconds were to try and prevent the deaths of their charges. This was not always possible.

Brantome noted that it was common enough for men, even skilled ones, to kill one another due to their fury and hate.

In the 16th century two feuding factions, the Calderani and Jani, in Italy engaged in a vendetta against one another over a loan. In the course of the vendetta, fourteen men had died and two women, who had killed one another in a duel. To settle the matter, the two families picked six champions to fight on the outskirts of town with swords and daggers and no armor. When it was all over, one man remained.[134]

Sackville nearly died in his encounter with Lord Bruce. In 1609, James Steward and George Wharton killed one another in a duel in London. In 1610, Sir Hatton Cheke and Sir Thomas Dutton, were fighting with rapier and dagger on a beach in Calais.

"Stripping to their shirts in a cold morning, they ran with that fury, on each other's sword, as if they did not mean to kill one another, but strive who should first die."[135]

In 1712 Mohun and Hamilton fought one another at Hyde Park with small swords and killed one another, leaving their seconds to continue the fight.[136]

Adam Simmons of the Phoenix Society of Historical Swordsmanship uses a rapier and dagger.

---

133   Ibid 66.
134   Ibid 146.
135   D.A. Kinsley, Blades of the British Empire, (Lulu: 2012), 480.
136   Stephen Banks, Duels and Duelling, (London: Shire Publications, 2012), 23.

The duel between Steward and Wharton in 1609 became the subject of a London ballad. In the ballad the men meet and terms are worked out, including the removing of doublets in case armor was hidden beneath.[137]

Castiglione's advice to gentlemen in the 16th century is clear on the matter of bravery.

But when he finds himself so far engaged that he cannot withdraw without reproach, he ought to be most deliberate, both in the preliminaries to the duel and in the duel itself, and always show readiness and daring.

Nor must he act like some, who fritter the affair away in disputes and controversies, and who, having the choice of weapons, select those that neither cut nor pierce, and arm themselves as if they were expecting a cannonade; and thinking it enough not to be defeated, stand ever on the defensive and retreat, — showing therein their utter cowardice. And thus they make themselves a laughing-stock for boys.[138]

---

137 http://ballads.bodleian.ox.ac.uk/static/images/sheets/30000/25003.gif May 26 2016 Public Domain Art.
138 Baldassare Castiglione, Book of the Courtier, accessed May 23, 2016, https://archive.org/stream/bookofcourtier00castuoft/bookofcourtier00castuoft_djvu.txt

He goes on to cite an example of two gentlemen who fought in a cowardly manner, publicly shaming them and encouraging potential duelists not to fence necessarily with skill, but assuredly with great bravery.

There were even techniques that allowed for aggressive forward movement to end a duel quickly as possible. Salvator Fabris' 1606 treatise is divided into two books. The first covers principles of the rapier that were, for the most part, traditional. The second covers how a man might kill his opponent by drawing his sword and running at him without hesitation.

George Silver despised this Italian method, which had become so popular as to make its way into England. In his *Paradoxes of Defense*, Silver decries the manner in which Italians fight and how easy it is to harm one another.

> If two valiant men fight being both cunning in running and that they both use the same at one instant, their course is doubled, the place is won of both sides and one or both of them will commonly be slain or sore hurt.
>
> And if one of them shall run, and the other stand fast upon the Imbrocata[139] or Stocata[140], however, the place will be at one instant won of one side and gained of the other and one or both of them will be hurt or slain.
>
> If both shall press hard upon the guard, he that first thrusts home in true place, hurts the other, and if both thrust together, they are both hurt.

In Italy, this desire to be aggressive to the point of recklessness continued into the 18th century. In 1763, Angelo said this of the Italians,

> …by an immediate advance of their left foot to the right; and they thrust straight thrusts at random, or make passes and voltes[141]: they have much dependence on their agility and parade of the left hand; for that reason, when two Italians fight together they often are both hit together…[142]

William Shakespeare was aware of the Italian tendency towards recklessness, guided by their sense of honor. Mercutio, in *Romeo and Juliet*, comically notes that his friend Benvolio would draw his sword at such minor offenses as a man cracking nuts too loudly or having hazel eyes. Mercutio ends up being confronted by Tybalt and refuses to back down. Benvolio warns Mercutio that he should not fight, or if he must, to do so in a private place. Mercutio will have none of it, and bravely draws his blade, despite chastising Benvolio just a moment before on the rashness of men and dueling.

When dueling with swords gave way to pistols, the act of standing close to an opponent and accepting and giving fire without flinching perhaps makes more sense in light of Castiglione's admonishments of cowardly fighting, which Europeans took, sometimes fatally, with the utmost seriousness.

In Brantome's commentary on dueling, in nearly every encounter he compliments the men when they fight valorously, even if they perished.

---

139   A thrust from above.
140   A thrust from below.
141   A turn of the foot around the body, called and inquartata in the 17th century Italian treatises.
142   Domenico Angelo, The School of Fencing with a General Explanation of the Principal Attitudes and Positions Peculiar to the Art. with Hungarian and Highland Broad Sword and The Angelo Cutlass Exercises, (London: Land's End Press, 1971 org. 1765), 85.

Death, however, was not always the result of a duel. Simply showing up was enough to satisfy most, while a single wound could bring a duel to a swift, and not fatal, end.

When in the late 1500s Captain Bourdielle dueled with a friend, Cobios, over some unknown quarrel, he was able to cut his opponent in the hand. Cobios dropped his sword. This was, traditionally, not a noble blow.

> "Pick it up again, I am not in the habit of fighting men without arms," Bourdeille said.
>
> "I couldn't hold it, my hand is so cut," replied Cobios.

With their honor satisfied, Bourdeille put aside his rapier and helped his friend get to a surgeon to bandage his wound. The decision was to fight again later, soon as the wound had healed![143]

In a similar example, two friends were dueling when one was wounded enough that he could not continue.

"That's enough for old friends like us!"

The other, however, asked that they both wear bandages, so as to impress everyone with their deed.[144]

Surrender in a duel was possible and depending on the nature of the duel had different consequences. In the early 16th century the victor could still claim the defeated as a prisoner and ransom him to his family in the same manner as knights of the medieval era. More often, mercy was granted and the two parted ways. By the end of the 16th century it was considered poor-form to take a man prisoner and it was expected to, with great courtesy, set him free.[145]

Chivalry, in the form of fair play, in the duel was not universal, though, and more likely to take place between friends who decided to engage in a duel for the manly sport of it. Cheating, as it were, was not universally derided either. When a duelist wore mail the color of flesh, Brantome, lauded his cleverness. When a duelist allowed his foe to pick up a dropped weapon, the talk of the town was if giving up such an advantage was Christian courtesy or foolishness. Contemporaries were divided on the matter.[146]

Chivalry was also not always accepted. A Scotsman, stabbed in a duel, was asked if he had had enough. He refused to end the duel and was stabbed again. Still, the Scotsman refused to end the duel, and his opponent was forced to stab him two more times and end the man's life.[147]

Unlike a judicial duel, a private duel did not involve courts of any sort. No crime had to be committed for a challenge to be issued in a private duel. While the causes of a judicial and a private duel might

---

143   George H. Powell, Dueling Stories of the 16th Century: From the French of Brantome, (London: 1904), 126-127.
144   Ibid 127.
145   Frederick R. Bryson, The Sixteenth-Century Italian Duel, (Chicago: University of Chicago Press, 1938), 81.
146   George H. Powell, Dueling Stories of the 16th Century: From the French of Brantome, (London: 1904), 129.
147   Ibid 131.

be similar, such as an accusation of a lie, the most common cause was of a real or perceived insult.[148] Insults were not grounds for a judicial duel, but they became the mainstay for getting into a private one. Such insults were made doubly sensitive, and potentially deadly, if a woman were involved. For a noble, or gentleman, a lady's honor was as sacred as his own. V.G. Kiernan further lists root causes of the private duel as politics, women, alcohol, boredom and a means of displaying bravery.

Italians in the 16th century tried to explicitly pin down what were acceptable reasons for dueling, or if a duel would even be sufficient. To give a lie was called a *mentita*. If a person accused another and had proof, this was not a lie. So, if a person were called a traitor, and really was a traitor, a duel would not regain his honor because he was in fact a traitor. If a *mentita* was given by mistake, but the accuser refused to retract his claim, a duel would make him no less a liar.[149] The wrangling over what form of insult or lie could be dealt with by a duel were many. When reading the corpus of material, it appears that private dueling should have been rare given the many stipulations. However, in Italy and later throughout Europe, dueling was a mania.

The private duel was a right, according to the nobility and anyone claiming the title of gentleman. And defending this right meant partaking in a duel!

Any man who claimed noble blood, from small-time landowner to powerful magnate, could challenge his peer, as could any gentleman challenge another who matched his status. This was a time-honored tradition. So it was that kings could, and did, challenge one another to single-combat, but a knight could not challenge a king.

Thus, Charles V of the Holy Roman Empire was well within his rights to challenge Francis I of France to a duel, but it would have been absurd for a common soldier, or even a noble, to try the same. The same was true among the gentlemanly class, who would never deem to challenge a farmer to a duel, and, had they done so, it would have been quite the compliment to the farmer!

Various dueling codes included examples of means of refusing a duel. Grounds for refusal included those of class, called *rifiutare*. Duels could not be accepted from religious men or scholars, nor Jews. Duels could also be refused by means of *ributare*, where the challenger was deemed unworthy of honor. Thus, if an angry priest tried to call a gentleman out for a duel, he would be refused on the grounds of *rifiutare* and if a pirate tried he would be refused on the grounds of *ributare*.[150]

Because the duel was a right, engaging in one was a means of defending the privileges of the class. Author V.G. Kiernan in his *The Duel in European History* proposes that the private duel was part rite of passage for young men and part class declaration. For a young man living in the 16th through 18th centuries, fighting a private duel showed his bravery and established him as a true gentleman, who while not above the law, was willing to flout the law in the name of honor. This defiance of the law was also a way for the class to push back against the encroachments of the state. It was not without its risks.

Vincent Saviolo's late 16th century treatises on fencing includes acceptable reasons to duel and also warns the readers that to duel might lead to injury or harm at the hands of the monarch. His suggestion

---

148 In ranking of causes for a duel, a lie trumped all others. This derives from the judicial dueling days when perjury was one of the most serious of offenses and continued on as the great crime of lying and the greatest insults- in being called a liar. However, at the root of all lies was an insult. Thus, the lie and the insult were linked.
149 Frederick R. Bryson, The Sixteenth-Century Italian Duel, (Chicago: University of Chicago Press, 1938), 4.
150 **Ibid 13.**

was to duel in a private place and that, yes, it was risky to duel, but honor was more important than life.[151] Saviolo's attitude was not unusual and despite the risks, duelists defied their monarchs.

Ben Johnson, an English playwright and contemporary of William Shakespeare, was noted for his satire, which landed him in trouble with the law, and his temper, which landed him in a duel in 1598 in which he killed actor Gabriel Spencer. Johnson related the duel, years later, claiming Spencer had a longer sword and that after being wounded in the arm, Johnson was able to kill him.[152]

This was a private duel and so it was illegal. Unlike Sackville, who dueled and killed Lord Bruce fifteen years later, Johnson was not an upper-class English gentleman. Johnson was a playwright and about as low on the social ladder as a man could get. Furthermore, the sitting monarch at the time was Queen Elizabeth, whose agents the year prior had arrested Johnson for his part in performing an insulting play called the *Isles of Dogs*.

Johnson was arrested after his duel and would have been hanged as a murderer, but with a bit of legal sleight of hand he was tried by an ecclesiastical court instead of the state one.[153] He was stripped of his possessions and branded on the thumb, but he avoided the hangman's noose. The cause of the duel was never stated, though Johnson, unsurprisingly, claimed that it was Spencer who initiated it.

The state and church made dueling illegal and immoral, but the nobility, and by extension anyone who claimed to be a gentleman, clung to their privilege even into the early 20th century. It was a scourge that baffled contemporaries, and their efforts to stop it had middling success.

In France, dueling was punishable by death as early as 1566. It would be one of several harsh-sounding, yet rarely enforced edicts.[154]

In the late 16th century, a Frenchman murdered his rival, rather than duel him, and quickly became wanted by the authorities. Wandering about Europe, he fought several other duels and avoided being murdered only by staying on the move. When religious war broke out in France, he was pardoned for his crimes so long as he raised a certain number of men to fight on behalf of the Crown. This he did and his numerous homicides were forgiven.[155]

Henri IV condemned thousands of French duelists and then promptly pardoned them. His casual attitude toward dueling led to the death of upwards to one-third of the French nobility.[156]

Cardinal Richelieu called dueling a pernicious evil and disastrous madness, yet even with the power of the Catholic Church and the state at his fingertips, 17th century France remained a hotbed of private dueling.[157] He, along with King Louis XIII, was one of the few French rulers willing to use the headsman's axe to curtail dueling.

---

151 Markku Peltonen, The Duel in Early Modern England: Civility, Politeness and Honour, (Cambridge: Cambridge University Press, 2003), 77.
152 Helen Ostovich, Holger Schott Syme, Andrew Griffin, Locating the Queen's Men, 1583-1603: Material Practices and Conditions of Playing, (Farnham: Ashgate Publishing, 2009), 91.
153 He was able to recite portions of the Bible and claim Benefit of Clergy.
154 V.G Kiernan, The Duel, (Oxford: Oxford University Press, 1988), 74.
155 George H. Powell, Dueling Stories of the 16th Century: From the French of Brantome, (London: 1904), 123-124.
156 Frederick R. Bryson, The Sixteenth-Century Italian Duel, (Chicago: University of Chicago Press, 1938), 131.
157 Mika LaVaque-Manty, "Dueling for Equality: Masculine Honor and the Modern Politics of Dignity", University of Michigan, (2006): accessed May 18, 2016, http://www-personal.umich.edu/~mmanty/research/Dueling.PT.pdf

In 1627, the Comte de Bouteville-Montmoreceny, who had already survived 21 duels, engaged in his last. In broad daylight, in a well-respected square in Paris, Bouteville, who had snuck back into France to defy Louis XIII's ban on dueling, fought the Marquis de Beuvron. The duel was as exciting as it was scandalous because each had brought two companions who were all for defying the king.

The duel took nearly an hour, with spectators noting it was more akin to a street brawl. The fight demonstrated the blend of the gentlemanly duel, with its niceties, and self-defense, with its brutal efficiency. The men thrust, hacked, kicked and punched; on the other hand, the fights remained one on one. Brutal as it was, there was a level of fairness upheld.

Beuvron eventually found a dagger at his throat. Bouteveille, however, said the man had fought gallantly and let him live. Chivalry was not dead! The seconds brought along were not so lucky, and one of them was mortally wounded. Like rats off a sinking ship, the duelists bolted from the scene.

Bouteveille and one the seconds were captured by Louis XIII's guard and placed into custody. Louis XIII was tempted, and pressured, to spare the men, but Cardinal Richelieu indicated that to do so was to undermine royal authority. The two were beheaded, in what for France was a rare crackdown on the duel, and one that did not endure.[158]

In the next generation, Louis XIV went to great lengths to stamp out dueling in France. While somewhat successful, even the Sun King had setbacks. At one point, he sent a loyal noble to disrupt a duel. Instead, the noble joined in! [159]

In Italy, the birthplace of the private duel, 16th century anti-dueling laws were common as they were disregarded. In Milan, duelists could be hanged and quartered. In Naples, the punishment for dueling was the death of the duelists as well as their seconds.[160]

The military were perhaps the greatest proponents of the private duel. By Italian custom, all men who wished to duel should be in theory soldiers. Gentlemen, for example, were expected to rally to the king's standard in times of war, so they were in essence soldiers at all times. Officers and common soldiers alike were considered socially acceptable when it came to the duel, but class differences still remained. A common soldier might challenge another, but he could not challenge his general. He could challenge a lower-ranked officer, but only in peacetime.[161]

In England, the duel was with some success repressed among every class except the military. The same was true for the rest of Europe. The military continued dueling, so that in the 19th century, upwards of two-thirds of all duels took place between military men, often with the nod of approval from the commanders.[162]

During a military campaign, and with soldiers in general, the duel was endemic. Gustavas Adolphus, the king of Sweden, found an ingenious solution to his officers dueling during the Thirty Years War. Any men could duel, but they had to do it in front of the army, and the victor would be hanged immediately afterwards.[163]

---

158 Ben Hubbard, From Spartacus to Spitfires: One-on-One Combat through the Ages, (Canary Press, 2011).
159 Alfred Hutton, The Sword and the Centuries, (Staffordshire: Wren's Park Publishing, 2003 org. 1901), 193.
160 Frederick R. Bryson, The Sixteenth-Century Italian Duel, (Chicago: University of Chicago Press, 1938), 103.
161 Ibid 16.
162 Ben Hubbard, From Spartacus to Spitfires: One-on-One Combat through the Ages, (Canary Press, 2011).
163 Stephen Banks, Duels and Duelling, (London: Shire Publications, 2012), 21.

In England, Francis Bacon, working in conjunction with King James I, was attempting to prosecute a pair of duelists and said of dueling,

> It is a miserable effect when young men, full of towardness and hope, such as the poets call *aurora fillii*[164], sons of the morning, in whom the comfort and expectations of their friends consist, shall be cast away and destroyed in such a vain manner…
>
> So as your lordships see what a desperate evil this is; it troubles peace, it disfurnishes war, it brings calamity upon private men, peril upon the state and contempt upon the law.[165]

Meanwhile in France, though duels were illegal, some monarchs allowed them to take place. Henri IV, when the Pope asked about his tolerance toward dueling, responded,

> The heat and courage which is common among those of this nation who during this happy time of peace…find themselves without employment.[166]

In other words, France, having ended its religious wars, had bored gentlemen who had no other way to display their courage than dueling.

In 16th century Italy to be caught dueling was to be executed, yet lawyers found clever means of excusing their clients. Castillo in 1525 and Alciato in 1541 believed that, yes, dueling was illegal by modern law, but when it took place in private places the participants were actually under Lombard law where dueling was legal, never mind the fact that such private duels lacked a crime, judges, barriers and so forth. Lawyers continued to excuse dueling, citing not only ancient law but natural rights. Was it not natural to defend one's self? Self-defense would long be a cover under which dueling existed well into the 19th century.[167]

Thoroughly perplexed, Italian writers in the 16th century stated numerous logical reasons why dueling was wrong. It was an affront to the Church, God would not necessarily pre-ordain the winner, it was open to abuse, and went against common sense. The duel was for honor, yet one Italian duelist said that most duels arose over gambling debts and quarrels involving women. Yet, dueling flourished, to which writers explained that, although evil, it was necessary and only natural that a man defend his honor as he would his life. One writer shrugged and noted that, although evil, dueling at times gave spectators great joy.[168]

During the Enlightenment, the most educated of Europe were dismayed by the duel, though showed a deep understanding of it. Montesquieu said that in France he felt pity towards a man challenged to a duel. He could end up stabbed through the heart, victorious and then escorted to the scaffold, or banished from the society of men for refusing to fight.[169]

---

164   A reference to dying, honorably in war, opposed to dishonorably in a duel.
165   Daniel Derrin, Rhetoric and the Familiar in Francis Bacon and John Donne, (Teanick: Farleigh Dickinson University Press, 2015), 92.
166   Barbara Holland, Gentlemen's Blood, (London: Bloomsbury Publishing, 2004), 33.
167   Frederick R. Bryson, The Sixteenth-Century Italian Duel, (Chicago: University of Chicago Press, 1938), 104.
168   Ibid 89-91.
169   V.G Kiernan, The Duel, (Oxford: Oxford University Press, 1988), 171.

Tom and Stephanie Farmer, of the Knoxville Academy of the Blade, demonstrate small sword techniques. Women duelists, while rare, were not unheard of. La Maupin was a legendary opera singer and courtesan, as well as an avid duelist, challenging, and defeating, numerous men.

Montesquieu was perhaps overstating his case. France had passed yet another law in 1723 stating that the penalty for dueling was death, yet by 1753 not a single duelist had ever found himself with a rope about his neck.[170] Cardinal Richelieu might have been willing to summon the executioner, but Louis XV was not so bold.

Samuel Johnson, praised for his reason, admitted that a duel might be necessary much in the same way that Montesquieu had.

> He, then, who fights a duel, does not fight from passion against his antagonist, but out of self-defense; to avert the stigma of the world and to prevent himself from being driven out of society.[171]

Enlightened men tried, without success, to stem the tide of dueling, which took its toll on the nobility and gentlemen more than on the common masses. In France, a tribunal of military men, the Tribunal de Marèchaux, was formed to act as a court of honor. The goal of the tribunal was to be a place outside of law where respected men mediated between nobles and gentlemen and prevented a duel.

Rousseau explained why this process failed. The duel was a matter of cultural importance, especially to the nobility. Men who chose to go to a tribunal, even of esteemed peers, would be branded as

---

170 Ibid 167.
171 Barbara Holland, Gentlemen's Blood, (London: Bloomsbury Publishing, 2004), 3.

cowards by society, because gentlemen, like it or not, approved of the duel. A century ahead of his time, Rousseau said the only thing that would end dueling was if public opinion could be turned against it.

Always an avid dreamer, Rousseau devised a way to steer public opinion away from dueling. First, he believed the tribunal had to have less an appearance of law, which had already failed to rein in the duel, and more the appearance of a mutually agreed upon meeting stage for aggrieved parties.

Second, the two would not be summoned to the court, but with great and solemn ceremony, asked to come. They would then be escorted, in full public view, so all could see they were choosing to go face their rival.

Finally, the aggrieved would act out their issues with one another in front of peers, whose goal would be to listen to each, and then try to devise compromise. If no compromise could be reached—Rousseau believed this would rarely occur—then the men would fight. The illusion of a potential duel was all that was needed to satisfy the public's demand of honor.[172]

Alas, not even Rousseau's contemporary philosophers could be rational enough to dispense with the duel.

Noted for his wit, Voltaire was a titan of the Enlightenment, but when a French aristocrat had him beaten in the streets, Voltaire challenged him to a duel. The noble had Voltaire tossed into prison for his trouble.[173]

Enlightened philosopher or not, Voltaire was a gentleman and subject to the burdens of honor, and the prejudices of society, as Rousseau noted.

Gentlemen were those of good breeding and education who didn't necessarily have land or title, but were respected by their peers as better than the uncouth masses. While the size of the nobility steadily declined as early as the 14th century, those who called themselves gentleman increased in number, and they took to dueling as much as their social betters.

This rising class upset the old because some of their fencing was considered not quite befitting of a *true* gentleman. In France this divide was keenly felt between the *noblesse d'épée* and the *noblesse de lettres* and the *noblesse de robe*. On paper, all were noble and called themselves gentlemen, but the first had always had their noble privileges, while the others bought it from, or were given it by, the king. In 1623, François Dancie complained about the upstarts who, though noble, were dueling with weapons he found unbecoming of a proper French noble.

> Nobles never wear a dagger, let alone carry one in the hand, this being more for a bloodthirsty villain than a gentleman, who would only use one if assigned in a duel.
>
> But, with the sword alone, they adorn and support themselves with the best company and accessory, the most recognizable to show its greatness in repelling the enemy, if he dared to confront it.

---

172   Patrick Coleman, Rousseau's Political Imagination: Rule and Representation in the Lettre a d'alembert, (Geneva: DROZ, 1984), 85-86.
173   "Voltaire," accessed May 20, 2016, http://www.visitvoltaire.com/voltaire_bio.htm

> Thus, I say that the sword is a great man's finest plume, without which he cannot be distinguished from the financier, merchant, or bourgeois, whom the insults of our times allow to dress as well as the great man.[174]

A proper gentleman had to dress correctly, speak well, know manners and be willing to defend his honor. By the 19th century, even well-respected politicians and artists, who had no noble blood, were engaged in duels over matters of honor on both sides of the Atlantic Ocean. For centuries, the middle class had sought to mimic their noble betters, they finally had achieved parity and with it the duties expected of men of honor.

The burden of a noble or gentleman's social class included the right, and also the duty, of the private duel. It was that duty that drew a very unlikely politician into such an affair.

Abraham Lincoln was challenged to a duel on September 22 of 1842. Because he was challenged, Lincoln had the right to set the terms of the duel, and he did so in a way to give himself so many advantages that his opponent, James Shields, would likely demure. Lincoln, a towering figure, insisted on the use of long sabers and that a plank of wood be placed longwise between him and Shields. The intent was that Lincoln could easily reach Shields, but Shields, a shorter man, would not be able to reach Lincoln.

Despite these restrictions, Shields agreed to the terms, and the duel was to be fought in Missouri, where dueling had yet to be abolished. The duel was called off at the last minute, which was not unusual and usually thanks to the cooler heads of the seconds.

Lincoln kept the affair as private as possible, perhaps regretting how close to death or murder he had come. His wife once recalled an officer asking her husband, "Is it true…that you once went out, to fight a duel and all for the sake of the lady by your side?" Lincoln replied, "I do not deny it, but if you desire my friendship, you will never mention it again."

As for the cause of the duel, Mary Todd and Abraham Lincoln had sent a letter to a local newspaper under the false name of Rebecca. The contents of the letter insulted Shields over a political matter to such a degree that he rooted out who "Rebecca" really was and demanded Lincoln fight a duel. Such a public insult was too great a blow to Shield's sense of honor to let it slide without a demand for satisfaction. Lincoln, pragmatic as he was, was still a gentleman and bound to the rules of his class.

In France, the painter Edward Manet slapped his friend Edmond Duranty with a glove, an insult and a reference to the tossing of the gauntlet from medieval days. A duel with swords was arranged in the forest of Saint-Germain in February 1870. After Manet inflicted a slight wound upon Duranty, Manet considered the matter resolved and the two went back to being friends.

The impetus for the duel was that Duranty, a writer, had not been flattering enough of one of Manet's works of art, which the artist took as a personal insult to his honor.

Duels in which no one died became increasingly more common, and the few deaths that did occur were treated as scandalous rather than the typical burdens of being a gentleman.

In the dying days of the duel, in the mid to late 1800s, swords remained popular in France because they were less lethal than pistols. Mark Twain was amused and said,

---

174   "French Fencing," accessed May 30 2016, https://columbiaclassicalfencing.com/2012/11/17/french-fencing-sources-on-using-the-unarmed-hand-to-parry-or-oppose-an-incoming-blade/

> This pastime (dueling) is as common in Austria to-day as it is in France. But with this difference—that here in the Austrian states the duel is dangerous, while in France it is not. Here it is tragedy, in France it is comedy; here it is a solemnity, there it is monkeyshines; here the duelist risks his life, there he does not even risk his shirt. Here he fights with pistol or saber, in France with a hairpin—a blunt one. Here the desperately wounded man tries to walk to the hospital; there they paint the scratch so that they can find it again, lay the sufferer on a stretcher, and conduct him off the field with a band of music.[175]

"The Code Of Honor--A Duel In The Bois De Boulogne, Near Paris" G. Durand, 1875. With seconds watching, two men duel with small swords. As was custom, their coats are off and they fight in their shirts. This was originally done to prevent anyone from wearing secret armor.[176]

The private duel, like the judicial duel before it, declined under religious and state pressure. However, the social pressure of being gentlemen trumped both, and it was only when public opinion turned against dueling that it truly declined, just as Rousseau had predicted.

While private duels in the 16th through 18th centuries were common enough, toward the middle

---

175   Autobiography of Mark Twain, Volume 1 By Mark Twain, Harriet Elinor Smith p 148
176   G. Durand - Harper's Weekly, New York: Harper Brothers, Vol. 19, No. 941 (9 January 1875), p. 41; this scan from : Das Wissen des 20. Jahrhunderts, Verlag für Wissenschaft und Bildung, 1961, Rheda, Bd.1 S.439 Public Domain Art.

of the 19th century, dueling was frowned upon by the public at large and seen as barbaric, both in Europe and the United States. When Hamilton was killed by Aaron Burr in a pistol duel in 1804, it was met largely with public outcry.[177] Had it happened fifty years earlier, it may have met with quiet and solemn applause.

When Burr was found not-guilty of murder by reason of self-defense, high society did not accept it. Dr. Timothy Wight, president of Yale College, delivered a sermon decrying the duel and its savagery. He was shocked that in Christian society murder was punishable by death, except if upper class men agreed to murder one another.[178]

When the Duke of Wellington, of Waterloo fame, partook in a duel in 1829, the newspapers did not celebrate him for meeting his obligations as a gentleman, but rather decried the practice of dueling, which could have carried off a national hero and sitting politician.[179] By this point, dueling was seen as something old-fashioned and irrelevant, except in France, where politicians like Clemenceau continued exchanging fire, and in Italy where swords were still used to settle differences. However, the general downward trend in dueling continued throughout the 19th century. The last fatal duels in Britain and the United States were in the 1850s.

While duels did take place in the 20th century, they were exceedingly rare outside of Italy, with a handful of notable exceptions. Duels were virtually extinguished during World War II.[180]

The private duel in Europe, and later in America, lasted roughly from the 16th century to the 19th, with the church and state and eventually society turning against the curious practice that allowed men, at least the "right" kind of men, to murder one another. Meanwhile, self-defense was yet another reason that people learned how to use weapons, one that was socially acceptable throughout European history.

Benito Mussolini in a friendly duel with a fascist officer in 1936. Mussolini had been involved in a real duel with an anti-fascist newspaper editor in 1921. The duel ended after 40 minutes when Mussolini's opponent was wounded and unable to continue.[181]

177 V.G Kiernan, The Duel, (Oxford: Oxford University Press, 1988), 306.
178 Ibid 305.
179 Stephen Banks, Duels and Duelling, (London: Shire Publications, 2012), 43.
180 A duel with swords did take place in France in 1967, though this was not a usual event.
181 http://www.theatlantic.com/photo/2015/11/today-in-history-november-23/417279/ May 14 2016 Public Domain Photograph.

Kyle Griswold of the Phoenix Society of Historical Swordsmanship in a tournament using the messer. The messer was a popular weapon for civilian defense in the Holy Roman Empire. Photo courtesy Jonathan Ying.

Self-Defense

Kyle Griswold uses the buckler on the author, demonstrating that in swordsmanship not just the blade is a weapon.

Europe was a violent place in the 14th and 15th century. The roads were isolated and a haven for bandits, such as robber knights. The countryside could erupt into familial warfare between rival estates. Cities, as they grew in size, were the most dangerous, and any alley might harbor a would-be assassin. It was a dangerous world.

Florence is a striking example of the violent crime that took place in 14th and 15th century Europe. The murder rate in Florence in the latter half of the 14th century was roughly double or more that of the most dangerous cities in the present-day United States[182]. An average of 50-70 people were murdered in Florence per year out of a population of 50,000.[183] In 2015, Chicago had 509 murders out of a population of 2.7 million. The odds of getting murdered in 14th century Florence were roughly 10 out of every 10,000 compared to 2 out of every 10,000 in 21st century Chicago.

Other cities in Europe during the 14th century also had exceedingly high murder rates. Utrecht, Krakow and Freiberg all had 5 murders per 10,000 people.[184] Most cities in the Low Countries, the

---

182   Based off FBI crime-stat reports from 2015.
183   Peter Spierenburg, A History of Murder, (Cambridge: Polity Press, 2008), 16.
184   Ibid 16. (Note that the murder rate while calculated for every 100,000 involves cities whose populations were as low as 30,000.)

Holy Roman Empire, Poland and Italy boasted similar bloody rates. Using modern comparisons, the FBI rated St. Louis as the city with the highest number of murders in the United States as of 2015 while most European cities of the 14th century boasted higher rates.[185]

Rates of assault were roughly double the homicide rate, with Krakow and Regensburg racking up 10 assaults per 10,000 people. Historian Pieter Spierenburg in his *A History of Murder* points out that these rates are only the known and documented murders and assaults. The real number of homicide and assault victims was likely much higher, especially in the European countryside where the law's reach was weak and records are lacking.[186]

Fiore de Liberi's treatise on the use of weapons, the *Flower of Battle*, includes references to armored judicial dueling within the barriers and unarmored private duels, in which the author himself fought five other masters. Elements of his work seem appropriate for dueling, tournament, perhaps mounted skirmishing and self-defense. Fiore's work was written in the early 15th century, but his experiences were likely derived in the 14th century at a time when Italy was flooded with mercenaries and violence was common, both in the streets and on the field of honor and war.

Examples of self-defense in the *Flower of Battle* include using a walking stick against a spear-wielding opponent, throwing branches, and defending against a dagger attack while seated and carrying only a marshal's baton. Most of Fiore's work seems applicable in a duel or in self-defense. The majority of his section on the dagger involves the defender having no weapon at all, a further clue to the context of the work, which clearly includes self-defense as well as dueling.

From the MS Ludwig XV 13, in the possession of the J. Paul Getty Museum. The master, wearing a crown, prepares to defend himself with a walking stick and a dagger against an opponent armed with a spear. Although two spearmen are shown, the text indicates they are attacking separately, thus indicating that the technique can work against both high and low thrusts.[187]

> Here they fight with daggers, God help us all.
> — Talhoffer

---

185 "FBI Statistics," accessed May 20 2016, https://www.fbi.gov/about-us/cjis/ucr/crime-in-the-u.s/2015
186 Peter Spierenburg, A History of Murder, (Cambridge: Polity Press, 2008), 16.
187 Digital image courtesy of the Getty's Open Content Program.

From the MS Ludwig XV 13, in the possession of the J. Paul Getty Museum. The student of the master, wearing a garter, has thrown a tree branch, closed with his opponent, beat aside his spear and planted a dagger in his chest.[188]

From the MS Ludwig XV 13, in the possession of the J. Paul Getty Museum. The student of the master, wearing a garter and seated, uses his marshal's baton to prevent an attack by a dagger.[189]

---

188   Digital image courtesy of the Getty's Open Content Program.
189   Digital image courtesy of the Getty's Open Content Program.

John Patterson and Charles Buschmann of the Phoenix Society of Historical Swordsmanship demonstrate Fiore's Posta di Donna and the German Vom Tag.

German treatises also include examples of martial arts whose setting leans more toward self-defense than a duel. Such examples include treatises on the use of the dussack, a wood or metal form of saber[190], or the messer, a large knife. These weapons were cheap and ubiquitous. In the Holy Roman Empire it was common for everyone to be armed on some level, it was just a matter of how.[191] Other examples include mixed weapon match-ups that indicate something other than a duel and indicate an affair more likely to occur in self-defense, such as a dagger used against a dussack as seen in Paulus Hector Mair's opus on weaponry from the 1540s.

> If you are easily intimidated, no fencing should you learn.
> - Liechtenauer's Zettel

---

190   Roger Norling believes the dussack was as much a weapon as war as any other. See the Dussack as a Weapon of War.
191   B. Anne Tlusty, The Martial Ethic in Early Modern Germany: Civic Duty and the Right of Arms, (New York: Palgrave Macmillan, 2011), 3.

A recreation from Paulus Hector Mair's Opus Amplissimum de Arte Athletica depicting men using dussacks. Dussacks were wooden or metal weapons that were used as training tools or for self-defense.[192]

Fiore's work from around 1410 was explicitly for the nobility, or at the very least, mercenary commanders; decades later, Vadi referred to it as the art of princes and kings. But other European treatises involving self-defense were written for the rising middle class, such as guildsmen and burghers.[193] Self-defense was, after all, something every man might need to know, not just the upper rungs of society. This was in itself liberating and something both Fiore and Vadi warned their readers about—to not let the peasants learn the art.

For noble and common alike, violence was a part of life that could come up unexpectedly. In Brantome's account of 16th century duels, an offhand comment notes that people were being ingloriously assassinated on street corners or in shady woods.[194]

Anywhere outside the sight of law was dangerous, the roads between the cities especially so, where bandits, some of them from the nobility, preyed on travelers. One such account comes from Bartholomäus Sastrow's 16th century account of his life.

---

192   Recreation by Mariana Lopez-Ródriguez.
193   Philippo Vadi, trans. Guy Windsor, Veni Vadi Vici, (The School of European Swordsmanship, 2013), 51.
194   George H. Powell, Dueling Stories of the 16th Century: From the French of Brantome, (London: 1904), 84.

A recreation from Meyer's 1560 treatise dedicated to Otton von Solms depicting a German and Pole with dussacks.[195]

Detail of the Field of Cloth and Gold attributed to Hans Holbien the Younger circa 1545. Crowds rush to see Henry VIII. Most of the gentlemen are armed with side swords[196] and in the case of a youth, a sword and buckler.[197]

---

195   Recreation by Ksenia Kozhevnikova.
196   Side swords in the mid 16th century were more akin to proto-rapiers, capable of both the cut and thrust. Many of the duels described by Batome used similar weapons.
197   https://commons.wikimedia.org/wiki/File:British_-_Field_of_the_Cloth_of_Gold_-_Google_Art_Project.jpg Public Domain Art.

Detail of the Field of Cloth and Gold. Two men fight by a public fountain while onlookers pay them no mind and a woman calmly fills her jug. This sheds some light on the common violence people encountered.[198]

> The brigands came up with them and entered into conversation. Suddenly one of them snatched the loaded pistol Lagebusch was carrying at his saddle-bow—the fashion of carrying two had not come in—fired it at Lepper, who was galloping back to the carriage, killing him there and then, while Lagebusch set spurs to his horse in time to warn Sonnenberg, who hid himself in the brushwood. My brother armed with a pole, and standing with his back against the carriage to prevent an attack from behind, offered a stout and not unsuccessful resistance. He managed to wound in the thigh an assailant who, carried away by his horse, bit the dust further up the road.
>
> But another miscreant, charging furiously, sliced away a piece of my brother's skull as big as a crown and at the same time dealt him a deep gash at the throat. As a matter of course, my brother lost consciousness; nay, was left for dead while the bandits sacked the carriage…[199]

In England during the same century, the casual use of violence was described in a letter from a son to his father. The letter describes daily life and politics, and then, almost as an aside, the son mentions the near-murder of his father.

> There is talk here how you and Howard fought together on the shire and that one of Howard's men struck you twice with a dagger, and so you would have been hurt but for a good doublet that you had on at that time. Blessed be God that you had it on.[200]

---

198   https://commons.wikimedia.org/wiki/File:British_-_Field_of_the_Cloth_of_Gold_-_Google_Art_Project.jpg Public Domain Art.
199   Jean Chandler, A comparative analysis of literary depictions of social violence in two important 16th Century autobiographies, from the perspective of the fencing manuals of the Renaissance. Acta Periodica Duellatorum. Volume 2015, Issue 1, 101–137.
200   Roger Virgoe, Private Life in the Fifteenth Century: Illustrated Letters of the Paston Family (London: Weidenfeld & Nicholson, 1989), 116.

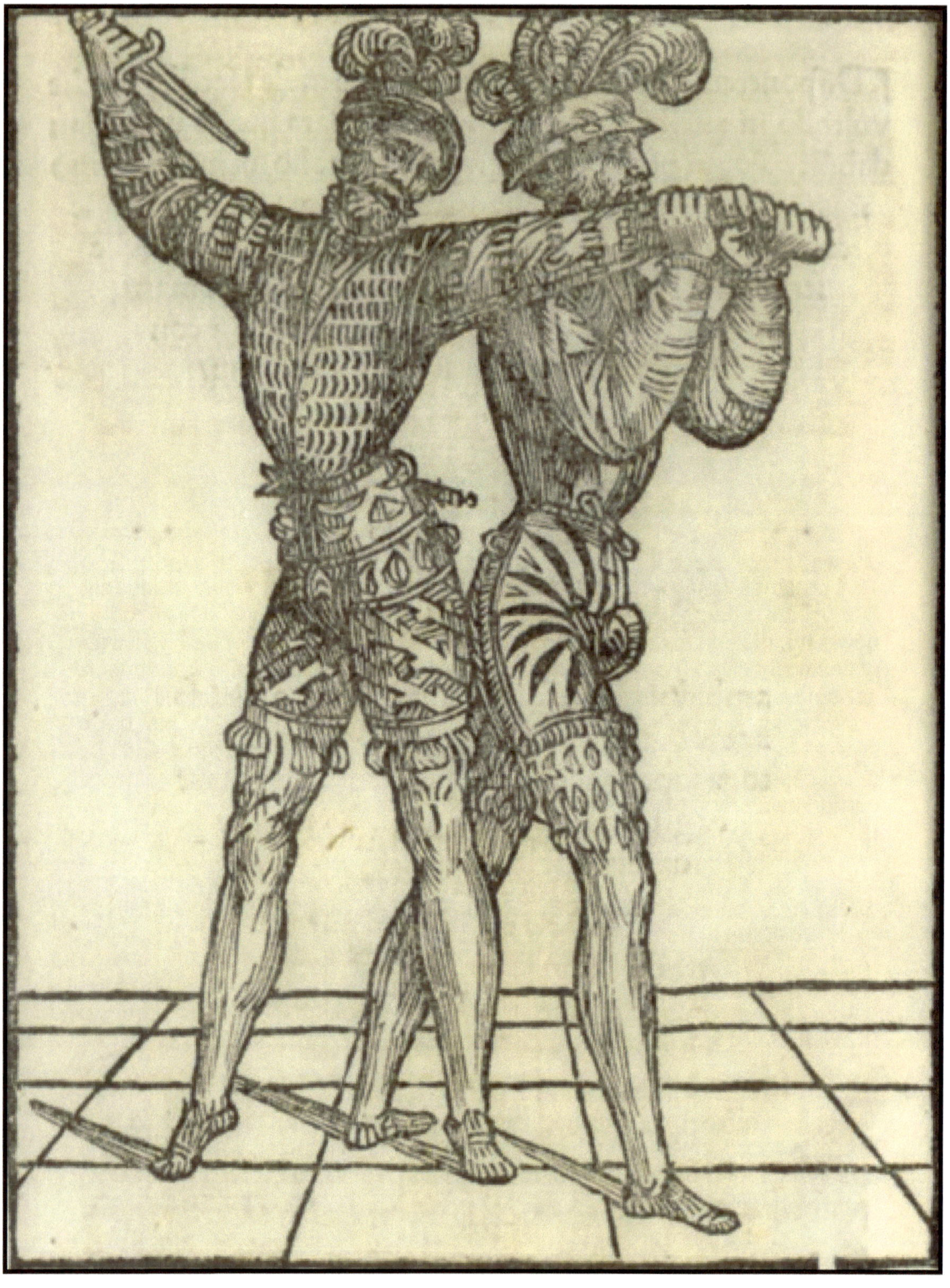

From Marozzo's Opera Nova, an unarmed defender prepares to break his opponent's arm before he can use his dagger.[201]

201 http://bibliodyssey2lj.livejournal.com/36774.html Public Domain Art.

By the 17th century, in Italy, treatises on the rapier were directed primarily at private dueling but in many instances strayed into the realm of self-defense. Nicoletto Giganti's second book covers likely street encounters, such as what to do when you're attacked suddenly or attacked by multiple opponents. In regards to the cloak he stated,

> It is very useful to understand how to wield the cloak and its characteristics, since there are many places where carrying a dagger is not permitted and therefore everyone uses a cloak for defense. On occasion others, despite having daggers by their side, when suddenly attacked, by nature leave their daggers, judging the cloak to be much better.[202]

And when it came to multiple opponents he advised,

> I would like to teach you how to defend yourself against cuts, in case of necessity, against two or three people. If you are attacked by two people, as often occurs, if you cut a *mandritto* at one, in that tempo the other will strike at you. While if you thrust at one, in that tempo you will take a thrust from the other. Therefore you will quickly find yourself dead, as has happened to many.[203]

He goes on further to detail techniques in mismatched affairs that are unlikely to take place in a duel, such as dagger against a man with dagger and rapier, or dagger against a polearm.

Salvator Fabris' 1606 treatises on the rapier, *Lo Schermo, overo Scienza d'Arm*, primarily details dueling, but he included a section on using daggers, throwing a cape, and wrestling and defending against a polearm for purposes that were, in his own words, "unexpected situations."

> …that even among honorable gentlemen some unexpected situations may arise that do not leave time to recur to longer weapons… [204]

In Italy, especially, the duel and self-defense could mingle. Familial vendettas were common, spanning many generations and inspiring Shakespeare's *Romeo and Juliet*. Mingled into family ties were politics. For example, an insult could drive two men to fight, resulting in one's death. This only spawns a desire for justice from his comrades, but should it be achieved, the cycle simply repeats. So dangerous was Italy that powerful families lived in fortress-houses to keep safe. Harvard professor Daniel Lord Smail noted that the feud, the vendetta, the duel and the lawsuit all stemmed from the same desires.[205] These desires were what made the Italian city-states dangerous places.

Benvenuto Cellini's autobiography from the 16th century includes numerous street encounters. While he often claims to be innocent, one must wonder at the sheer number of encounters and his numerous arrests. He even goes so far as to murder a city guard in revenge for the death of his brother.

> It was nightfall and the clock had just struck the hour. The arquebusier had finished supper and was standing in his doorway with his sword in hand.

---

202 Nicoletto Giganti, trans. Joshua Pendragon and Piermarco Terminiello, The Lost Second Book of Nicoletto Giganti, (London: Vulpes, 2013),122.
203 Ibid 47.
204 Salvator Fabris, trans. Tom Leoni, The Art of Dueling: Salvatore Fabris' Fencing Treatise of 1606, (Highland Village: Chivalry Bookshelf, 2005), 263.
205 Daniel Lord Smail, "Factions and Vengeance in Renaissance Italy: A Review Article," Comparative Studies in Society and History, 38.4 (Oct. 1996): 781-789.

> I crept upon him, grasping a Pistonian dagger, and aimed a sudden backstroke with the idea of cutting his head clean off. But he turned in a flash and the blow landed on the edge of his left shoulder, shattering the bone. He staggered up, was so dazed by the terrible pain that he let go of his sword and then took to flight.
>
> I went after him and caught him up in a few steps. Then I raised my dagger above his bent head and drove it exactly between his neck-bone and the nape of his neck.[206]

Cellini murdered the guard. This was no duel and it was a fact of life on the darkened streets of Italian cities.

Late 17th century material from the Low Countries, such as Nicolaes Petter's treatises on wrestling and defense, is more appropriate for an encounter on the street than a private duel. The treatise includes instructions for preventing an opponent from drawing his knife and performing a variety of wrestling holds against an armed or unarmed assailant.

Engraved by Romeyn de Hooghe in 1674, the defender grips the attacker's wrist and hand before he can draw his knife. From the works of Nicolaes Petter.[207]

Just as a judicial and private duel could share similarities, self-defense could be seen as a duel of the most informal nature. Mimicking their social betters, commoners in Europe engaged in brawls that were without proper challenges, seconds, or much preliminary agreement and yet were often fought with matched weapons as a sign of fair play and bravery.

In Amsterdam in 1681, a youth tired of being teased drew his knife and demanded his tormenter, Simon, do the same.

---

206 Jean Chandler, A comparative analysis of literary depictions of social violence in two important 16th Century autobiographies, from the perspective of the fencing manuals of the Renaissance. Acta Periodica Duellatorum. Volume 2015, Issue 1, 101–137.
207 http://wiktenauer.com/wiki/Nicolaes_Petter Public Domain Art.

> "*Sta vast*! Now it is you or me that gets a cut in his face," Simon said to the boy.

Alas, for Simon, he was stabbed in the chest. The witnesses gathered around, and as Simon bled out, the boy stayed with him till the end.[208]

To say Simon was killed in a duel is not quite right, nor was his death clearly due to an act of self-defense. The line is murky, just as it was when judicial dueling gave way to private.

In the same city, two gentlemen came upon two common men who were being harsh with their lady companions. The gentlemen, one armed with a rapier, objected to the violence, and the common men drew their knives in response. A fight ensued that could be seen either as the gentlemen defending a lady's honor or defending themselves against the sudden onrush of knife wielding attackers.[209]

Again in Amsterdam, this time in 1704, a young man named Hendrick Block took particular joy in harassing Warnaar Warnaarse. Warnaarse was the gardener of a local powerful burgomaster, Nicolaes Wisten. Block was a local troublemaker.

Block repeatedly hurled verbal insults at Warnaarse and beat him with such interesting bludgeons as a dead seagull. During one instance when Block was menacing Warnaarse yet again, the latter produced a stick to defend himself. Block drew a knife in return and cut Warnaarse's robe and chin. From there, Warnaarse took the matter to the authorities. Block was arrested and, under torture, which was still a shockingly common practice, confessed to his crimes. His use of a knife against a man with a stick earned him little sympathy from the court, even though Warnaarse was the first to take up a weapon. A knife was not an appropriate response for a stick. For Block, self-defense was not accepted as an excuse to draw his knife.[210]

However, self-defense remained a viable legal means of committing violence. While judicial and private dueling lost favor and were suppressed by church and state, the right to self-defense was integral to European and later American society. Self-defense could also be used as a legal means of dueling. When men who were arrested for dueling were taken to court, their best chance at not being hanged or beheaded was to claim self-defense.

Self-defense as a legal claim was always a possibility. However, it was not permission for wholesale murder. John David Michaelis wrote in the 18th century of the strange burdens of the English state when it came to the issue of self-defense as a legal crime. Michaelis asks his readers, if a monarch pardoned a man for dueling, under the guise of self-defense, did that not undermine the monarch's legal system and was it not despotic toward the families of the deceased? Furthermore, did the nobility have the right to murder? According to Michaelis, no, and yet despite his objections and appeals to reason, they often did.[211]

In an infamous duel between two English aristocrats in 1712, the challenged parties killed each other, and the seconds became involved in the fray. Colonel Hamilton, one of the seconds, claimed self-defense and was found guilty in Old Bailey court, not of murder, but of manslaughter. He was released and faced no further punishments.[212]

---

208 Peter Spierenburg, A History of Murder, (Cambridge: Polity Press, 2008), 85.
209 Ibid 89.
210 Ibid 65-66.
211 John David Michaelis, Commentaries on the laws of Moses (Volume 4), (Ann Arbor: University of Michigan Press, 1814), 452 -453.
212 Stephen Banks, Duels and Duelling, (London: Shire Publications, 2012), 24.

Legal lines were difficult to pin down as even pre-arranged private duels could turn into something quite unexpected.

In 1591 two Frenchmen decided to fight a duel and agreed to meet at a private location. The first, Fredaigues, arrived with a groom to hold his horse. His opponent, Romefort, arrived with an armed friend who was disguised as a groom. Their intent was to ambush and kill Fredaigues, but the fight was swift and hard. Fredaigues killed Romefort in one pass and was able to retreat back to his horse before Romefort's companion could get involved. Mounting his steed, Fredaigues charged, and the would-be assassin fled.[213]

The Baron de Soupez planned to challenge several people to a duel, but ended up assassinating them instead. In one case, he disguised himself, and along with two hired swords, attacked his man in the streets and then fled. Du Gua, a friend of the victim, proclaimed the Baron his mortal enemy.

Not bothering with a duel, the Baron repeated his trick. He had two hired men watch the door of Du Gua's lodgings and then snuck inside to kill him. Dui Gua awoke and was able to jump out of a window and take up a pole for defense, but with a few quick thrusts from the Baron's sword, he was mortally wounded. Brantome noted that the Baron was the type of man who earned infamy for his way of killing, but was able to get away with it more often than not.[214]

The Comte de Martinego had a similar experience when, rather than challenging a rival to a duel, he simply brought along a pair of soldiers, kicked the man's door in and murdered him.[215]

Vicomte of Touraine arrived to fight a duel with Duras, when from out of hiding came five thugs armed with swords. Vicomte was able to fight them off, receiving many cuts in the process. He was nearly overwhelmed when out from the woods sprung a buck. The animal charged the assailants and Touraine survived. Angered, he planned to sneak into Duras' house and murder him. For his part, Duras claimed he had nothing to do with the ambush.[216]

In Italy, Count Claudio saw four men about to duel one another. He tried to dissuade them, and, for his trouble, they attacked him as a "spoil-sport." The count masterfully handled his sword, killing two and asking the others to desist. Instead, they kept after him, so he killed a third and asked again. The lone survivor agreed to give up the fight and was taken to a surgeon to bandage his wounds. Brantome further added that Count Claudio eventually found employment for the man.[217]

In all of these cases, the matter at hand may have started off as a duel but turned into self-defense.

The treatises on dueling used the cover of self-defense to justify themselves. Castiglione's *Libro de Cortegiano* of 1528 warns a gentleman to defend himself and not seek out needless conflict.

> Nor should he be too ready to fight except when honor demands it; for besides the great danger that the uncertainty of fate entails, he who rushes into such affairs recklessly and without urgent cause, merits the severest censure even though he be successful.[218]

---

213 George H. Powell, Dueling Stories of the 16th Century: From the French of Brantome, (London: 1904), 40.
214 Ibid 118.
215 Ibid 120.
216 Ibid 110.
217 Ibid 132-133.
218 Baldassare Castiglione, Book of the Courtier, accessed May 26, 2016, https://archive.org/stream/bookofcourtier00castuoft/bookofcourtier00castuoft_djvu.txt

Giganti's pair of rapier treatises of the early 17th century do not say his art is meant to win a duel, but that it is to learn the art of self-defense. He even gives an example of a situation where his art might come in handy and be seen as self-defense. On daggers he noted,

> Furthermore in places where carrying the dagger is permitted, if a gentleman exchanges words with an enemy who is also armed with a dagger and does not know how to defend himself, if they fight he will be in great danger, as will his opponent. [219]

The first fencing treatise printed in the Dutch language was by Johannes Georgius Bruchius and is titled *Grondige Beschryvinge van de Edele ende Ridderlijke – ofte Wapen-Konste*. Bruchius is quite clear that his rapier manual is not about how to murder another man. While his techniques might very well be used in a duel, and the images depict single-combat between men with matched weapons, he wrote in his introduction,

> …Nobody should think that I have assembled this work to teach another how he can injure his neighbor whenever he fancies to. That is not in the least my objective. I only seek that an honest man may know how he will be able to protect his own body, when jumped by another and forced to do so, to the disadvantage of his assailant, as is approved by both the divine and human laws. [220]

In the 16th to 17th centuries, homicides in Europe were overwhelmingly caused by stabbings, usually from a sword or dagger. In Amsterdam sixty percent of all homicides were caused by either daggers or rapiers between the 1660s and 1670s, but by the 18th century, when the sword was worn less often, that number had dropped to between 17 and 29 percent.[221] People simply didn't stab each other as often as they used to, as the pistol became just as fashionable for dueling, robbery and assault. Overall, though, the chance of getting murdered for any reason in the 18th century was lower than it had been in the prior centuries.

Still, examples of street encounters do occur in 18th century treatises on the sword. Domenico Angelo's 1763 fencing manual *L'Ecole des Armes* includes an example where two opponents face one another, one armed with a small sword and cloak, the other with a lantern—hardly an item one would take to a duel. He explains,

> Though there are severe punishments inflicted on those who are found sword in hand with a dark lanthorn, yet there are some to be met with from time to time; therefore I think it necessary to show the manner of defense against it.[222]

Angelo gives further insight on the nature of self-defense in Italy, where he said men did not leave the house without a dagger, even though in many regions it was illegal to walk around with one.[223]

---

219   Nicoletto Giganti, trans. Joshua Pendragon and Piermarco Terminiello, The Lost Second Book of Nicoletto Giganti, (London: Vulpes, 2013),129.
220   Reinier van Noort, Of the Single Rapier, (Glasgow: Fallen Rock Publishing, 2015), 28.
221   Peter Spierenburg, A History of Murder, (Cambridge: Polity Press, 2008), 100.
222   Domenico Angelo, The School of Fencing with a General Explanation of the Principal Attitudes and Positions Peculiar to the Art. with Hungarian and Highland Broad Sword and The Angelo Cutlass Exercises, (London: Land's End Press, 1971 org. 1765), 96.
223   Ibid 87.

The use of a lantern depicted in the 1763 fencing manual L'Ecole des Armes by Domenico Angelo. Angelo created a fencing school in London that became famous and was passed down to future generations of Angelos[224]. The text, written by his son, indicates a night time street encounter in which a man uses a lantern to try and blind his opponent.

While 14th century Europe was dangerous, the homicide rate dropped steadily from that point on. Monarchs strengthened their rule, cities developed police forces of some sort and courts enforced their rulings, by hanging if necessary. Perhaps most importantly, society tolerated inter-personal violence less and less.

In the Holy Roman Empire originally it seemed everyone was armed, from peasant to knight, but every community had different rules about it. The right to bear arms could also be restricted or even temporarily reduced. A man in one town thrust his sword into a wooden post, and so he lost the right to carry a sword. A noble tried to limit the right to bear arms of a town he took possession of, but the town, citing ancient law, ignored his decrees.[225]

While on the roads and in the countryside there was little legal oversight on arms, the cities could be incredibly strict. As mercenaries and state-funded armies replaced civilian militias, the rules on who can and can't carry weapons changed. *Benvenuto Cellini* in his autobiography gave such an example in the 16th century.

> [While in Milan] We carried our daggers at our backs in Walloon fashion, which caused us to be summoned before the authorities. How did we dare to appear in public armed with daggers—a crime which was punished with hanging in

---

224	Ibid 96.
225	B. Anne Tlusty, The Martial Ethic in Early Modern Germany: Civic Duty and the Right of Arms, (New York: Palgrave Macmillan, 2011), 1-3.

> Italy? In consideration of our presumed ignorance of the law, mercy would be shown to us this once, but we ought to take it as a warning.

England was less draconian about the right to bear arms. In London in the 16th century, it was common for men to carry arms, giving rise to the term "swashbuckling" for those who carried side swords and bucklers. Nobles wore side swords, while young and old alike were to be found with a dagger.[226]

However, partially in an effort to rein in the people's frivolity, Queen Elizabeth passed edicts that limited the lengths of the newly popular rapier. She also tried to ban certain types of clothing and shoes in a largely failed effort to limit luxuries.[227]

In the 17th century, the carrying of weapons in England continued to decline. In Essex, the most common weapon was whatever people had readily available when roused to anger, including sticks, stones and pots. Only two deaths occurred in Essex due to a sword during the century.[228] While the nobility and those who called themselves gentlemen might be routinely dueling one another with swords, the population at large was steadily safer.

Self-defense receded as a skill that had to be learned to the point that in the 19th century authors of self-defense treatises lamented the lack of interest in them, much in the same way 16th century authors lamented the lack of interest in the use of swords. This was, however, not without good cause. In the 14th century, European cities on average had a murder rate of 50 people per 100,000, but at the close of the 18th century that number had dropped to 10 per 100,000, and by the end of the 19th century it dipped as low as 1 per 100,000.[229]

As V.G. Kiernan described it, duels and self-defense were common affairs because, "everyone carried weapons for self-protection in disorderly streets and on unpoliced highways; in any sudden fracas swords or daggers would come out like claws."[230] Yet, by the 18th century and beyond, the streets were not so unruly and the highways not so unpoliced.

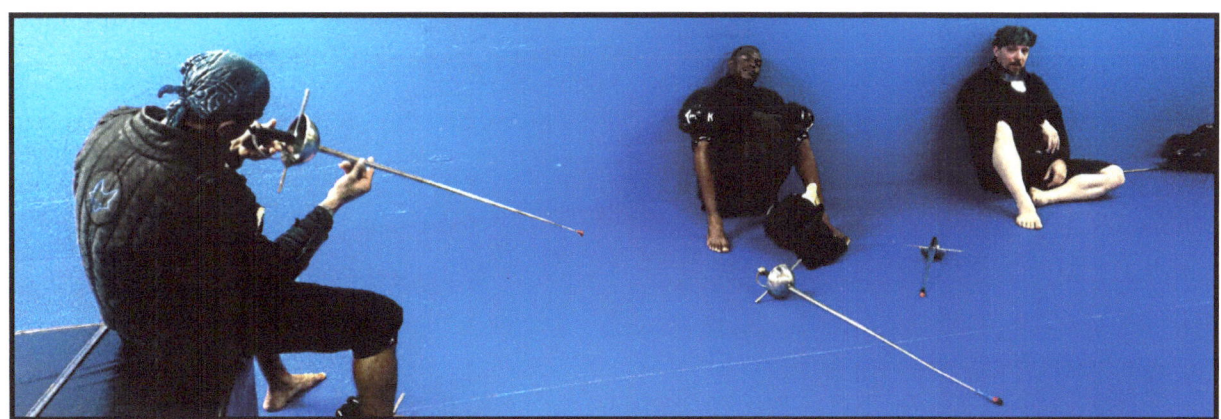

McKenzie Ewing, Marcus Lewis, and Jonathan Shores of the Atlanta Freifechter at rest after training.

226   V.G Kiernan, The Duel, (Oxford: Oxford University Press, 1988), 80.
227   Robert Chambers, Chamber's Journal of Popular Literature, Science and Arts, (1877), 142.
228   V.G Kiernan, The Duel, (Oxford: Oxford University Press, 1988), 81.
229   Manuel Eisner, Long-Term Historical Trends in Violent Crime, accessed May 20, 2016, https://soci.ucalgary.ca/brannigan/sites/soci.ucalgary.ca.brannigan/files/long-term-historical-trends-of-violent-crime.pdf 87.
230   V.G Kiernan, The Duel, (Oxford: Oxford University Press, 1988), 61.

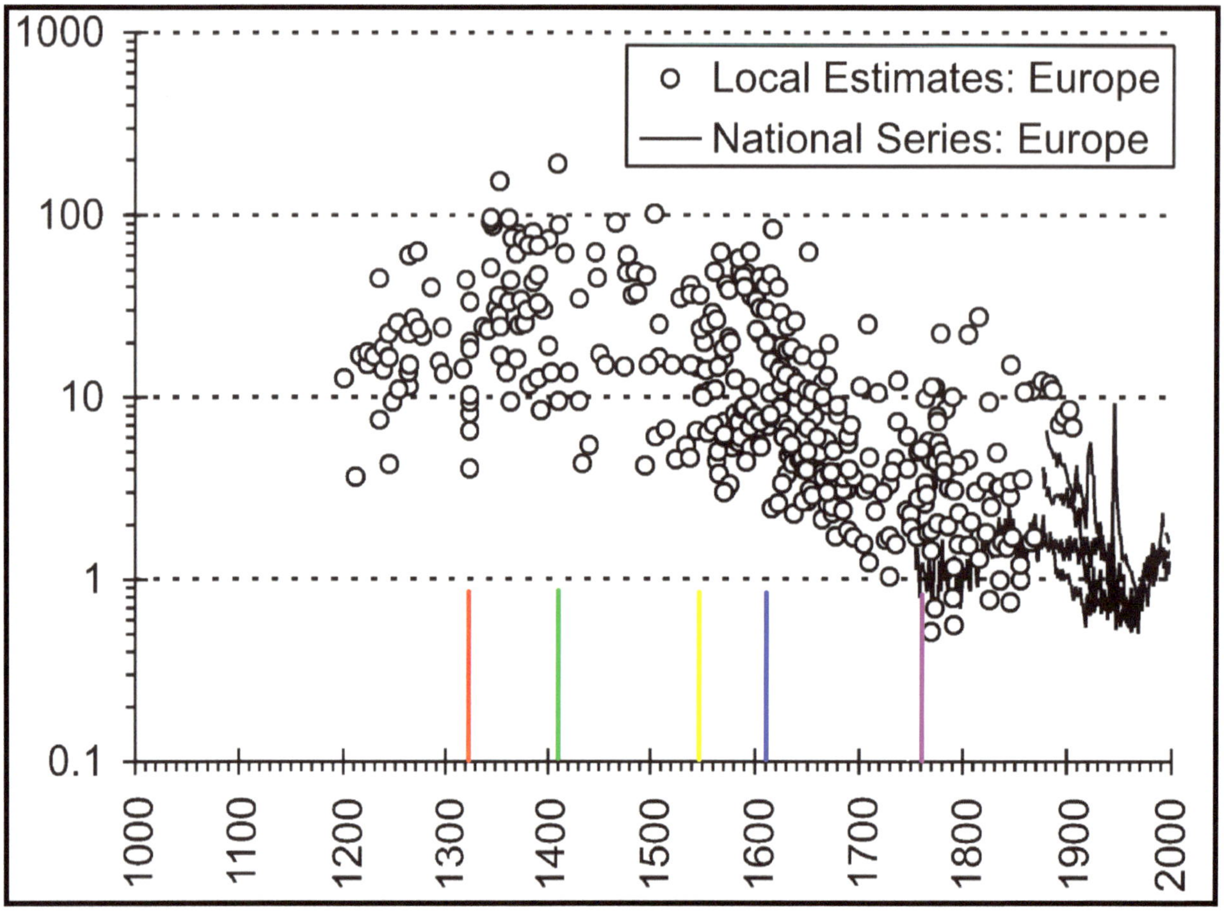

Chart depicting Europe's falling homicide rate. Deaths include duels, but not war-time casualties or atrocities. The colors, added by the author, indicate the following treatises. Red – MS I.33, Green – Fiore de Liberi's Flower of Battle, Yellow – Palus Hector Mair's Codex Icon, Blue – Nicoletto Giganti's Rapier treatises, Purple—Domenico Angelos' L'Ecole des Armes.[231]

Russ Mitchell in the attire of a common soldier of the Hungarian Palatine in the 15th century.

---

231   Manuel Eisner, Long-Term Historical Trends in Violent Crime, accessed May 20, 2016, https://soci.ucalgary.ca/brannigan/sites/soci.ucalgary.ca.brannigan/files/long-term-historical-trends-of-violent-crime.pdf 95.

Tournaments

Tournaments were derived from the early days of sanctioned combat. At first, large melees were fought on foot within wooden barriers, often called the lists. These were not friendly encounters, and it was not unusual for men to die—sometimes a great many men. Later, horses were introduced and eventually greater ritual and regulation. This was a trend mirrored in judicial dueling, which also became ever-regulated until it ceased to exist. Tournaments were also increasingly regulated and ritualized, but rather than vanish like the judicial duel, they became forms of entertainment.

However, at their earliest, they were deadly affairs meant to mimic the bloody reality of war. Sometimes they even took place between warring armies or rival cities.

In the 12th century, Roger Hoveden said in reference to tournaments,

> A youth must have seen his blood flow and felt his teeth crack under the blow of his adversary and been thrown to the ground twenty times. Thus he will be able to face real war with the hope of victory.[232]

In 1240, sixty knights supposedly died at a tournament near Cologne that spiraled out of control for unknown reasons. In England, the following year, the Earl of Pembroke was killed in a tournament at Hertford. Enraged, his retainers took up arms against those deemed responsible for his death and even more men died.[233] A century later, tournaments were less dangerous, but by no means safe, with eighteen knights dying in Rome's coliseum in a tournament.[234]

Rules were gradually put in place and different types of combat were developed. A tournament included Deeds of Arms, called *faits d'armes*, which included such combat as; group combat, single-combat, and jousting as well as non-combative sports, such as trying to lance a ring from horseback.[235]

At a tournament the fighting could be done with sharp weaponry, à *outrance*, or with blunted weapons, à*plaisance*. Safe zones, *recets*, were set up and barriers of wood erected to keep the fighting contained in the lists. Within the lists, the fighting could be in earnest, involving multiple weapons. These tournaments even included the taking of prisoners and the demand of a ransom.[236] An outside observer might think they were witnessing a medieval battle were it not for the barriers of wood hemming the participants in.

> Zounds, a dog, a rat, a mouse, a cat to scratch a man to death! A braggart, a rogue, a villain that fights by the book of arithmetic!
> - Shakespeare

---

232   Thomas S. Henricks, Disputed Pleasures: Sport and Society in Preindustrial England, (Westport: Praeger, 1991), 26.
233   Ibid 27.
234   Frederick R. Bryson, The Sixteenth-Century Italian Duel, (Chicago: University of Chicago Press, 1938), XXII.
235   Terms varied throughout the centuries and by region with French and Latin phrases often being contradicted within the source material according to Clephan.
236   Ibid 28.

Wearing period armor, two opponents face one another in the lists using the half-sword. Armor advancements from the late 14th century on quickly made cutting an opponent difficult. It was far better to grab the sword by the handle and blade to try to thrust or close and topple the opponent.[237]

William Marshal and his Flemish friend Roger de Jouy turned tournaments into a profitable venture in the 12th century. Traveling around Normandy, they entered every tournament they could. The tournaments they engaged in were performed mounted, and each side's objective was to take prisoners and, failing that, claim their horses. Everything that could be milked for money was—horses, people, armor and weapons.

Marshal and de Jouy took as many prisoners as they could and split the profits between them, amassing a small fortune. At times, they were even on opposite sides of a tournament but still split their winnings, while deftly avoiding one another.

Contemporaries noted that the sport, if it could be called that, was filled with irregularities, including getting informants to point out the younger inexperienced knights who would be easy pickings for the experienced men.

---

237 Photo courtesy Trevor Clemons, Rachel Schuster, Steve Smith, Joshua Warren and Brian Scott Wilson.

On his death bed, with pride and a grin, William Marshal claimed to have taken five hundred knights prisoner during his tournament career.[238]

The French method of the tournament was to fight on horseback with the lance, which became known as jousting, or tilting. In a joust, only two opponents fought, separated by a wooden barrier. The jousters used blunted lances and attempted to unseat their opponent or break a lance. Whoever broke the most lances or unseated the most men became the champion. In times of peace, they were not meant to be fatal and called *Hastitludia Pacifica* and in times of war, the game could be played more earnestly in what 14th century chronicler Froissart called *Justes Mortelles et à Champ*.[239]

King Alfonso XI of Castile in 1330 had rules for jousting, which included rules such as,

> Firstly, we declare that the knights who must joust should run four courses, and no more. And if in these four courses one knight should hit the other, splintering his lance, and the knight upon whom that lance splintered did not break his own lance by striking his opponent, he shall be vanquished, for he did not break his lance.[240]

Rituals varied, but in all cases there was much pomp and ceremony involved in the tournament as well as tremendous costs to the host. In France, days were taken to introduce the participants, each who wore colorful decorations atop their armor. During this time, judges ensured everyone who was participating was a man of proper breeding and that their weapons and armor were in order.[241] Costs were enormous though, and in some cases unbearable. In Bruges, a guild of nobles and their supporters called the White Bear had the privilege of hosting tournaments. However, by 1487 the guild was dissolved under the mounting costs of such elaborate and largely ceremonial affairs.[242]

Tournaments drew in swarms of knights, to the point that feudal monarchs tended to worry about them. Having hundreds of knights gather under a noble, even for a game, was unsettling. In his biography on William Marshal, Historian David Crouch noted that the powerful French dukes and counts who hosted the tournaments did so, in part, to remind the monarchy that they could, if it pleased them, gather an army.[243]

In the 14th century rules were added to make tournaments safer than they had been in the prior century.[244] Two knights, for example, would agree in advance on how best to fight one another in what was called a *pas de la fontaine des pleurs*. In these Deeds of Arms, the goal was generally not to kill one another, but rather to display the prowess of the knights. Even bringing in equipment that was too warlike might be barred, such as a horse armored in spikes.[245] A traditional encounter might include three passes with a sword, lance and axe, or the throwing of a sword or spear, or three

---

238   David Crouch, William Marshal: Knighthood, War, and Chivalry, 1147-1219, (Abingdon-on-Thames: Routledge, 1992), 100.
239   Robert Coltman Clephan, The Mediaeval Tournament, (Ann Arbor: University of Michigan Press, 1919), 10.
240   Noel Fallows, Jousting in Medieval and Renaissance Iberia, (Woodbridge: Boydell Press, 2010), 209-210.
241   F. Kottenkamp, The History of Chivalry and Armor, (Mineloa: Dover Publications, 2007 org. 1857), 96-98.
242   Bert Gevart, Reinier van Noort, Evolution of Martial Tradition in the Low Countries: Fencing Guilds and Treatises, (Boston: Brill, 2016), 383.
243   "Noel Fallows, Jousting in Medieval and Renaissance Iberia, (Woodbridge: Boydell Press, 2010), 209-210.
244   This was not a universal trend. Poland continued to joust with sharp lances into the 17th century.
245   Catherine Emerson, Olivier de La Marche and the Rhetoric of the Fifteenth-century Historiography, (Woodbridge: Boydell Press, 2004), 202.

blows with a dagger and so on. Fighting could take place either on foot, mounted or both.[246] Judges watched over the fight along with the host who was usually a king or some high ranking noble, such as a Duke, Baron or Margrave. After every blow, the presiding lord could stop the combat, separate the knights and have them go at it again. The host could entirely end combat by tossing a white baton or staff into the lists. This was done usually before a fight became too dangerous. The winner was determined by the judges and the two would make some form of physical contact as a form of reconciliation before departing.

Some duels were far more serious, or what was called a *luite ds mortelz ennemis*.[247] Even these rarely ended with a fatality.

Reece Nelson and Ben Bruce demonstrate one of the more fatal techniques to be used against an armored opponent.

Ben Bruce encounters a half-sword technique.

246   Ibid 204.
247   Ibid 205.

A Passage of Arms or *pas d'armes* was a slightly different form of tournament. While normally a local lord or king would host a tournament of their own volition, in a *pas d'armes*, a knight and his retainers would seek permission to set up at a given area and seek single combat from any worthy challenger.

In a *pas d'armes*, two opposing combatants fought with an array of weaponry, but killing one another was not as important as displaying skill and bravery, much in the same way as a *pas de la fontaine des pleurs*. A *pas d'armes*, just like all tournaments, took place in a marked-off area. This was called the lists, the barriers, or the *Champ clos*. However, they were not always public affairs, as they could take place in remote areas or over a period of many days.

Legendary knights left their homeland and sought challengers to capture and bring back to their lady loves. While many of these legends were just that, there were plenty of knights who sought a Passage of Arms in the search of fame and potentially reward.

The Spanish knight Suero posted himself at a bridge and barred any knight from passing. He ended up defeating all comers and capturing several French, German and English knights who in turn were ransomed as was custom.[248]

In 1445, a knight in the service of the Duke of Milan, Galiot de Balthasin, was granted permission to leave Italy and search out other knights to do combat with. However, the Duke of Milan asked that Galiot not issue any challenge but merely agree to one if presented the opportunity.

While visiting the Duke of Burgundy, Galiot's situation became known. He was a knight looking for a *pas d'armes*, but forbidden from challenging anyone. Within the Duke of Burgundy's court was a knight sympathetic to Galiot's plight, the Lord of Ternant. Ternant wore a badge upon his chest of his lady, which was a general challenge to all comers. They had but to touch, or tear off the badge. To touch it was to ask for *pas d'armes*; to tear it off was to ask for a duel to the death.

With the Duke's permission, Galiot gently touched the badge and was granted the fight he wanted. This was not a judicial duel, for no crime had been committed. Nor was it a private duel because Galiot had been respectful in touching the badge and his fight would be witnessed by many, including the ruling authority. It was a *pas d'armes*, and the challengers agreed to fight with multiple weapons, though with no real intent of harming one another.

The two decided to face one another on foot, armed with spears, swords and axes and then on horseback with lances and swords. Masters of the List, armed with sticks to part the two knights should things get too dangerous, acted as referees. Further adding to the level of safety, the fighters were only to deliver a set number of blows.

In this particular Passage of Arms spectators watched the knights battle. The two knights paused between fights, put on different surcoats, fought again, paused, put on yet different surcoats and continued fighting. The *pas d'armes* could be a fashion show as well as a test of martial skill.

Galiot and Lord Ternant fought, blows were rained down and no one was harmed, thanks to their skill and superior armor. The Duke tossed a white staff down at the end of the combat on horseback and the two knights presented themselves to him. All were pleased, and the *pas d'armes* was complete.[249]

---

248   Frederick R. Bryson, The Sixteenth-Century Italian Duel, (Chicago: University of Chicago Press, 1938), XXII.
249   Alfred Hutton, The Sword and the Centuries, (Staffordshire: Wren's Park Publishing, 2003 org. 1901), 3-8.

While intended to be bloodless, a *pas d'armes* could lead to injury. In 1449, a knight in the service of the Duke of Burgundy, Lalaing, was given permission to travel abroad and seek out challengers. In Scotland he was obliged, but in England Henry VI refused to allow it, perhaps not wanting to pay for the spectacle.

Just as Lord Ternant had been sympathetic toward Galiot, within the English court, an esquire, Thomas Qué, was eager to fight Lalaing. The two agreed to leave England and fight in the presence of the Duke of Burgundy, the same who had allowed Galiot and Ternant to fight. Showing a level of bravado, they agreed to fight with whatever armor they chose and with poleaxe and sword until one had fallen.

The Duke granted the Passage of Arms, but Qué arrived with a poleaxe that was larger than Lalaing's. There was some debate, but the mismatched pairing was allowed and combat commenced. The lighter armored and armed Lalaing was able to land heavy blows onto Qué, but as Alfred Hutton put it, "The man was strong of limb, with much good old British beef and ale in his composition."

Qué was able to deliver a strike to Lalaing's hand, damaging it to the point that the knight could barely hold his poleaxe. Sensing victory, Qué attempted to use a heavy, over-the-head blow to finish the fight. Deftly, Lalaing closed the distance and with his uninjured hand was able to slip his arm under Qué's raised arm, grasp the back of his helmet and topple him into the mud. Qué had been wearing a bascinet with a beak, which became stuck in the moist ground. Thus ended the *pas d'armes* with Lalaing as the victor, though at the cost of a hurt hand.[250]

Lalaing went on to fight many more such challenges and in one case, at the Passage of the Fountain of Tears, so named for a nearby statue of a weeping woman, he waited for a month willing to fight anyone. Many tried, but Lalaing defeated them all, though he killed no one. When he returned to the Court of Phillip of Burgundy he was accepted into the Order of the Golden Fleece, a chivalric order of great renown.[251]

In 1453, Lalaing was killed by cannon fire during a revolt, a sign of the times to come for the knightly class.[252]

Francesco Lodá and Tim Kaufman in a rapier and dagger tournament. Photo courtesy of Véronique McMillan of the Triangle Sword Guild.

---

250   Ibid 12-15.
251   Matthew Galas, "The Deeds of Jacques de Lalaing: Feats of Arms of a 15th Century Knight," ARMA, accessed May 23, 2016, http://www.thearma.org/essays/Lalaingg.htm#.VGl3e5V0yUm.
252   Joseph Calmette, The Golden Age of Burgundy: The Magnificent Dukes and their Courts, (New York: W.W. Norton, 2001), 100.

From Fiore de Liberi's the Flower of Battle, the student wearing the golden garter locks his opponent up. He can topple and strike him at will. This is a play similar to that performed by Lalaing against Qué in their Passage of Arms.[253]

253   Digital image courtesy of the Getty's Open Content Program.

Jean Froissart's 15th century depiction of a joust that took place in Spain between Reginald de Roye and John Holland in 1387. Barriers keep the combatants contained, while elevated stands let guests of note watch the action below. Not all mounted combat involved a lance.[254]

---

254 https://commons.wikimedia.org/wiki/File:Joust_John_Holland_Reginald_de_Roye.jpg Public Domain Art.

Having entered the lists, two champions separated by a barrier tilt against one another. A lance lies broken in the foreground while spectators on elevated platforms watch. The knights wear armor, specifically for jousting, and wear elaborate decorations. It was not unusual for there to be wardrobe changes during a tournament.[255]

255   Arnholot, http://www.erfgoedbankhoogstraten.be/php/dia1.php?s=600&trefwoord=dia Public Domain Art.

During the 16th century the pageantry of tournaments and jousts increased and they became forms of celebration or royal entertainment. While the joust still existed, the days of knights dominating the battlefield had long since given way to more modern field armies using pikes, halberds and gunpowder. Jousting and tournaments were still a part of Renaissance culture, but they were less about military training and more about reviving and romanticizing the martial past.

A joust in the 16th century. Such affairs were largely bloodless, though not without danger. A barrier separates the jousters who are tilting, while barriers also keep the spectators out of the way.[256]

Spain continued to participate in tournaments well into the Renaissance, adding rules and games. In 1548 the *Doctrina del arte de la cavalleria* was written by Juan Quijada de Reayo and commissioned by Beltrán de la Cueva. Beltrán was a famous captain who impressed Emperor Charles V and Henry VIII of England. Juan Quijada was a military commander and an avid competitor at tournaments, competing in games and earning prizes, such as a golden sword in 1549.

The games included fighting one on one, in which each combatant had to deliver specific strikes in an almost ritualized fashion. The fighters had to deliver three blows with the pike, land five strokes with the sword, deliver three blows each with the head and shaft of the lance, cast one spear, deliver seven strokes with a two-handed sword, and land nine blows with an axe.[257] No one was killed. So the martial games of

---

256   Heinrich Wirrich 1571 https://commons.wikimedia.org/wiki/File:Heinrich_Wirrich_-_Proper_description_of_the_Christian_wedding_-_WGA25782.jpg Public Domain Art.
257   Noel Fallows, Jousting in Medieval and Renaissance Iberia, (Woodbridge: Boydell Press, 2010), 47-48.

the 1200s, in which up to sixty men might die, had become far safer by the 1500s, though not without risks.

In 1485, the younger brother of King James III of Scotland had been forced to flee to France. There, he was killed in a joust by the Duke of Orleans. A splinter from the lance penetrated his helmet. He would not be the first, or the last, to meet such a fate.[258]

Paulus Hector's Mair de Arte Athletica II from the 16th century was a massive treatise containing all manner of weaponry, including the use of weapons meant for jousting, such as blunted lances. Unseating an opponent or breaking a lance earned points.[259]

Axel Pettersson and Kristine Konsmo at a workshop teaching Historical European Martial Arts. Photo courtesy of Véronique McMillan of the Triangle Sword Guild. Axel has been a major influence on the modern HEMA movement in terms of coaching, tournaments and gear-design.

---

258   Katie Stevenson, Chivalry and Knighthood in Scotland 1424-1513, (Woodbridge: Boydell Press, 2006), 81.
259   https://commons.wikimedia.org/wiki/File:Paulus_Hector_Mair_Tjost_fig2.jpg Paulus Hector Mair Public Domain Art.

A joust in France. Today, an active community re-creates the martial games of the Medieval Era and Renaissance. Photo courtesy Harrie Gielen, Wikicommons.

Henry VIII, the king of England, enjoyed tournaments and jousting in particular. He saw tournaments as a way to revive a flagging martial spirit in his nobility. Henry VIII was a man who was willing to act and not just talk. In 1524, he participated in a joust and was severely injured. George Cavendish, the usher to Cardinal Wolsey, recounted the event.

> On 10 March the king, having a new armor made to his own design and fashion, such as no armorer before that time had seen, thought to test the same at the tilt, and ordered a joust for the purpose. The lord marquis of Dorset and the earl of Dorset and the earl of Surrey were appointed to be on foot: the king came to one end of the tilt and the duke of Suffolk to the other.

Then a gentleman said to the duke: 'Sir the king is come to the end of the tilt.' 'I see him not,' said the duke, 'by my faith, for my headpiece blocks my sight.' With these words, God knows by what chance, the king had his spear delivered to him by the lord Marquis, the visor of his headpiece being up and not down or fastened, so that his face as quite naked. The gentleman said to the duke: 'Sir the king is coming.'

Then the duke set forward and charged with his spear, and the king likewise unadvisedly set off towards the duke. The people, seeing the king's face bare, cried hold, hold; the duke neither saw nor heard, and whether the king remembered his visor was up or not few could tell. Alas, what sorrow was it to the people when they saw the splinters of the duke's spear strike the king's headpiece. For most certainly the duke struck the king on the brow right under the guard of the headpiece on the very skull cap or basinet piece to which the barbette is hinged for strength and safety, which skull cap or basinet no armorer takes heed of, for it is always covered by the visor, barbette and volant piece, and thus that piece is so protected that it takes no weight. But when the spear landed on that place there was great danger of death since the face was bare, for the duke's spear broke into splinters and pushed the king's visor or barbette so far back with the counter blow that all the King's head piece was full of splinters. The armorers were much blamed for this, and so was the lord marquise for delivering the spear blow when his face was open, but the king said that no one was to blame but himself, for he intended to have saved himself and his sight.

The duke immediately disarmed and came to the king, showing him the closeness of his sight, and he swore that he would never run against the king again. But if the king had been even a little hurt, his servants would have put the duke in jeopardy. Then the king called his armorers and put all his pieces of armor together and then took a spear and ran six courses very well, by which all men could see that he had taken no hurt, which was a great joy and comfort to all his subjects present.[260]

The king was not harmed, but later in life he complained of headaches and other issues that may have been exacerbated, if not outright caused, by his athletic lifestyle, which included jousting. Not all kings were as fortunate as Henry VIII when it came to jousting. Although heavy armor and blunted, breakable lances made jousting safer than it may have ever been, there were still risks.

King Henri II in 1559 partook in what was supposed to be a friendly and safe joust. While tilting against Montmorceny, a member of the Scottish guard in the king's service, Henri II was unhorsed. Many illustrious people were in attendance, including Mary, Queen of Scots. Requesting one more joust, the king tilted against Montmorceny a second time.

This time, the king was more than unhorsed. Montmorceny's lance exploded, which was a design feature to make jousting safer, but a sliver of wood entered the king's helmet and penetrated his eye, reaching the brain. The king fell from his horse, mortally wounded. Montmorceny begged the king to cut off his hand and head. Henri, weak, but still conscious, refused and complimented his Scottish guard.

---

260 http://englishhistory.net/tudor/king-henry-viii-jousting-accident/ May 21 2016

The English ambassador, Nicholas Throckmorton, was an eye witness to the king's condition and wrote,

> I noted him to be very weak, and to have the sense of all his limbs almost benumbed, for being carried away, as he lay all along, he moved neither hand nor foot, but lay as one amazed.
>
> The king died soon after, leaving his Medici wife, Queen Catherine, in charge of France at a critical time when the Reformation was sweeping its way across Europe. The king's death was shocking enough that the joust was ended as a pastime in France.
>
> In one unusual episode, a gentleman named Marivaut was grieved by the assassination of Henri III. He determined to die and so challenged anyone and everyone to a fight in the lists. An opponent was found and they decided to fight in armor with lances on horseback in a joust. This was not unusual, but when Marivaut donned a helmet that did not protect his face, his opponent was incredulous.
>
> Marivaut insisted they commence with the joust and was promptly killed when a lance struck him in the head.[261]

Tournaments and jousts also had political value even as their martial purposes became questionable. In 1520, France and England, long-time enemies, put aside their differences temporarily at a spectacular tournament called the Field of the Cloth of Gold. Cardinal Wosely arranged for the tournament, and vast sums of money were spent by England and France. Two camps were built, one for the English and the other the French, with a field between them. The tournament started with Henry VIII of England riding toward Francis I as if to engage in single-combat. Instead, the two kings met in the center of the field and raised their feathered caps—and the celebrations began. They hugged and showed mutual affection immediately.

Over twelve thousand people attended a three-week festival, which quickly turned into an arms race of pageantry. The two kings each dressed in increasingly expensive costumes, and the nobility in each camp spent money lavishly. The name, Field of the Cloth of Gold, was earned as the English and French camps dazzled onlookers in their bid to outshine the other.[262]

Henry VIII and Francis I appeared to get along—so much so that as the two watched some men wrestling, Henry suddenly took Francis by the collar and asked for a match. Henry VIII was large and Francis I slender, but the French king was able to throw Henry. Henry wished to wrestle again, but the French and English nobles dissuaded him in fear of a friendly match turning deadly earnest. In a show of trust, Francis appeared alone in the English camp to visit Henry. If the English king was brooding over the wrestling match, the surprise visit by Francis I, without guards, delighted him.

Jousts were had, though the two kings did not face off against one another as had been agreed beforehand. Instead, they charged against their nobles. The objective was to break the lance against the opponent, or unseat him. Henry VIII was able to break five lances, while Francis I managed four. A chronicler at the time, Jacques Dubuois, was more dramatic about the event.

> They bend forward upon their horses and are poised for the blow… they collide and exerting themselves with all their might, crash into each other with a noise like thunder that resounds to the very stars.[263]

261   George H. Powell, Dueling Stories of the 16th Century: From the French of Brantome, (London: 1904), 69-70 Brantome, whose narrative is likely embellished, noted this story was told to him secondhand.
262   Glenn Richardson, Generous to a Fault, (New Haven: Yale University Press, 2013), 141-177.
263   Ibid 141-177.

Later, the kings entered the lists for foot combat. Rules were put in place to keep the swords lighter in weight to prevent serious harm. Henry VIII at one point had a sword invalidated because of its size. Francis I was concerned that no gauntlets could hold up to the blade.[264]

A day of fighting and no one was seriously hurt, which was, at this point in time, the desired outcome of all such tournaments.

Despite a personal affinity between the English and French monarchs, the nobles were not as warm to one another. The English were wary of the French and fearful of Henry's temper, while the French nobility panicked when they found out their king had risked visiting the English camp without any supervision. While the monarchs may have been genuinely friendly and perhaps intrigued by one another, a lasting peace between England and France was not to be. A month later, due to his alliance with Charles V of Spain and the Holy Roman Empire, England went to war with France.

Further tournaments were held for political purposes, though none quite as spectacular and expensive as the Field of Cloth and Gold.

The Field of Cloth of Gold possibly painted by Hans Holbien the Younger around 1545. Despite the great mass of military men in the painting, no one wears armor except the jousters. Such suits were, as the tournament was, an appeal to the past. The opposing tents can be seen, each in gold, and to the far upper right the jousting lists, complete with a barrier to separate the horses.[265]

> And this book of Frencing will save many men mens' lives, or put common quarrels out of use because the danger is death...
> — Giacomo di Grassi

---

264 John Block, editor, Scottish Notes and Queries, (Aberdeen: 1897), 45.
265 https://commons.wikimedia.org/wiki/File:British_-_Field_of_the_Cloth_of_Gold_-_Google_Art_Project.jpg Public Domain Art.

Larger than life, Henry VIII and Francis I embrace beneath a golden tent. Detail from the Field of Cloth and Gold.[266]

When the 16th century arrived, the days of the joust being a viable means of settling affairs or training the military had passed. The 17th century saw its rapid decline, but the occasional joust or tournament still took place. James I, for all his complaints about dueling, could be seen jousting as a form of entertainment.[267]

John Evelyn's personal letters describe a 17th century joust. He was impressed by it, or rather by the pageantry around it, but the entire affair was without danger and called a *War of Love*, in which the prizes were the favors of the witnessing ladies.[268] Years later, he described another joust, this one held in Rome, which was just as friendly.

266   https://commons.wikimedia.org/wiki/File:British_-_Field_of_the_Cloth_of_Gold_-_Google_Art_Project.jpg Public Domain Art.
267   V.G Kiernan, The Duel, (Oxford: Oxford University Press, 1988), 45.
268   Douglas D.C. Chambers, David Galbraith, The Letterbooks of John Evelyn, (Toronto: University of Toronto Press, 2014), 353.

> There had been in the morning a joust and tournament of several young gentlemen on a formal defy, to which we had been invited; the prizes being distributed by the ladies, after the knight-errantry way. The lancers and swordsmen running at tilt against the barriers, with a great deal of clatter, but without any bloodshed, giving much diversion to the spectators...[269]

The Enlightenment of the 18th century had made armor, save for helmets and the occasional breastplate, all but obsolete, and only the Poles and Russians were still using lances. Whatever martial value tournaments and jousting had, it was largely extinct by the 1700s.

The joust and tournament as a form of entertainment remained, though, and in the 19th century Britain conducted a reenactment of a tournament organized by the Earl of Eglinton. Today, jousting and tournaments still take place in Europe and in the United States in the form of Renaissance Fairs and reenactments.

This armor was made in Milan in the late 16th century for Don Alonso Perez de Guzman el Bueno, duke of Medina Sidoni. It is richly engraved and provided protection for its wearer as well as symbolized his extreme wealth. The armor had different pieces made for it so it could be set up for warfare or tournaments. Courtesy Walters Art Museum.

---

269   "Diary of John Nevely", accessed May 30, 2016, https://archive.org/stream/diaryofjohnevely024466mbp/diaryofjohnevely024466mbp_djvu.txt

The joust between the Lord of the Tournament and the Knight of the Red Rose by Hodgson, depicting the reenactment of a tournament hosted by Archibald the Earl of Eglinton.[270]

Axel Pettersson giving advice to Peter Haas at a Historical European Martial Arts tournament. Photo courtesy of Rebecca Glass.

270   https://commons.wikimedia.org/wiki/File:The_Joust_between_the_Lord_of_the_Tournament_and_the_knight_of_the_Red_Rose.JPG Public Domain Art.

War

War provides a backdrop to the fencing treatises of the 14th to 18th centuries. The treatises of Historical European Martial Arts are not about military tactics, military strategies, and so forth, except perhaps when they cover skirmishing or single-combat. Yet, war lurks in the background of the material.

War lends another layer of context to the source material. In Fiore de Liberi's work there are numerous means to place an opponent in a lock, making them all but helpless. Such a tactic may seem strange. Why not just kill the man and not risk a lock? There are many possible answers, and warfare in Italy during the 14th and 15th centuries provides a plausible answer.

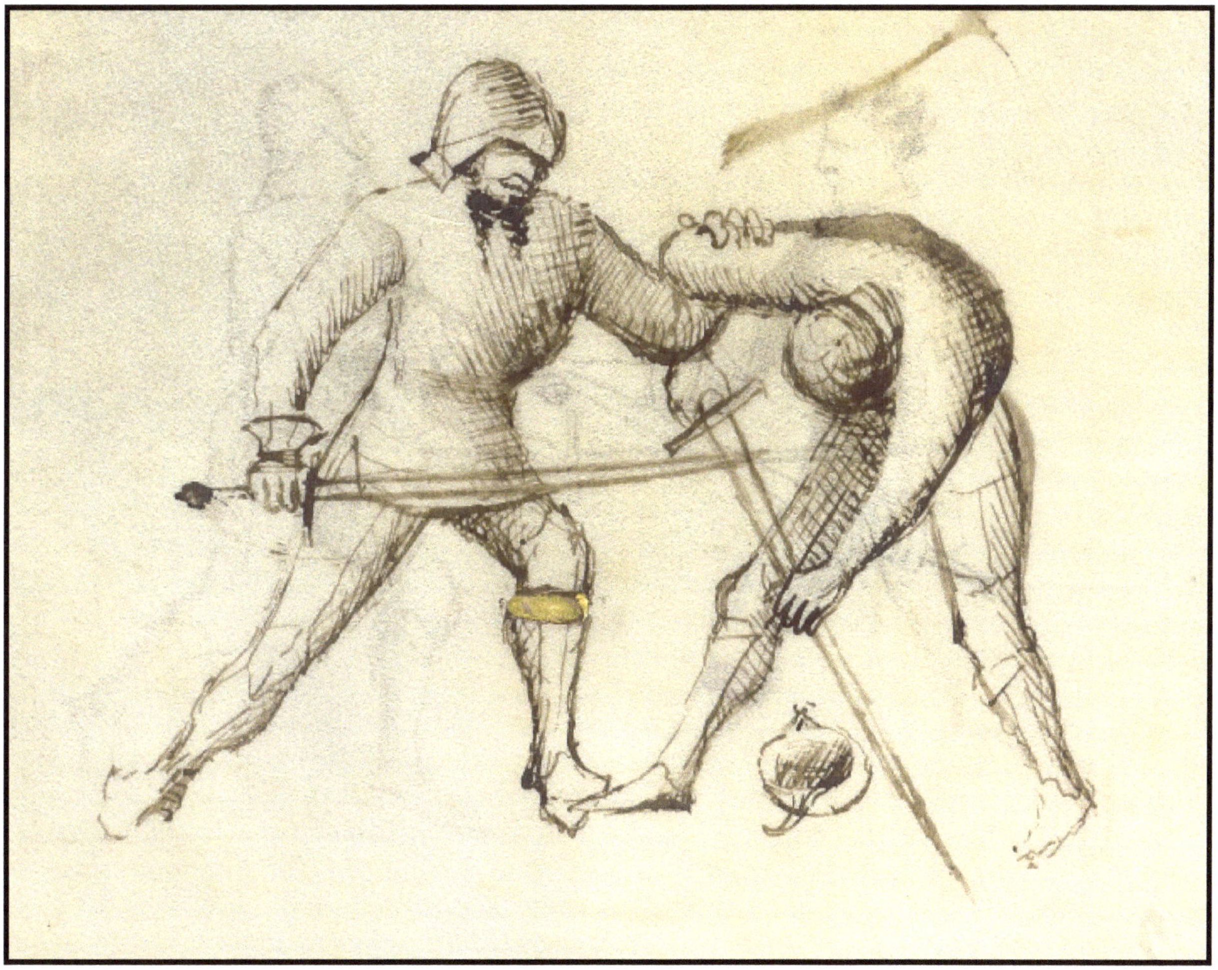

From Fiore de Liberi's the Flower of Battle. The lower-lock is achieved and the student, wearing a golden garter, has his enemy at his mercy. If a person wanted to take a prisoner for a ransom, this technique would be profitable.[271]

---

271   Digital image courtesy of the Getty's Open Content Program.

Christopher Nelson and Jay Simpson of the Phoenix Society of Historical Swordsmanship demonstrate one of Fiore de Liberi's locks.

In Italy, during Fiore's lifetime, mercenaries rampaged throughout the peninsula. While battles could be bloody affairs, it was far more sensible to take prisoners than kill them. Prisoners could be ransomed; corpses could at best be looted. The "bloodless" nature of warfare was not unique to Italy; it was customary, especially among the knightly classes.

The disarms and locks in the *Flower of Battle* were quite plausibly a means to take a prisoner for later ransom. Such was customary in Fiore's day. Then again, perhaps they were a means to defeat an opponent in a sanctioned duel without killing him. Fiore's students engaged in duels, but they did not kill their opponents. It is hard to say for certain, and the history has to stand as a guide for modern interpreters.

Leaping far ahead to 1599, George Silver, in his *Paradoxes of Defense,* was critical of the Italian rapier, precisely because of its drawbacks on the battlefield. Complaining about Spanish, French, and Italian rapier techniques he said,

> ...strange vices and devices of Italian, French, and Spanish fencers, little remembering, that these apish toys could not free Rome from Brennius's sack, nor France from the King Henry the Fifth and his conquest.

He continues, with a critical comment about the foreign Italians who had come to England peddling a type of swordsmanship he found better for murder than defense of self and nation:

> But that which is most shameful, they teach men to butcher one another here at home in peace, wherewith they cannot hurt their enemies abroad in war. For, your honor well knows, that when the battle is joined, there is no room for them to draw their bird-spits, and when they have them, what can they do with them? Can they pierce his corslet with the point? Can they unlace his helmet, unbuckle his armor, hew asunder their pikes with a Stocata, a Reversa, a Dritta, a Stramason or other such tempestuous terms?
>
> No, these toys are fit for children, not for men, for straggling boys of the camp, to murder poultry, not for men of honor to try the battle with their foes.
>
> Thus I have (Right Honorable) for the trial of the truth, between the short sword and the long rapier, for the saving of the lives of our English gallants, who are sent to certain death by their uncertain fights, and for abandoning of that mischievous and imperfect weapon, which serves to kill our friends in peace, but cannot much hurt our foes in war, have I at this time given forth these Paradoxes to the view of the world. And because I know such strange opinions had need of stout defense, I humbly crave your Honorable protection, as one in whom the true nobility of our victorious ancestors has taken up residence.[272]

Of his own methods, using a shorter stouter sword, Silver was confident that his techniques were as applicable in self-defense as they were on the battlefield.

War was ever present in Europe from the 14th century well into the modern era and was the ubiquitous backdrop of the fencing treatises even if they were not dedicated to it as much as they were to dueling. Salvator Fabris, for example, noted that the ramparts were very far from the dueling techniques in his book.[273]

The following is a brief overview of the major wars and conflicts of Europe from the 14th to 18th century; however, it is at best just a quick glimpse. A detailed recounting would require several books unto themselves. Needless to say, Europe was engaged in near unending wars, both large and small.

> Fencing (Right Honorable) in this new fangled age, is like our fashions, every day a change, resembling the chameleon, who alters himself into all colors save white.
>
> - George Silver

---

272 George Silver, "Paradoxes of Defense", accessed May 22, 2016, http://www.pbm.com/~lindahl/paradoxes.html

273 Salvator Fabris, trans. Tom Leoni, The Art of Dueling: Salvatore Fabris' Fencing Treatise of 1606, (Highland Village: Chivalry Bookshelf, 2005), 263.

Froissart's depiction of the Battle of Poitiers where the English longbow once again turned back the French in 1356.[274]

14th Century

War was near continual in Europe from the 14th century to the 18th century. The nature of war and its participants, however, varied greatly.

In the 14th century European warfare had turned inwards. The crusades to the Middle East of the 11th century had died out by the late 13th century. Disasters struck Europe from all angles starting in the mid-13th century and accelerating into the next. Historian Barbara Tuchman in her work on the 1300s, *A Distant Mirror*, added the fitting subtitle- *The Calamitous 14th Century*.

---

274   https://commons.wikimedia.org/wiki/File:Battle-poitiers(1356).jpg Public Domain Art.

From the East came the Mongols and the Turks. Mongol conquests had stretched from their steppe homeland and blazed across Asia and into Europe. Russia had fallen under Mongol rule, leading to Russian client-states watched over by Mongol overlords. While the initial tidal wave of the 1200s was over, and the Mongol Empire well on its way to fracturing, the threat they posed to Europe endured.

Poland had sustained and survived three separate Mongol incursions in the 1200s and in the 14th century had to contend with continual smaller-scale raids.

Byzantium had been severely weakened by the 4th Crusade when the Venetian Doge was able to redirect it and sack Constantinople in 1204. The damage to the Byzantines was fatal, and the Ottoman Turks tore chunk after chunk of the Byzantine Empire away throughout the 14th century. The inheritors of the Roman Empire were dwindling fast and finding Europe uncaring about their plight, while their Ottoman neighbors were unerring in their desire for conquest.

England and France entered into the Hundred Years War. In 1337, Edward III of England claimed the throne of France via his mother, the sole surviving child of the dead French King Phillip IV. The French denied the claim, reviving Salic law and denying the right of women to inherit property, thrones included. Undeterred, Edward III invaded a country larger than his, but was able to win key battles, thanks to the power of the longbow.

At Crecy in 1346 and Poitiers ten years later, the English longbow devastated the French armored knight both on horseback and on foot. While the heavy cavalry charge was supposed to be unstoppable, the English did not oblige the French by standing in open fields. Instead, the English picked elevated positions with narrow fronts where they could focus their firepower and blunt French assaults.

So fierce was the English arrow-fire that upwards of 90,000 arrows landed on the French army in a three minute period at Crecy and Poitiers.[275] Such volume of fire overwhelmed the numerically superior French army. When the French King, John, was captured at Poitiers, the war entered a quiet period. Peace was hardly universal, though. English and French soldiers alike made their living off of war, as well as the countless mercenaries from Europe who had flocked to France. Rather than accept peace, these soldiers formed large international bandit companies and besieged Pope Innocent VI in Avignon, France.

Unable to dislodge the mercenaries with spiritual power, the Pope paid a ransom instead, with a caveat that the mercenaries leave for Italy. In the 1360s, hordes of mercenaries, including the Englishman John Hawkwood, entered Italy. Italy was flooded with foreign mercenaries who drifted from contract to contract, supplied by one of the many warring city-states. Their name became *condottieri*, after the word "contract."[276]

> The halberd, a very old weapon first invented by the fighting women called Amazons.
>
> - Paulus Hector

---

275   Peter Reid, Brief History of Medieval Warfare, (New York: Running Press, 2008), 49-56.
276   William Caferro, John Hawkwood: An English Mercenary in Fourteenth-Century Italy, (Baltimore: Hopkins University Press).

John Hawkwood was a veteran of the Hundred Years War. When the war paused, rather than return to England, he joined and eventually led a mercenary company. He would spend the rest of his life in Italy fighting for and against numerous city-states.[277]

Italy in the 14th century was not a united body, nor had it been for some time. It was, nominally, under the rule of the Holy Roman Empire, but the Emperor rarely crossed the Alps, leaving Italy to the Pope, who had fled to Avignon, and a motley collection of Imperial princes and rival merchant-guild republics.

Spain was not unified and the stronger Catholic Kingdoms, such as Castile, were battling against fellow Catholics and Muslims in an effort to unify the Iberian Peninsula. Progress was steady but slow, and would not be complete until 1492.

Central Europe was also inwardly focused during the 14th century. The Holy Roman Empire stretched over a vast amount of territory, but the Emperor had little power. Ecclesiastical cities, free cities, petty kingdoms and more made the Empire unruly at best and rebellious at worst.

A final scourge to the 14th century was the Black Plague, brought from the East by the Mongols and

---

277 https://commons.wikimedia.org/wiki/File:John_hawkwood.jpg Public Domain Art.

eventually winding its way into Italy and then the rest of Europe during the mid-1300s. Cities were devastated, some losing upwards of half their population. The death toll was in the millions and led to social strife throughout Europe.

In 1381, the English peasants rebelled under Wat Tyler. In France, two separate revolts broke out: one in 1358 called the Jaquerie and another in 1382 called the Harlee after the Black Plague.

Overall, armies were largely medieval in nature, relying on armored cavalry and infantry. Recruitment was at the local level, where a knight would arrive with his retainers to form a lance, a noble would arrive with his personal army and the king with his. Control of these armies was a difficult process as the king of France discovered when his knights, without orders, charged through his own Genoese mercenaries.[278]

Chivalry still existed as an ideal, but a cynic could perhaps see through it. Nobles took one another prisoner in battle. This, courtesy of chivalry, was on the one hand an example of Christian mercy, but it was also economic and a form of insurance. Taking a prisoner would lead to a ransom, and by taking a prisoner, one could expect similar kind treatment should their situations ever be reversed.

Changes were taking place, though, as seen in the Hundred Years War where the range of the longbow upended traditional tactics. Gunpowder was still in its infancy, but Europeans were fast adapting the new technology to siege tactics and the use of hand-held weapons. Foot soldiers were also taking on greater roles and taking on mounted knights. In the Battle of the Golden Spurs, Flemish rebels were able to defeat a French mounted army in 1302. The Flemish were on foot and armed with goedendags, clubs affixed with iron spikes. They did not take prisoners.[279] Not taking prisoners would become more common, especially in cases where common foot soldiers were set against the mounted nobility.

If ever there was a time that matched the biblical apocalypse, it was the 14th century, in which plague, famine, war and death were all around.

Lee Smith of Blood and Iron in a tournament using the rapier and dagger. Photo courtesy of Jonathan Ying.

278 John A. Wagner, Encyclopedia of the Hundred Years War, (Westport: Greenwood Press, 2006), 107.
279 J. F. Verbruggen, The Battle of the Golden Spurs, (Woodbridge: Boydell Press, 2002 org. 1957), 249.

Depiction of battle from the Holkham Bible, showing the use of weapons, including sword and buckler, in the early 14th century.[280]

15th Century

Warfare in the 15th century was a time of transition from the old to the new, or in some cases back to the old. New weapons such as gunpowder were developed, with cannons in particular changing the nature of war. The Swiss revived Greek-phalanx style infantry tactics. Armor dramatically improved, covering soldiers in metal plate with fewer and fewer gaps. Armaments and armor rapidly improved, each trying to match the other.

The Mongol Empire steadily broke apart, and the invaders from the East were defeated as much by themselves as anyone else. The Grand Prince of Moscow, Ivan III, ceased paying the Mongols tribute in 1480, but continued to keep up friendly enough relations, all while annexing territory and laying the foundation for the Russian state centered upon Moscow. Fractions of the Mongol horde remained in Europe, including the Golden Horde, but these Mongol states receded in power and size.

In 1453, Byzantium ceased to exist when the mighty walls of Constantinople were breached by the Ottomans and their Sultan, Mehmed II. To accomplish this feat, massive cannons were needed. Ironically, they were built by the Hungarians, who soon after the fall of Constantinople would face the Turkish onslaught.[281]

---

280   Simon Schama, A History of Britain: At the End of the World? 3000 BC - AD 1603, (London: BBC, 2000), 219.
281   Steven Runciman, The Fall of Constantinople: 1453, (London: Cambridge University Press, 1990), 77–78.

The Roman Empire was truly dead, and the Ottoman threat to Europe persisted into the following centuries. Mehmed II expanded his influence into Europe and the Middle East, posing a continual danger to anyone unfortunate enough to border his lands. Most of the Balkans fell, leaving Hungary and tough mountainous kingdoms, such as Wallachia, as the bulwark against further Ottoman encroachments. Meanwhile, the Mediterranean ocean was contested between Europeans and the Ottomans.

After the fall of Constantinople in 1453, the Ottoman Empire expanded in all directions. For a time, Wallachia and Hungary held back the tide into Europe, but eventually the Ottomans would besiege Vienna, Austria, twice.[282]

Poland emerged as a powerful state in the 15th century. Poland, a Catholic country, had been at odds with pagan Lithuania. In the 13th century, German Teutonic Knights moved into the Baltic to bring the crusade to the pagan East. This suited Poland for a time, but when the Lithuanians converted, the Teutonic knights had no intention of stopping their conquest.

The Lithuanian king Jagiełło married the Polish queen Jadwiga and created one of the largest

---

282 https://commons.wikimedia.org/w/index.php?curid=3508743 By André Koehne Creative Commons 3.0

nations in Europe. Upon her death, Jagiełło became the sole ruler of a united Lithuania-Poland and marched against the Teutonic knights. A tremendous battle was fought at Grunwald in 1410 and the Teutonic army was soundly defeated. Although the Teutonic order was not destroyed, it was pushed back and would no longer pose a serious threat. Poland entered a period of relative peace and prosperity.

The Battle of Grunwald in 1410 marked the emergence of a powerful Polish state. Here, the Polish King Jagiełło *holds aloft a Teutonic standard. Painting by Jan Matejko 1878.*[283]

For England, the glory days of the Hundred Years War were nearly revived when Henry V won the Battle of Agincourt in 1415, again, thanks in large part to the tried and true longbow. The French King, Charles VI, was forced to accept peace, and Henry married his daughter. A son was born and,

---

283   https://commons.wikimedia.org/wiki/Battle_of_Grunwald#/media/File:Jan_Matejko,_Bitwa_pod_Grunwaldem.jpg Public Domain Art.

legally, it seemed the Hundred Years War would end in England's favor. The reality was far more complex. The French nobility did not want an English king, and misfortune on the battlefield did not change their minds.

A strange situation was that the English could win battles, but not the war, and the French could lose battles, but not the war. The English, realizing this early on, responded with grand raids into France called *chevauchee*. These raids were successful at first but by the 15th century were costing more than they were netting.[284] Henry's surprise victory at Agincourt, and the completeness of it, allowed for an opportunity to truly win the war, not just rake in loot and ransom.

However, it was not to be. Henry V died of illness in 1422, and the French did not accept his one-year-old son. When King Charles VI died, his son Charles VII, claimed the throne of France and proceeded to drive the English out.

Rather than march his army into the hail of arrows the English so customarily greeted the French with, Charles VII instead built up an impressive artillery train. Using modern cannons, Charles VII was able to defeat English fortresses and regain the initiative. Joan of Arc's appearance brought fresh vigor to the French armies, and for the first time in the long war, French victories became common.

With the English without a strong ruler, Charles VII's only other serious rival to the French throne was Burgundy. That problem solved itself when Charles the Bold, the Duke of Burgundy and great-grandfather to the Holy Roman Emperor Charles V, was killed in 1477 at the Battle of Nancy. Swiss foot soldiers armed with halberds butchered him and his invading army. Charles the Bold's body was found naked and heavily mutilated, which for the time was a scandalous end to a man of his station.[285] However, the facts were that the common soldiers had little regard for men of high birth, which put both worry and fear into the nobility. Charles' death marked the end of the Burgundian state, and the lands of Charles the Bold were contested by France and the Holy Roman Empire for years to come.

England's King, Henry VI, grew up under the thumb of his advisors, and when in 1453 all English territory in France was lost, except for Calais, he had a mental collapse. The king's weakness inspired his enemies. The king was deposed, but this led to further instability as two houses claimed the throne of England—the house of Lancaster, of which Henry VI was a part, and the house of York, whose leader was Edward.

The War of the Roses pitted the rival houses against one another, culminating at the Battle of Bosworth in 1485. The King at the time was Richard III of the house of York. The Lancastrian line had died out, but were replaced by Henry VII of the house of Tudor.

Richard III, wanting to end the war once and for all, led an armored cavalry charge straight for Henry VII. If he could kill Henry, then he could kill the Tudor cause. Richard's charge came within a lance thrust of ending the war, but Henry VII was able to find shelter among his mercenaries. Richard's cavalry force was surrounded and pushed back toward a marsh by a combination of mounted and foot soldiers.

Richard's horse lost its footing and he fell from it, but he refused to surrender or retreat, crying out,

---

284   David Nicole, The Great Chevauchée: John of Gaunt's Raid on France 1373, (New York: Osprey, 2011), 73.
285   Thomas A. Brady Jr., Politics and Reformations: Histories and Reformations, (Boston: Brill, 2007), 191.

"God forbid that I retreat one step. I will either win the battle as a king or die as one."[286]

He died as one. His body was mutilated and only recently re-discovered. Richard was the last English king to die on the battlefield, and his failed cavalry charge marked the end of England's reliance on armored knights.

Josh Warren of Broken Arm Swordsmanship in 15th century armor. Josh depicts a man-at-arms in Burgundian service. Armor in the 15th century steadily increased in its plate coverage thanks to armor making advancements. Compared to riveted chain links, plate was lighter and offered better protection, but required more skill to make. Photo courtesy Ann Warren, armor by Patrick Thaden and Josh Warren.

In Italy, mercenary warfare continued between the petty states and city-states. No one city could gain the upper hand on the other. The Pope's return to Rome from Avignon simply added another layer of complexity to the situation. Change occurred when the ruling despot of Milan, Ludovico, sought to use France as a way of tipping the balance of power in his favor. Instead, when Charles VIII invaded in 1494 with the intention of securing familial rights in Naples, he turned Italy into a

---

286   Michael Jones, Philippa Langley, The King's Grave, (New York: St. Martin's Press, 2013), 206.

warzone between various major states. Ludovico quickly discovered the French had no intention of making Milan masters of Italy and, worse, that Milan, despite a serious military reputation in Italy, could not contend with the much larger French army. French entry into Italy drew the Pope and the Holy Roman Empire into the fray. The Papacy had just left France and were now poised with France coming to them. The Holy Roman Empire was nominally in charge of Italy, but with French encroachments, they were forced to play a larger role.

Mercenaries continued to be employed in ever-greater numbers, and the situation remained highly complex. The French invasion was turned back by a unified body of Italians, but no sooner had the French left that the Italians returned to their typical in-fighting. The pattern would not change.

The many states of Italy in 1494. Further complicating the situation was the Ottoman threat to the East, France to the West and the Holy Roman Empire to the North.[287]

Spain was finally united by King Ferdinand and Queen Isabella. Together, they drove the Muslims out of the Iberian Peninsula with the fall of Granada in 1492. The victory had a global impact. Christopher Columbus, in the service of Spain, discovered the New World that same year. At the close of the 15th century, Spain was poised to be the most powerful state on Earth.

---

287   https://commons.wikimedia.org/wiki/File:Italy_1494_v2.png Creative Commons Share and Share Alike.

Peasant rebellions continued, though for different reasons than in the prior century. Jan Huss, a religious reformer from Prague, capital of Bohemia, was summoned to account for his issues with the Catholic Church and was burned at the stake for his trouble in 1415. The Holy Roman Emperor, Sigismund had granted Huss safe passage, but had allowed him to be burned. Complicating the matter, the Emperor's brother happened to be Wenceslaus, the King of Bohemia.

Huss' death sparked religious anger not only at the Catholic Church, but also at the King of Bohemia for allowing it to happen. The close relationship between the king and the Emperor reeked of conspiracy. Riots broke out and the King of Bohemia, Wenceslaus, died in 1419 after some of his representatives were tossed out of a tower window—supposedly from the shock of it all.[288]

With no heir of age, the king's widow, Sophia, was made regent, but the riots became a full-fledged rebellion.

The Papacy and Emperor threw armies at the Hussites but were turned back time and again. The Hussites used a ring of wagons, supplemented by gunpowder weaponry, to defeat the more traditional Imperial armies. As with many peasant armies, such as the rebels of Flanders and the Swiss at Nancy, the Hussites did not take prisoners.

Though victorious on the battlefield, the Hussites lacked a strong leader, and their cause was divided by internal factions. The more radical elements were defeated by those Hussites seeking compromise and peace within the Empire and the Catholic Church. This was achieved in 1434, but decades of warfare had left Bohemia still ravaged nearly 50 years after the rebellion.[289]

The 15th century saw tremendous changes in warfare. Author Geoffrey Parker goes so far as to say it was the end of the 15th century that brought about a military revolution to Europe, one in which traditional tactics gave way to the new. The armored knight was less viable, while the armored foot soldier was more so. Ranged weaponry took on an increasingly important role, and gunpowder dramatically changed the course of war, especially when it came to sieges. The state further increased its power by steadily eroding the military power of the nobility in England and France, while Poland went the opposite direction, empowering local magnates. The removal of Byzantium and the addition of a strong Poland, rising Russia and powerhouse Spain all dramatically changed European politics.

> Sometimes, even after you have so wounded an opponent, he is able to withdraw his sword and wound you. Your mistake in this case will be either failing to pass all the way to the opponent's body or failing to take the tempo correctly.
>
> - Salvator Fabris

---

288 International Journal of Humanities and Social Science Vol. 2 No. 4 [Special Issue – February 2012] 115 God's Warriors from the Czech Kingdom – the Terror of Central and Eastern Europe in the First Half of the 15th Century Doc. PhDr. David Papajík, PhD. P 120

289 Frederick Engels, "The Peasant War in Germany" contained in the *Collected Works of Karl Marx and Frederick Engels: Volume 10* (International Publishers: New York, 1978) p. 428.

A Hussite Wagenburg. Hussites, armed with flails, swords, axes, maces and gunpowder weapons, as well as crossbows, were able to defeat the more traditional Imperial armies. The religious rebellion, which included atrocities on both sides, was a taste of what was to come in the 16th century.[290]

16th Century

Gunpowder continued to change the way European wars were fought. Geoffrey Parker's central thesis in his *The Military Revolution* is that gunpowder led to three innovations that made Europe different than the rest of the world. These innovations were, in his mind, a revolution that spread, not unlike the Renaissance did.

First, gunpowder allowed field armies to deliver gunfire in the form of small and large arms on the battlefield. While early 16th century handheld firearms were primitive, by the close of the century the musket had come into being and would dominate European battlefields for another hundred years with little change. Cannons, meanwhile, improved dramatically, with Europeans discovering the optimum sizes to use for specific tasks.

---

290   https://commons.wikimedia.org/w/index.php?curid=1177786 Public Domain Art.

Second, the advancements in gunpowder led to radical redesigns of fortifications. Castles simply could not withstand the modern weaponry as had been seen in the closing years of the Hundred Years' War. To adapt, newer fortresses were built using steep ramps and sharp angles. An arms race between fortress designers and cannon-makers continued steadily.

Third, gunpowder was adapted to ships. Older methods of fighting at sea, which consisted of ramming and boarding actions, gave way to long-range gunnery. This was developed and improved upon by Europeans. The technological edge the Europeans had in naval terms cannot be overstated. Newer ships could travel longer and longer distances, allowing colonization of the planet, while the gunpowder weaponry meant there was little anyone outside of Europe could do to stop them.[291]

These three innovations led to greater societal changes. Wars became larger and more destructive—and required more effort to maintain. The nobility, who in the 14th century were responsible for raising troops, could not meet the demands of modern armies. Gradually, the nobility became the officers under increasingly larger state-run armies. There were exceptions, but the trend continued towards centralization of military power in the hands of the monarch. Meanwhile, the practice of using local militias for defense was used less-often.

The Ottoman Empire pushed farther into Europe. Wallachia and Hungary both fell to the Ottomans, whose fairly modern armies overwhelmed their feudal opponents. After the fall of Hungary, in the Battle of Mohacs in 1526, the Ottomans were a thorn in the side of the Holy Roman Emperor, Charles V. In 1529, Vienna, the capital of Austria and Charles V's personal domain, was placed under siege by Suleiman the Magnificent.

Rain, fierce resistance and, finally, snow forced the Ottomans back. This setback was exacerbated at sea 40 years later when an alliance of Catholic nations defeated the Ottoman navy at the Battle of Lepanto in 1571.

In Russia, Ivan IV, or Ivan the Terrible, strengthened the monarchy and made diplomatic inroads to the rest of Europe, including trade relations with England, which culminated in a marriage proposal to Queen Elizabeth I. She politely declined.

War and famine, however, brought ruin to the country, and Ivan IV grew suspicious of a rebellion. He harshly punished his nobles for even a whiff of treason and earned a reputation for cruelty against his own people.

He went through a total of seven wives, and killed his own son, by accident, in a dispute.

Ivan's heir was thus dead, and the next in line to be Tsar was Feodor I. Feodor was possibly mentally disabled, and he dampened relations with England. He sought to draw in other Europeans, but Russia remained a distant, backwater country to the rest of the continent. He died without an heir—ending the main line of the Rurik dynasty and inviting severe political instability in the next century.

Poland in the 16th century went through a curious transition that was mimicked in Bohemia and Hungary. In these Eastern European kingdoms, the nobility was able to gain the power of electing the king. While theoretically this was to be hereditary, it did not have to be. Because of the elective

---

291   Geoffrey Parker, The Military Revolution: Military Innovation and the Rise of the West, 1500-1800, Second Edition (New York, NY: Cambridge University Press, 1996). Chapter 1

nature of Poland's monarchy, it was possible for a man to be king of Poland and somewhere else. Poland would boast monarchs who also sat on the thrones of France, Transylvania, Sweden, Russia, and Saxony.[292]

Throughout the late 1500s, the Polish nobility exerted greater control over the monarchy, making Poland an unusual republic that fused with Lithuania to become the *Rzeczpospolita*, or Commonwealth.

Unlike the armies of Western Europe, the Polish armies remained reliant on cavalry but adapted to the changing nature of war by lengthening their lances and carrying firearms.

For France, the 16th century was a period of external and internal threat. While England had been, more or less, dealt with during the Hundred Years' War, the Hapsburgs came to be the bane of France. When Charles V became King of Spain and the Holy Roman Emperor, France was surrounded on all sides.

The French were aggressive to this encroachment and challenged the Hapsburgs wherever they could, including in the Low Countries and Italy, while at the same time offering support to anyone who would fight the Hapsburgs, even religious opponents. In 1536, Francis I and the Ottoman Suleiman the Magnificent formed a mutually beneficial alliance. Charles V, who had surrounded France with his domains, in turn found himself surrounded, with the French on one side and the Ottomans on the other.

Francis I used Protestantism as a tool to weaken the Holy Roman Empire, but the door swung both ways. French nobles, eager for independence, adopted Protestantism, which led to religious strife similar to that within the Holy Roman Empire.

In 1559, Henri II was killed in a joust, and France fell under the rule of his wife, Catherine Medici. A devout and ruthless Catholic, she invited Huguenots (French Protestants) to Paris, only to have them locked in the city and massacred. Religious war plagued France, and was not settled until Henri IV took the throne and granted Protestants rights and protection in the Edict of Nantes in 1598.[293]

Hal Siegel of Therion Arms in 14th century attire. Photo courtesy of www.TherionArms

292   Many of these monarchs could not balance two thrones and in some cases did not want them. Henri de Valois abandoned the Polish throne for the French one, while the Kings of Sweden found themselves just the Kings of Poland, and Władysław IV was able to only rule Russia in name and only for a short time.
293   Supposedly 6000-10,000 nobles died in duels during Henri IV's reign. James I thought Henri's death at the hands of an assassin was justice for his promotion of the duel.

Francois Dubois' depiction of the St. Bartholomew Day's Massacre where Protestant Huguenots were killed by Catholic mobs. All manner of weaponry is shown, including rapiers, spears, arming swords, sabers, clubs and firearms. Catherine Medici, dressed in black, can be seen in the upper left inspecting the dead bodies before they are tossed into the Seine River.[294]

During the 16th century, England was dominated by two figures. Henry VIII was the second son of Henry VII, who had won the War of the Roses. Henry VIII desired a strong dynasty, but when his Spanish wife did not produce any male heirs, he sought a divorce. The Pope denied him this, and Henry VIII took the drastic step of creating his own religion.

The Anglican Church was on the surface Catholic but replaced the Pope with the king. Henry VIII granted himself a divorce. This did not come without a cost. Henry VII had betrayed Spain and so had betrayed the Hapsburgs—and his invention of a new religion caused a great deal of religious turmoil at home.

Henry VIII's second wife bore him no sons, and so he found an excuse to execute her and spent the rest of his life hopping from wife to wife in hopes of a male heir. He had one legitimate son, but Edward VI was sickly.

In the late 16th century, Henry VIII's daughter from his second marriage took the throne. Queen Elizabeth enhanced England's power by defeating the Spanish Armada and expanding England's influence, with piracy, overseas. Her long reign was not without its crises, but was largely stable and successful.

---

294   https://commons.wikimedia.org/wiki/File:Francois_Dubois_001.jpg Public Domain Art.

Italy in the 16th century was divided as it always has been, but after the first Italian Wars, others followed—this time involving France, the Holy Roman Empire and Spain. The wealthy city-states were at the mercy of the much larger foreign nations. Italian writers were in shock that the most educated and cultured people in Europe were powerless in the face of foreign armies. Machiavelli attributed this weakness to the Italians' skillfulness in duels but lack of sense when it came to armies.

> Although military excellence seems to be extinct in Italy, this arises from the fact that the old methods were not good and there has been no one who knew how to devise new ones. We have great excellence in the members, if only it were not lacking in the heads. In duels and engagements between small numbers, see how superior the Italians are in strength, in dexterity, in resource. But when it comes to armies, they make no showing; and it all proceeds from the weakness of the heads.[295]

Italian battles were not about Italy as much as they were about the desires of other nations. In 1525, the Battle of Pavia saw the Renaissance armies of France go up against the German and Spanish forces of the Hapsburgs. During the battle, the French king, Francis I, was captured and placed in the care of his long-time enemy Charles V. Italians mattered very little in the epic battle fought on their soil, which was truly about the struggle between Charles V and Francis I.

The Battle of Pavia 1525 depicted on a Brussels tapestry. The battle included pike, shot and artillery, marking it rather modern in nature.[296]

In Spain, the discovery of the New World by Christopher Columbus in 1492 allowed for massive expansion. Spanish colonies dotted North and South America and the Caribbean, as well as parts of Africa and Asia. Wealth poured in from the colonies but led to inflation throughout Europe that was not fully understood. Charles V became King of Spain, but was also the Holy Roman Emperor.

---

295 Niccolo Machiavelli, The Prince (Mineola: Dover Thrift, 1992), Chapter XXVI.
296 https://commons.wikimedia.org/wiki/File:Battle_of_Pavia.jpg Public Domain Art.

This single powerful monarch had too much to control, and when he stepped down, he gave his son Spain and his brother the Germans.

In 1588, under the reign of Phillip II, the Spanish Armada was defeated by the English navy, setting the stage for an end to Spain's meteoric rise.

The Holy Roman Empire was devoured from within and without.

War took on incredibly destructive overtones with the onset of religious strife. The Catholic Church had been flagging under the weight of both its own corruption and of European politics, in which monarchs were exerting ever more control. Reformers, such as Jan Huss, were silenced or burned.

When Martin Luther decried the practices of indulgences with his *95 Theses*, the stage was set for an upending of society.

Luther was protected by various northern princes within the Holy Roman Empire and opposed by the papacy and by Emperor Charles V. While there was an attempt to get Luther to come to terms at the Diet of Wurms, nothing came of it except Luther's insistence that he was right and the Catholic Church could not prove him wrong.

War broke out between the Protestants and Catholics within the Empire. Charles V at the same time was plagued with assaults from France and the Ottomans, as well as the Pope in Rome, who was quick to side with France in hopes of undermining Imperial authority.

The Pope's decision to side with Francis I would lead to a largely German army of Protestants sacking Rome in 1527. Pope Clement VII was captured and placed into the hands of an angry Charles V to go alongside the captive French monarch, Francis I.

In what took tremendous willpower and a serious toll on the Emperor's well-being, Charles V was able to bring his many enemies to heel. In doing so, he did not win lasting victory as much as establish a temporary peace.

Cuis regio, eius religio was the policy set down in 1555, which temporarily brought stability to the Holy Roman Empire. The various rulers of the Empire could pick the religion of their people and the Emperor would accept that.

The 16th century brought about the Reformation, which led to political turmoil and war throughout Western Europe. Eastern Europe was largely spared such issues, with Poland having tremendous religious toleration and Russia being Orthodox and not having the same problems as the Catholic Church.

Gunpowder dramatically changed the nature of warfare, but by no means made swords and lances obsolete. The costs of war, both literally and in human suffering, rose at the same time as inflation due to excesses of gold and silver brought in from the New World.

> If you want to avenge yourself, break the four openings with skill
> - Liechtenauer's Zettel

Charles V sits upon his throne with his various enemies tied to his foot and well under his control, including Suleiman the Magnificent, Pope Clement VII, Francis I, and various Imperial electors.[297]

17th Century

Many of the political issues of the 16th century flared up once more in the 17th century. The dynamics of France set against Spain and the Holy Roman Empire remained. Religious issues thought settled, returned and were more destructive than before.

Warfare continued along the same trends as before, with gunpowder taking on an increasing role. In Western Europe, pike and shot became the mainstay of armies, and the cavalry's role was less about an armored breakthrough and more about securing the flanks and, with fortune, getting behind the enemy. The use of professional soldiers over militias continued, with one commander in 1622 saying dismissively of local levies,

---

[297] https://en.wikipedia.org/wiki/Charles_V,_Holy_Roman_Emperor#/media/File:Charles_V_enthroned_over_his_defeated_enemies_Giulio_Clovio_mid_16th_century.jpg 5-27-2-2016 Public Domain Old.

> "If one wishes to skirmish with [kitchen maids] in white aprons, then any of them is good enough; but to go into the field, storm fortifications, they are useless fops."[298]

Armor largely vanished from the battlefield during the 17th century, save for helmets and breastplates. While there were some attempts to maintain fully-armored cavalry, the gun proved simply too strong and armor too expensive.

European culture flourished, but war was common and massive economic hardships only increased.

The Ottoman Empire made a final bid to conquer Europe, besieging Vienna in 1683. As before, the city held out and reinforcements arrived, culminating in Poland's mounted army crashing into the Ottoman camp.

In 1687, the Holy Roman Empire defeated the Ottomans at the second Battle of Mohacs. Although in the first battle, the Ottomans had superior technology, in the second, the Hapsburgs commanded an army far more modern than the Ottomans were prepared for. Hungary was largely liberated, leading to a Hapsburg dual state of Austria and Hungary that would survive the collapse of the Holy Roman Empire.

While the Ottomans were defeated, they remained in Europe as a continual presence into the 20th century. Their empire was on the decline throughout, with pieces of it breaking away or being liberated, such as Hungary in 1699.

For Russia, the early 17th century was disastrous. The death of Tsar Feodor I led to the Time of Troubles, a period of massive instability in Russia. There was no clear heir, and false heirs and warring nobles tore the country apart. A Polish noble, for a time, had the chance to rule after taking Moscow, but no one could settle Russia. War, famine, Polish intervention and pretender kings crippled the land.

In 1613, a Grand Assembly of Russian nobles elected Michael Romanov to be Tsar. The Poles were driven out and Russia had a period of recovery.

The close of the century brought Peter the Great to the throne. Peter, wanting to learn about the rest of Europe, traveled incognito. He worked in shipyards, hosted raucous parties, explored and, most importantly, learned how far behind his country was compared to others. Throughout his reign, which stretched into the 18th century, Peter modernized Russia, creating a navy, using military tactics similar to France's, building the city of St. Petersburg and the Winter Palace and challenging Sweden for the Baltic.

Poland experienced a Golden Age during the first part of the 17th century under the Commonwealth. Polish nobles had tremendous power over their king, and each powerful magnate was largely independent.

Poland did not involve itself overly much in the Thirty Years' War and allowed a fair degree of religious tolerance with few issues.

Wars with Russia proved costly, and dynastic struggle with their Swedish king led to war. In the

---

298   B. Anne Tlusty, The Martial Ethic in Early Modern Germany: Civic Duty and the Right of Arms, (New York: Palgrave Macmillan, 2011), 4.

Deluge, Sweden and Russia invaded Poland in the mid-1600s. This war caused untold damage that was comparable to the excesses of the Nazis in World War II. Poland was ravaged and survived but had lost the Ukraine to Russia.

A resurgence of Polish power came when they relieved the city of Vienna in 1683 under King Jan Sobieski, but this was a brief moment. As neighboring states, such as Prussia, Austria and Russia, centralized their authority, Poland remained de-centralized and unable to prevent the encroachment of their enemies.

King Jan Sobieski meets with Emperor Leopold I. Polish assistance saved Vienna and irrevocably turned back the Ottomans from further encroachment into Europe.[299]

In terms of their military, the Polish army was divided roughly in two. The Royal Army was built along Western lines with a reliance on pike and shot; the other half was larger and used traditional cavalry tactics but adapted them to the modern battlefields. Polish hussars, for example, used lances that were hollow, light-weight and just a bit longer than the pikes of the foot soldiers.[300]

In the 16th century, Charles V dominated politics and war. In the 17th century, the French King Louis XIV, the Sun King, did the same. Louis increased royal power, exerting divine right and setting a model for other monarchs through Absolutism. The nobles were placed firmly in his control and became employees, of a sort, or were kept as guests at the Palace of Versailles, under the watchful eye of the king.

---

299   https://commons.wikimedia.org/wiki/File:Grottger-Jan_III_Sobieski_i_Leopold_I_pod_Schwechat.jpg Public Domain Old.
300   Richard Brezezinski, Polish Armies 1569-1696, (London: Osprey, 1987), 23.

Richard Marsden and John Patterson of the Phoenix Society of Historical Swordsmanship demonstrate a 17th century Polish duel, in which many Western customs were followed- though not always!

French religious policy reversed, with the Edict of Nantes being revoked and Protestants ordered to convert or leave the country.

Louis XIV's wars were numerous and fought against France's traditional enemy, the Hapsburgs. Louis XIV, like Francis I before him, sought many ways to pick, prod and strike at the Imperial domains of the Hapsburgs. Such was Louis' might that large alliances were formed to prevent French expansion.

His stance against dueling, in Voltaire's opinion, was just another effort to control the masses rather than any moral outrage at the practice.[301] It was also that desire to control all things that made the Sun King a tremendous figure in his age, whose armies were always on the march and whose long reign left a lasting mark.

England during the 17th century did not deeply involve itself in the Thirty Years' War but had its own issues in the mid-1600s with civil war. Charles I was a dual monarch, King of England and Scotland. He had tried to rule England without Parliament and increase his authority over the entire British Isles. When he attempted to force Scotland to practice Anglican-style Christianity, it was too much. Scotland rebelled and when the king tried to force taxes and loans, Parliament rebelled. The English Civil War saw both armies equipped with pike and shot. Royalist victories lacked follow-through and Parliamentarian victories failed to capture the king.

The Parliamentarian army reformed itself, becoming the New Model Army, which used such innovations as standardized training and weaponry. However, they were independent of

---

301 V.G Kiernan, The Duel, (Oxford: Oxford University Press, 1988), 97.

Parliamentarian control and would later be used against them. Furthermore, the leadership of the army was Puritan in nature, which put them at odds with those seeking religious tolerance.

Charles I was captured, and attempts to negotiate with him failed. He was tried by a very much reduced Parliament and executed in 1649. This was a shocking state of affairs in Europe, but England's island status made invasion difficult, and the ravages of the Thirty Years' War made it all but impossible.

For a time, England existed under a Commonwealth headed by a Lord Protector, Oliver Cromwell, who was a strict Puritan. Cromwell increased his power over the state as Parliament after Parliament failed to govern. His death came without a clear plan of succession and Charles I's son, Charles II, was allowed to return to England. The monarchy was thus restored in 1660.

The United Provinces of the Low Countries formed in the late 16th century and had become an economic and naval powerhouse in the 17th century. However, the Dutch were small and surrounded by hostile neighbors. A series of spectacular naval victories and drastic measures at home kept the country from being divided up by larger countries. The Dutch fought both the English and French, sometimes at the same time. William of Orange eventually made peace with England and married Charles II's niece, Mary.

After Charles II's death, his brother James II inherited the throne and followed too closely in the footsteps of his father for comfort. Parliament overthrew him and instituted a Constitutional Monarchy that was ruled jointly by William of Orange and James' daughter Mary. The Glorious Revolution of 1688 put Great Britain on the road toward democratic rule in stark contrast to the Absolutism so common on the continent.

The Italians during the 17th century remained powerless in their own affairs. As had been the pattern since the late 1490s, France and the Holy Roman Empire, and later Austria, waged war back and forth over who would control the peninsula.

While Spain had been a powerhouse in the 1500s, the 1600s brought trouble. The defeat of the Spanish Armada in 1588 severely weakened their naval ambitions. The Hapsburg wars with the Valois dynasty of France brought little success. Meanwhile, Spanish attempts to control the New World and Asia failed as Dutch, English and French colonies appeared.

Spanish holdings in the Low Countries slipped, and their military tactics were outperformed by newer German, Dutch and later Swedish methods.

The Spanish used *tercios*, which were large blocks of pikes supported by arquebus-armed soldiers. Although it was a very effective method, military treatises, including Dutch and German, recommended smaller formations of men that were more tactical on the battlefield.

The 17th century destroyed the Holy Roman Empire in all but name. Charles V's peace broke when his grand-nephew, Ferdinand II, engaged in the Thirty Years' War. From 1618 to 1648, Imperial armies filled with mercenaries and even led by them did battle against Protestants and the French. The results of the war were destructive.

> And guard yourself from all parries which the simple fencers execute...
> - Ringeck

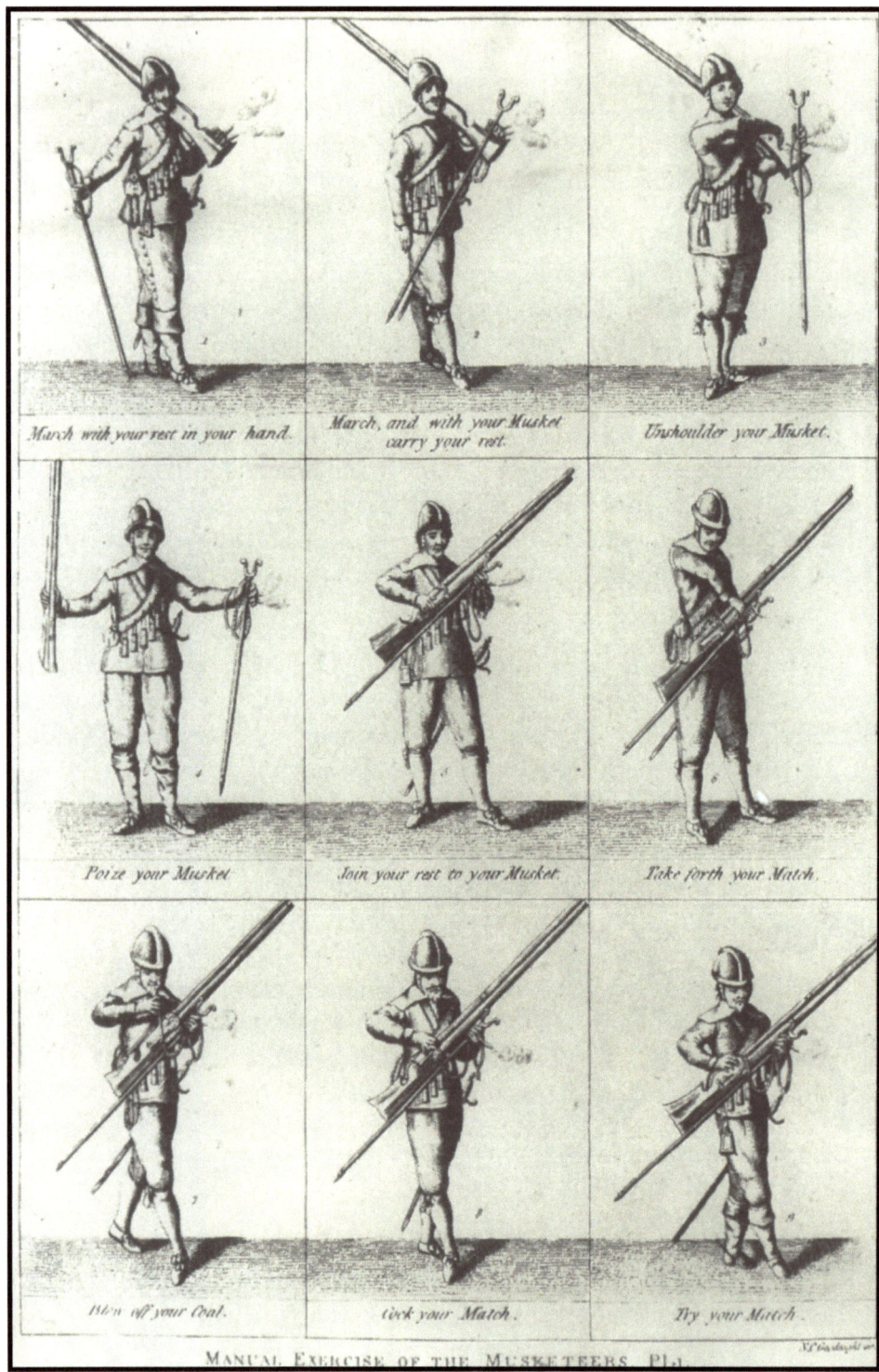

Military treatises from the 17th century gave instructions on the use of arms, such as the handling of an arquebus.[302]

The Empire was shattered, and though it existed on paper, the reality was that after the Peace of Westphalia, there was no Holy Roman Empire. Instead, there was Hapsburg Austria in the south and a variety of German kingdoms in the North, including Prussia.

---

302   https://commons.wikimedia.org/wiki/File:Manual_of_the_Musketeer,_17th_Century.jpg Public Domain Art.

Sweden demonstrated tremendous power during the war, led by Gustavus Adolphus, but when he was killed in battle, Swedish influence in the war diminished. Sweden's tactics, however, endured, which used lines of men who delivered a volley of gunfire before charging. The Swedish method of thinner lines and longer fields of fire supplanted the older methods of massed formations of pikemen.

18th Century

The horrific nature of the wars of the 17th century brought about an attempt to sanitize and rationalize warfare. Armies modernized and developed tactics that would endure for a century.

Infantry, armed with muskets and equipped with bayonets, were supported by field artillery, moved into position by teams of horses and cavalry of the heavy and light variety. Only heavy cavalry wore armor, and even then, this was relegated to a breastplate and open-faced helmet.

Officers of the military were to be gentlemen while the common soldiers were to be brutally beaten automatons. Linear tactics were also dominant in naval warfare, where European ships would line up to deliver tremendous broadsides.

Although in the 17th century mass reprisals against the civilian population and wholesale massacres over religious issues were the norm, the wars of the 18th century were conducted in fields, almost by agreement, far from populated centers.

While the rules and customs of 18th century warfare may seem foolish, they were a direct response to the horrors of the 17th century.

Russia eclipsed Sweden in the early 17th century as a major power. The Swedish King, Charles XII, and the Russian Tsar, Peter the Great, conducted a long-running war over the Baltic. Sweden lacked the population to engage in such a war, and their monarch lacked the ability to sue for peace—ever.

Charles XII was killed in a siege, and Sweden at last sued for peace with a victorious Russia. The Treaty of Nystad ended the Great Northern War in 1721. Russia from this point on became a major European player, with a modern-style army that could handle other European states. Russian expansion continued from the Baltic into Poland, which was carved apart in the late 1700s.

Poland ceased to exist during the 18th century. A weak government combined with aggressive neighbors led to a series of treaties that ultimately saw Poland carved up between Prussia, Russia and Austria. The Polish army was still mostly mounted and used the lance, which had been abandoned in Western Europe.

France, England, Prussia, Russia and Spain all engaged in wars with one another. These wars were not epic religious struggles, nor plans to conquest entire countries. Instead, the wars were for what usually amounted to small gains. The War of the Spanish Succession, the War of the Austrian Succession and the Seven Years' War changed the map of Europe only slightly, though, overseas, Britain wrested away Canada and India from the French.

Rebellions were common, including the Spanish Catalan and the Scottish Jacobite uprisings.

The armies of Europe looked and behaved similarly, with a few notable exceptions. Prussia's King Frederick the Great, for example, placed a line of soldiers behind his main line to use in oblique movements. He also drafted soldiers in their thousands so that Prussia was an army that had a country rather than a country with an army! When the Scottish rebelled, they went to war using broadswords and small shields called a *targes*, fighting in a style reminiscent of prior centuries.

Strategy was less about battlefield tactics and more about forcing fortresses to surrender, or getting the enemy to engage in a pitched battle on unfavorable ground. Behind all of it was discipline. Armies that could line up, shoot and be shot at were victorious, and armies that could not fled under withering musket fire or the bayonet charge.

The nations of Europe racked up huge debts in the 18th century to fund their wars. These debts led to instability. The American and French Revolutions of the late 18th century were both products of heavy taxation due to the wars. In turn, these Revolutions sparked long-lasting wars and the rise of Napoleon in Europe, as well as a new and major power in the form of the United States across the Atlantic.

Prussian soldiers march in rows ready to deliver a volley of musket fire.[303]

> Whosoever wants to engage in the knightly art of fencing, in whichever arms they may be, fighting mounted or on foot, he must have these attitude or attributes, to whit, if he wants to perform the plays, he shall have four qualities, that is strong as a courageous lion, keen-eyed as an eagle, fast as a lynx and cunning as a fox.
>
> - Paulus Hector Mair

---

[303] https://upload.wikimedia.org/wikipedia/commons/9/9a/Hohenfriedeberg_-_Attack_of_Prussian_Infantry_-_1745.jpg Public Domain Art.

Weapons

Weapons used in the fencing treatises were varied. As warfare and attitudes toward dueling changed, weapons altered as well.

From the 14th to 16th century, the weapons depicted in the treatises could be used in a variety of settings, ranging from a judicial duel to self-defense to the battlefield.

The 16th century Italian masters were seeking a universal system in which their methods could be applied anywhere. However, the trend was more and more directed at civilian armament rather than military.

Christopher Nelson of the Phoenix Society of Historical Swordsmanship with a longsword. Longswords were popular in the 14th and 15th century.

The latter part of the 16th century and the 17th century saw a change as the wearing of a sword became more common and the private duel, *a la mazzza*, took hold.[304] The side sword became popular, followed by the rapier. The weapons used by civilians for daily wear were not as applicable on the battlefield and were more suited for dueling and self-defense. Fabris outright states that his method, and thus the rapier, is for dueling, while Bruchius demurs stating that the weapon is best used for self-defense. Neither speaks of the battlefield. This lack of battlefield application was a fact George Silver latched onto in his complaints about the Italian rapier that was becoming popular in England in the late 16th century. Silver's single-handed broadsword was, in his view, a far better weapon because it could be used in a variety of settings.

Despite Silver's complaints, the rapier became the mainstay weapon of civilian wear throughout Western Europe. In Poland, the saber was still worn as a symbol of the nobility's privileges, but rapiers were not unheard of.

The rapier's decline came about at the end of the 17th century. A smaller, lighter weapon—the small sword—became popular. These weapons were not for the battlefield but were entirely for civilian dress. They were light-weight, compact and manageable so that tasks that could be cumbersome with the rapier, such as sitting in a chair, were made easy. The 18th century treatises, like Angelo's, were set in a duel, with a few applications for a fight in a self-defense setting.

Laws on the right to carry arms varied, with local communities having restrictions. This is not to say people were not allowed to have weapons, as violent as Europe was, it was entirely normal to be armed. Urban areas could even require it, as the population might be expected to take up arms. The 16th century saw a change in these attitudes. Professional soldiers, mercenary or state-funded, largely replaced militias. Cities and towns attempted, with various success, to limit the weaponry of the populace.[305]

Categorizing weapons is a task outside the scope of this book. Broad terms are used for the sake of brevity and the modern era has added generic terms where historically there may have been none.[306] Classification of weapons can be difficult, partially because the common parlance today was not the same used in the past. A "sword" in a German treatise might mean a longsword while a "sword" in an Italian treatise might mean a rapier. For ease of discussion, popular modern terms are used to classify weaponry.

> ...[If dueling is not stopped] every man shall bear the sword not to defend, but to assail, and private men begin to presume to give law to themselves, and to right their own wrongs, no man can foresee the danger and inconveniences that may arise and multiply there upon.
> - King James I of England

---

304 As the middle-class grew in power they took to wearing swords. In the medieval era this would have been something only a knight or noble could do.
305 B. Anne Tlusty, The Martial Ethic in Early Modern Germany: Civic Duty and the Right of Arms, (New York: Palgrave Macmillan, 2011), 10-11.
306 Ewart Oakshott has a typology which categorizes various swords.

Rapiers and daggers. Rapiers were popular in the 17th century. Period terminology could be rather vague and 19th, 20th and even 21st century researchers continually search for the best way to classify historical weaponry.

14th Century

The earliest fencing treatise is *MS I.33*, which depicts monks using single-handed swords and bucklers. The weapon has various names, including one-handed sword, single-handed sword, short sword, or arming sword. The sword and buckler remained a popular combination throughout Europe even into the 17th century, though Fabris said it was not used by gentlemen.

MS I.33. Monks form guards with their sword and buckler. The sword is held in one hand and can be used to cut or thrust, while the buckler was a small shield for the hand.[307]

---

307 https://commons.wikimedia.org/wiki/File:Ms_I33_fol_32r.jpg Public Domain Art.

Charles Buschmann and Adam Simmons of the Phoenix Society of Historical Swordsmanship demonstrate guards, or wards, from I.33.

15th Century

The treatises of the 15th century mostly concern themselves with the longsword. The longsword is a weapon that could be held with one hand or two and had a variety of shapes depending on the time period. Blades, overall, grew more slender so as to be used to thrust as armor became more protective from the cut. Overall, they weighed less than three pounds, with exceptions being those blades meant for armored combat.[308]

> Note, this is when you come to him with the onset: you shall not watch or await his cut as he executes it against you. Because all fancers who watch and wait upon another's cut and wish to do nothing else than parry, they permit such art little joy because they often become struck with it.
> — Ringeck

---

308   A Medieval Italian pound was an approximate measure equal to 300-350 g, or 0.66 to 0.77 standard pounds. Fiore indicated the sword, for armored combat, should be 5 to 7 [Italian] pounds, so taking the upper and lower values as bounds, this gives a potential range of 3.3 to 5.4 lbs.

A longsword depicted in Fiore de Liberi's the Flower of Battle.[309]

Other weapons that were common included the dagger or rondel[310], poleaxe, spear and lance as well as the use of the sword in one hand. All of these can be found in the *Flower of Battle* by Fiore de Liberi. German manuscripts, like Paulus Kal's include the longsword, but also the short sword, messer, a large knife, and the dueling shield.

---

309   Digital image courtesy of the Getty's Open Content Program.
310   A rondel was a dagger that was more akin to an ice-pick, and suitable for going through armor, or padded coats.

Masters from the Flower of Battle. The first depicts a master preventing an attack with a dagger, while the others show guards to form when using the poleaxe, spear or lance. Fiore also covers the use of a large bladed polearm on foot, the staff, and even tree branches.[311]

> ...this knightly art of manhood was afforded and established by the learned and wise, also by the kings and princes as leaders of lands and kingdoms, which was done for the reason that land and people, widows and orphans would be kept in peace, calm and liberty, protected and saved from tyrants.
>
> - Paulus Hector Mair

311 Digital image courtesy of the Getty's Open Content Program.

From Talhoffer, two men engage in a judicial duel. They toss spears before they rush in to close.[312]

16th Century

The treatises of the 16th century were mostly written in German, Italian and even in Latin. The sheer volume of weaponry they show is tremendous.

The longsword, single-handed sword, dagger, spear, staff, poleaxe and lance remained popular, as well as the dussack, a wooden or metal weapon that was used in one hand, the messer, halberds, long staves, greatswords and sides-words, which included longer, thinner blades and were proto-rapiers with names such as *espada ropera*. There were also more traditional side swords, such as the broadsword favored by George Silver. For sporting purposes, the Germans developed a training longsword called a *federschwert*.

The term "rapier" itself can be difficult to place in the source material. Italian texts did not specifically use the word. They used "sword," no matter what was depicted, while English translations of Italian texts called out the rapier as a unique type of weapon. What is important to know is that in the 16th

---

312   Image courtesy the Royal Library of Copenhagen.

century, side swords that could cut and thrust were fashionable and over time had more complicated hand guards and gradually became longer and thinner.

In Poland, Russia and Hungary, the saber was the customary sidearm throughout the 16th century. They were larger weapons, whose knuckle-guards, if they had them, consisted of a chain attached to one of the large quillions.

Dussack of the 16th century.[313]

---

313 Image courtesy RJ McKeehan.

A soldier armed with a halberd, side sword and buckler.[314]

---

314 https://commons.wikimedia.org/wiki/File:Weiditz_Trachtenbuch_031-032.jpg Public Domain Art.

From a Dutch fencing manual of the late 1500s depicting the rapier and dagger. Early rapiers were stouter and not as long or thin as later period ones.[315]

17th Century

For gentlemen, the rapier was the dominant weapon throughout the 17th century, and many treatises on their use in a duel were produced. Salvator Fabris, Capoferro, and Giganti were three Italians who wrote about the rapier and were followed up by non-Italians who mimicked their systems, such as Joannes Georgius Bruchius of the Netherlands and Joachim Köppen from Magdeburg. Treatises for the rapier were also created by the Dutch, Spanish, Germans, French and English. The weapon could be seen worn at the hip throughout most of Western Europe and was as much fashionable as it was functional.

Not all rapiers are the same, and over the 17th century they tended to become longer and thinner, to the point that Gérard Thibault d'Anvers noted that men had lost the ability to gracefully draw their swords. Laws were even passed to try to limit their lengths.[316]

---

315   https://commons.wikimedia.org/wiki/File:VAULT_Case_MS_Fol.U.423.792_11r.png Public Domain Art.
316   Robert Chambers, Chamber's Journal of Popular Literature, Science and Arts, (1877), 142.

Other weapons or defensive items were to be found as well, such as the dagger, which could accompany a rapier, as could a buckler, shield, or cloak.

The greatsword remained as a viable weapon, though likely for a bodyguard or solider and not a gentleman walking about town.

Outside of Western Europe, the saber remained popular in Poland, Russia and the Ottoman Empire. The guards changed, using a metal knucklebow and times a ring for the thumb. In the late 17th century the saber became somewhat fashionable in Italy according to Francesco Marcelli in his treatise.

Greatswords in the 17th century were so large that they were not worn in sheathes, but carried over the shoulder like one would carry a polearm.[317]

---

317 https://commons.wikimedia.org/wiki/File:Bremer_Soldaten_-_Koster-Chronik_-_17._Jahrhundert.jpg Public Domain Art.

Richard Marsden of the Phoenix Society of Historical Swordsmanship with a saber, in 17th century Polish attire. The szabla was the name for the saber in Poland. It was a requirement for all nobles, called szlachta, to wear.

18ᵗʰ Century

The 18ᵗʰ century saw the last swords to be worn by civilians in the form of the small sword and spadroon. The small sword was exclusively a thrusting weapon and easier to manage on the hip than a rapier. Like the rapier, the small sword and its stouter cousin, the spadroon, were a part of fashionable attire and could be used to settle differences between gentlemen. Unlike the rapier, they were not overly long or heavy.

The pistol, by this point, was becoming the more common weapon to duel with, especially as the century progressed.

Few other weapons were worn by civilians in the 18ᵗʰ century, though a walking stick or hidden dagger would not be uncommon.

In most of Western Europe, gone were the days of wearing any form of protective gear, such as a buckler, or walking about town with a large weapon, such as a greatsword.

In some cases, such as with the Highlander Scots, the older weapons could be found. They wore daggers and large single-handed swords with basket hilts, called broadswords, backswords or claymores, and they carried a small shield called a targe. The Spanish, meanwhile, according to Domenico Angelo, were still wearing rapiers, and in Poland, the saber was still worn by the nobility until the dissolution of the 1790s.

Military men wore spadroons or sabers and would continue to wear swords well into the 19ᵗʰ century.

Under the gaze of seconds, one duelist defeats another, using a small sword, with a passata soto.[318]

---

318   1897 The Graphic hand colored wood engraving titled, "Types of Old Swordsmanship: A Duel with Small Swords in 1760." Public Domain Art.

Lee Smith of Blood and Iron coaches his students. Lee has won over dozens of tournaments and pursues HEMA as a professional career. His effort to have excellence in HEMA is boundless and his school continues to produce top-rated historical fencers.

Jake Norwood of Capital Kunst des Fechtens instructs Joseph Brassey of Grit-City HEMA. Jake has been a tremendous promoter of the modern HEMA movement, bringing world-wide attention to the art, helping to organize major events as well as compete in them. Photo courtesy of Mandy Michels Photography.

Skye Hilton of the Davenriche European Martial Artes School adjusting her armor.

The Masters and Their Treatises

The word "nation" does not easily apply when discussing Historical European Martial Arts because the concept of nation did not fully exist. While a great many of the 15th century treatises were written in German and, colloquially, are called German, the term is not quite right. Germany did not exist as a nation in the 15th century, nor would it until the latter half of the 19th century. Italian works may indeed be written in Italian, but there was no unified Italian nation, just as there was no unified German nation.

John Patterson and Charles Buschmann of the Phoenix Society of Historical Swordsmanship demonstrate Fiore's Posta di Choda Longa and the German Ochs guard.

It can be tempting to lump everyone from a region into a national style, however, this is a bit too simplistic. While all fencing from the region of Italy might be called, the Italian School of Fencing, this is in error because there are large differences to what Italians were doing in the 15th, 16th and 17th century ranging from style of presenting information to the terminology that was used. Furthermore, in the case of the Italians, their style of fencing spread throughout Europe and influenced other traditions.

The concept of nation did exist, even if the states did not. In the 16th century, Meyer refers to the German attitude toward fencing and Machiavelli speaks of the Italians as a people. Many of the treatises call out national traits when it comes to fencing. Silver derides the Italians, while Henning speaks poorly of the Polish. Pride for a nation could also be grounds for a duel as national honor did exist. There were national differences in fencing, even if the political boundaries were not as unified as they are today.

Father Jezierski put it best in the 18th century when describing fencing and nationality:

> It seems that, just as merriment has its own outward ways of expression, where the national character is exhibited in various dances, so the movements resulting from anger influence the ways one uses steel.[319]

The word "master" today has a connotation of expertise, but historically a master was simply one who taught. Within a guild context, he was one who had been judged by his guild-brothers as competent enough to teach others and judge other men who desired the title of master. Generically, anyone who taught fencing was called a master, and the term fencing-master was just as likely to draw up negative images as positive.

The masters themselves varied in who they were, but there are general trends that can be seen in their treatises. The masters provided text to work from that includes guards, which are places to wait and plays, which are techniques. Pictures were not always provided, but when they were, they often showed guards while the plays were depicted as complete. The material they had to work with was not cheap. Before the printing press, treatises were manuscripts written on vellum. Art and text was sparse by necessity. This expensive process was eased by the invention of the printing press in the mid 15th century, but it was not immediately adopted and artwork remained a costly endeavor. Today, in which photography and printing are cheap, the masters may have shown hundreds of pictures and written pages of text explaining a technique, but in the past they were limited by the materials available and high costs.

The masters were confronted with how to express martial arts in the written word sometimes with or without pictures. Even simple concepts proved difficult to explain, while other concepts were considered so basic as to be ignored.

Meyer in his treatise apologizes for discussing footwork, given the marketplace was sure to teach it, while later rapier treatises sometimes say nothing at all specifically about footwork. Holding a sword, a rather core concept of swordsmanship, is barely mentioned in earlier sources and glossed over in later ones.

Masters were confronted with difficult concepts to write about. How should the distance between the fighters be measured? There was no universal form of measurement until the modern era and even the use of exact local measurements was of little use. Henning noted that, given God made everyone differently, what exactly was a pace?

Treatises use different terminology for distance. Fiore de Liberi for example uses the terms *gioco largo* to discuss plays done at a wider distance and *gioco stretto* to discuss plays done at close range,

---

319   Translated by Daria Izdebska.

such as grappling. The German masters use different terminology, such as the *zufechten*, to discuss a distance where a fighter was a step away from being able to hit his opponent, and also a step away from being out of range. The *krieg* was where fighters were much closer to one another and where the binding of blades occur, while the *abzug* was the withdraw. In the 16th century, the concepts of fencing distance were melded with Aristotle's view of distance and time called measure and tempo. 16th and 17th century Italian masters refer to being out of measure, or unable to reach the opponent even with a step. Being in wide measure and able to reach the opponent with a step or lunge. Finally, being in close measure, where grappling was a distinct possibility.

Time was another concept masters approached in different ways, if at all. For the Germans, *vor*, 'before' and *nach*, 'after' sufficed, with further terminology used to discuss what to do when blades crossed. Italians of the 16th century used Aristotle's concept of time as moments of action. These moments were called tempo. To cut required two tempos by raising and lowering the arm, while to thrust took one, by extending the arm. To seize a tempo was to attack while an opponent provided an opening by moving or being still. Meanwhile, in England, George Silver divided time up into true and false times to determine which actions were the quickest. A hand, for example, could move faster than a foot.

The masters were not necessarily themselves duelists. Fiore mentions the five duels he fought, but the majority of the other masters make no mention of dueling. Some had military experience, such as L'Ange, while others were noted for their fencing performances such as Thibault, and most make no mention at all about their practical experiences.

They were generally not of noble birth. Fiore was a likely knight, but most of the other masters were of common blood no matter if they called their art knightly or not.

They were dependent on others. The masters sold the art of fencing, and though Manciolino likened other schools and masters to selling the art as if it were a whore, he was chasing patronage like the rest. Successful masters, like Fiore, Fabris and Thibault were invited into the courts of Dukes, Kings and Princes, or like Meyer, died in pursuit of such an opportunity. A majority of the treatises are dedicated to a noble patron of some sort.

They were secretive. Liechtenauer wrote in a poem that without explanation is undecipherable. Fiore kept his art a secret and only decided to put his system into writing so as to be remembered and only then by an elite few. Brantome in the late 16th century noted that the Italians kept secrets that even he could not pry out from them, while L'Ange's fencing treatise ends with a list of secrets he would not teach except in person.

The masters knew what few did. In the early traditions, the masters gave advice on how to fence against unskilled or wildly swinging opponents. Fiore calls them villains or *villiens* in reference to commoners. The Germans called those who swung with too much power *büffels*, or buffalos. In later traditions the masters, such as Giganti, remind their readers that though many gentlemen carry swords, few know how to use them.

Most of the masters did not write in English, and even if they did, it was in an older form. In today's world, this can make understanding their work difficult because a single word in the native language might have multiple meanings, all of them being relevant. Today's HEMA researchers and translators have to massage and tweak the archaic Latin, Italian, German and even English into something readable, which in turn brings forth interpretation.

The following is not an exhaustive list of the master's treaties, but rather, a selection to help further demonstrate themes and trends within Historical European Martial Arts.

Italy

A recreation of a binding of the swords from the Paris version of the Flower of Battle.[320]

The Italians boast one of the oldest fencing treatises available, that of Fiore de Liberi, whose four surviving copies were made in the early 15th century. This medieval system was meant for the highest classes of society and wasn't well-known outside their courts until Vadi, in his own words, revealed them and made them more a science and thus a perfect art. Fiore's and Vadi's works were not widely adopted, or if they were, there are no follow-up masters or records indicating as such.

The Italians are also credited with the customs of the private and unregulated duel in the 1500s, which Brantome called the duel *a la mazza*. It was the Italians who created much of the ritual, rules and informal regulations of private dueling throughout Europe by modifying prior legal combat. They were also the ones most likely to use trickery as a means of winning a duel.

Brantome, in his accounts on duels of the late 16th century, cites endless examples of the Italians' cleverness, which he was both disgusted with for its lack of honor and impressed by for its sheer ingenuity.[321]

---

320   Recreation by Ashton Warren.
321   Brantome recounts a variety of tricks in which, the duelist required he and his opponent use an unusual piece of equipment that, in the end, assisted one and not the other. Such items included, swords that easily broke, iron collars with spikes, rigid arm protection – all for the purpose of weakening an opponent in some unexpected way.

In Brantome's view, the crafty nature of Italians made their masters especially jealous of one another, a trait mentioned early in their fencing history and carried on. Offering money was not enough to get the masters to reveal their secrets.[322] Not all were so tight-lipped, though, and Manciolino, a 16th century fencing master, complained bitterly of fencing schools that sold the art of fencing bit by bit for their own profit, rather than for the noble cause of teaching self-defense.[323]

In the 16th century, the Italian duel and style of fencing, called today the Bolognese school, had spread. It was a cut and thrust system that included several masters and detailed instructions. Secretive as Italian masters could be, these printed works revealed their system and it became popular from Rome to London and Paris to Warsaw.

In the 17th century, several masters had books published on the Italian style of fencing following the advice of Agrippa whose core concepts would go on to dominate fencing theory for centuries. The cut and thrust system was largely abandoned in favor of a thrust-centric system using the rapier. The sheer amount of work printed by the Italians and those who mimicked them leaves modern readers with a fairly detailed window into what was the Italian method of fencing in the 17th century. The Italian impact on Europe in the realm of fencing cannot be understated and their influence on other European masters including the Dutchman Bruchius, the German L'Ange, the Englishman Swetnam, and the Frenchman Philibert de la Touche.

Secrecy and ingenuity were traits attributed to the Italians; the other was recklessness in dueling. The Italian Castiglione and the Frenchman Brantome lauded it, but England's George Silver was annoyed by it. In the 18th century, Angelo warned his readers about it.

In Spain, the Destreza master Alvaro Guerra de la Vega summarized the Italian style of fencing of the 17th century as one that was deceptive and very good at offense but not at defense.[324]

Fiore de Liberi: Flos Duellatorum, the Flower of Battle

Fiore de Liberi was an Imperial free-knight[325] from northern Italy. Given his writing and intended audience, he was likely attached to the Holy Roman Empire, who governed loosely over Italy by granting titles in exchange for lip service. In the case of Fiore's birthplace, the connection was far stronger with Aquileia being an actual part of the Holy Roman Empire until its conquest by the Venetians in 1420.

Fiore's formative years were in the late 14th century when Italy was filled with mercenaries called *condottieri*. In his own introduction, he states that if there were degrees offered to weapons masters, he would be a doctor several times over. He learned his trade by traveling and interacting with many Italian and German masters. Fiore said his skills were sufficient enough that he was asked at royal courts to teach his art, for both fighting in the barriers and in mortal combat. Outside his own writings, records are sparse, but he is found as a soldier, garrison inspector, mercenary captain and keeper of the peace.

---

322   George H. Powell, Dueling Stories of the 16th Century: From the French of Brantome, (London: 1904), 69-70.
323   Antonio Manciolnio, trans. Tom Leoni, The Complete Renaissance Swordsman, (Wheaton: Freelance Academy Press, 2010), 72.
324   Alvaro Guerra de la Vega, trans. Miguel Gomez, "Comprehension of Destreza", ARMA, accessed May 29, 2016, http://www.thearma.org/Manuals/destreza.htm#.V0tvIvkrKUk
325   He calls himself the son of a free knight, but translator Collin Hatcher notes that the exact translation is hard to pin down because spellings are different from copy to copy.

He was secretive of his art, insisting that his students came alone or with close relatives who swore oaths of secrecy. He also cautioned teaching the art to the peasants, indicating his art was for the nobility. The manuscript he wrote is dedicated to the Niccolò III d'Este, Marquis of Ferrara, Modena and Parma.

Fiore de Liberi claimed to have been involved in five duels, wearing only light leather gloves and a coat. All of these duels involved what he described as jealous masters who wanted his secrets, but he was not willing to share. Of all the duels, Fiore said he came away unscathed and acquitted himself honorably. He makes no mention if he killed or seriously wounded his five rivals.

The four surviving copies of his treatise, the *Flower of Battle* are the Getty, Morgan, Novati and Paris. They were written on vellum at great expense and the text is in either Italian or Renaissance Latin. Actual gold and silver was used in some of the treaties, and the Paris copy was hand-painted. These were expensive products in their day.[326] The current theory is that the Getty manuscript from the early 1400s is the oldest and perhaps the original while the other three are copies of it, or of each other.[327]

A recreation of the Paris version of the Flower of Battle. The crowned master prepares to defend himself from the dagger.[328]

---

326   Wiktenauer, "Fiore de'i Liberi", last modified August 16, 2016, accessed May 26, 2016, http://wiktenauer.com/wiki/Fiore_de'i_Liberi

327   Jay Leccese makes a strong case that the Morgan was copied from the Getty and that the Novati and Paris came from the Morgan.

328   Recreation by Ashton Warren.

Fiore de Liberi's purpose for creating a book was to be remembered in *Armizare*, the Art of Arms, but also because a student had once given him sage advice when it came to books:

> In addition let me just say that none of my students, including those mentioned above, have ever owned a book about the art of combat, except for Galeazzo da Mantova. And he put it well when he said that without books you cannot be either a good teacher or a good student of this art. And I can confirm it to be true, that this art is so vast that there is no one in the world with a memory large enough to be able to retain even a quarter of it. And it should also be pointed out that a man who knows no more than a quarter of the art has no right to call himself a Master.[329]

The *Flower of Battle* itself is a complete system covering wrestling, dagger, sword in one hand, sword in two hands, spear, poleaxe, and mounted combat, as well as some odds and ends, including tricks, such as the use of a hidden weight and rope within a poleaxe and blinding powder.[330]

The context of his works can be assumed to cross a wide spectrum of fencing, including judicial dueling, a Passage of Arms, self-defense and perhaps battlefield applications. Fiore simply says his art was for fighting in the barriers, for tournament purposes, and for mortal combat.[331]

A recreation of the Paris version of the Flower of Battle. Fiore depicts mounted as well as foot-combat.[332]

---

329   Translated by Collin Hatcher.
330   There is debate if the sword sections are the same sword, similar swords, or an arming sword and longsword.
331   Fiore depicts a mounted man chasing another back to his fortress, before stabbing him under the arm. Is this a military skirmish, a family vendetta, or some form of assassination on the highway? Fiore does not say.
332   Recreation by Ashton Warren.

Fiore's system includes many counter-attacks in which a crowned master awaits in a safe guard, and then intercepts an attack. From there, follow-on students wearing garters perform a variety of plays, with the occasional counter to a play from a crowned garter-wearing master taking place.

The system is largely applicable in or out of armor, though there are exceptions and there is an entire section dedicated to dueling in armor with the longsword.

Because his work is written as a system, plays from one part can apply elsewhere, and Fiore sometimes explicitly points this out.

While the *Flower of Battle* is comprehensive, it did not become a large, well-known system when compared to the German works. The likely reason for this is that Fiore's work was meant to be taught in secret to a rather elite and tiny group. The secretive nature of the art was echoed later by Philippo Vadi who used Fiore's work. There may also be a connection to *Cod. 5278*, a German manuscript that bears illustrative similarities to Fiore's treatises.

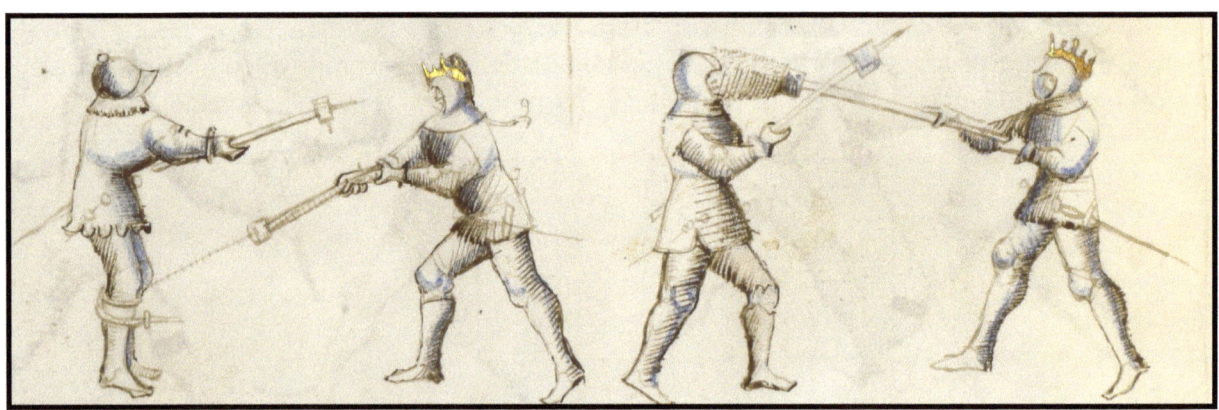

Tricks from the Flower of Battle include the use of a weighted rope to wind about the ankles and blinding powder.[333]

Philippo Vadi: De Arte Gladiatoria Dimicandi, On the Art of Swordsmanship

Little is known of Philippo Vadi and his treatise, which was created between 1482 and 1487, roughly 50 years after Fiore's writing. What is known is that Vadi was a medical student in Ferrara, the same place where copies of the *Flower of Battle* resided. At no point does Vadi reference Fiore de Liberi, but many of his techniques are clearly derived from Fiore and in some cases phrases are used almost verbatim.[334]

Vadi's work was dedicated to the Duke of Urbino and, echoing Fiore, warned his reader to keep it out of the hands of the low-born.

> Because heaven has not made these men in earthly flesh and beyond all cleverness and hard work and bereft of bodily agility, but instead they were

---

[333] Digital image courtesy of the Getty's Open Content Program.
[334] Philippo Vadi, trans. Guy Windsor, Veni Vadi Vici, (The School of European Swordsmanship, 2013),

> made without reason, like animals, just to carry heavy loads and do base and rustic works.
>
> And so for this reason I tell you that they are in every way alien to this science, and it appears to me that the opposite stands for everyone of perspicacious intelligence and lively limbs such as are courtiers, scholars, barons, princes, Dukes and Kings, who should be invited to this noble science...[335]

He goes on to say righteous men should learn his art so as to defend orphans. Although the printing press had been invented, it was still a relatively new invention and Vadi's work was made in the traditional way in manuscript form.

Though derived from Fiore, Vadi's work has plenty of unique commentary, guards, plays or modifications of Fiore's writings. A point he tries to express is that his method was new, even though it was taken from the older secret art of princes and kings. What made it new, in Vadi's eyes, was the application of science behind his techniques.[336]

Of fencing he says, "It is a true science and not an art." This is different from Fiore, who never uses the word "science" to describe fencing. Furthermore, Vadi introduces geometry and music (tempo) as an underpinning of the science behind the use of arms.

His work includes dagger, long sword, sword in armor, poleaxe and odds and ends similar to Fiore's *Flower of Battle*.

Vadi's advice is plentiful and includes elements that would be labeled as national characteristics of the Italians, such as bravery as well as trickery. Some of his advice is as follows:

> Know that cleverness always overcomes strength.
>
> Wisdom, strength and boldness act with him who desires honor in arms.
>
> You must have a bold heart, if a big man appears strong, using cunning will give you favor.
>
> Be as certain as death that your play is not courteous.
>
> Make yourself great in trickery, if you wish for success in this art that will bear you good fruit.[337]

Just as Fiore's work was limited in its audience, the same appears to be true of Vadi and there are no known follow-up masters to his work.

> As a young man I desired to learn armed fighting, including the art of fighting in the lists [36] with spear, poleaxe, sword, dagger and unarmed grappling, on foot and on horseback, armored and unarmored.
> - Fiore de Liberi

---

335   Ibid 51.
336   Ibid 10.
337   Ibid 48-50.

Vadi's version of Iron Door compared to Fiore's. The similarities are clear, though they are not identical.[338]

Antonio Manciolino: Opera Nova, New Work

Opera Nova was written in 1531. Its full title is *New Work by Antonio Manciolino, Bolognese, wherein are all the instructions and advantages that are to be had in the practice of arms of every sort; newly corrected and printed*. This indicates it is an update. The original, now lost, was likely penned in the 1520s.[339]

Of its author, painfully little is known, and his writings were not mentioned by subsequent fencing masters. Manciolino's work is unique because it is the first printed fencing book in Italian. It also departs from the structure of Fiore and Vadi, which used small instructions and pictures, to a much more verbose system of instruction supplied by text rather than imagery.[340] Manciolino's treatise has no fencing-relevant images at all, something that was common in other 16th century Italian works.

Opera Nova is divided into six books and covers the use of the sword and buckler, sword and shield, the sword alone, two swords, the sword and cape, the sword and dagger and the polearm. It

---

338   National Central Library of Rome Cod.1324 and Digital image courtesy of the Getty's Open Content Program.
339   Antonio Manciolnio, trans. Tom Leoni, The Complete Renaissance Swordsman, (Wheaton: Freelance Academy Press, 2010), 10.
340   Ibid 10.

also discusses how two can fence against two. No images are given, but the popular single-handed swords at the time were side swords which were able to cut and thrust.

Opera Nova was dedicated to the Duke of Sessa and tells its reader that the purpose of the book is to defend against a knowledgeable opponent and avoid a cruel death. In true Renaissance fashion, Manciolino references antiquity throughout his prose. The instructions include numerous guard positions that were named similarly to those in prior works, including guards such as Long Tail and Iron Door, which can be found in Fiore and Vadi. From these guards, Manciolino describes safe ways to attack or defend against an attack. While Italians might be categorized by other nationalities as valiant to the point of foolhardy, Manciolino reminds his reader that safety is paramount:

The skillful parrying of a blow is of no little profit or beauty and can be of equal or greater elegance than a good attack.[341]

The methods within are typical of the thrust and cut Italian style that eventually became popular throughout Europe and then was supplanted by a more narrow-stance and thrust-centric style.

The book was written at an interesting time when public dueling was giving way to private dueling, *a la mazza*, as Brantome called it. Manciolino discusses two forms of combat. First, the *Assaulto*, which was conducted with blunt weapons for practice and including the scoring of points. Second, the *spada filo*, or sharp sword, which was for mortal combat. The techniques within were meant to be universally applicable in a sport, or in life and death situations.

Manciolino taught in Bologna, which produced a series of masters that have been categorized today under the name the Bolognese, or Dardi,[342] School of fencing. This was not a single literal school, but a style of fencing that stemmed out of Bologna.

That said, schools for fencing did exist in Bologna. This was a new trend; in the past, a master, like Fiore, took on individual students, or was contracted by a noble court.

In his introduction, Manciolino gives insight into the state of affairs when it comes to these schools and his low opinion of them and most masters.

> As it is a human virtue to be of service to others and to admit that nobody is self-generated, so I believe it is steely greed to place in a school what is there only for one's own benefit instead of that of others.

He goes on,

> …The Art is not a whore to be sold at a price.[343]

ACHILLES MAROZZO: OPERA NOVA, NEW WORK

Marozzo's work, by the same name as Manciolino's, was also published just a few years later, 1536,

---
341   Ibid 74.
342   Lippo Dardi was a fencing master, born in the late 14th century and active in the early 15th century from Bologna. His works have since been lost, but he deeply influenced late 15th and 16th century Italian fencing. Ibid 9.
343   Antonio Manciolnio, trans. Tom Leoni, The Complete Renaissance Swordsman, (Wheaton: Freelance Academy Press, 2010), 72.

in the same city. Neither mentions the other in his work, but they share many similarities to what is the Bolognese School of fencing.

Unlike Manciolino, Marozzo mentions who taught him, and his works included some illustrations.[344] Furthermore, Marozzo's *Opera Nova* was reprinted many times and was a well-known fencing treatise in Europe.

Opera Nova was dedicated to Count Guido Rangoni and in the introduction gives advice on how not only to learn but to teach groups of students. Marozzo explains that teaching in secret is sometimes necessary, not because others might learn the techniques, but because the students might be embarrassed to practice in public in fear of making mistakes.[345]

The teachings of Marozzo were to be used in war and self-defense, but also explicitly in dueling. He goes so far as to explain how to issue challenges to another and what to expect.

Marozzo's choice of weapons includes the sword, the sword and buckler or shield, polearms (like spears), grappling and the greatsword.

Marozzo was not the last of the Bolognese School, just one of many that dominated the 16th century. Other similar masters included Angelo Vigianni and Giovanni dall'Agocchie. Author, researcher and historical fencer Tom Leoni considers that these men taught a similar style, but did not have, necessarily, a tight master-to-student relationship. Rather, their fencing method was common in Bologna and it spread elsewhere during the 16th century.[346]

Camillio Agrippa: *Trattato di Scientia d'Arme, con vn Dialogo di Filosofia*, Treatise on the Science of Arms, with a Philosophical Dialogue

Printed in 1553, Camillio Agrippa's work broke with the popular tradition of the Bolognese Schools. He was fascinated by geometry, and, besides being a fencing instructor, he was an architect and engineer. He did not hail from Bologna but Milan, in the far north of Italy. In his own words, his art was a "new discovery."[347]

Agrippa discounted the many named guards of the Bolognese School and came up with a simpler system of four primary guards that he ordered rationally from A through D. These guards were all point-forward, and Agrippa's solution to the many cuts and passes of the Bolognese system was to thrust while parrying at the same time, using an early form of rapier.[348]

This single-tempo attack and defense, done in one motion, was derived from an Aristotelian

---

344   Guido Antonio di Luca taught Marozzo and was, in Marozzo's estimation, responsible for a great many warriors. Though an author of writings, they have not been confirmed to have been rediscovered yet. May 30 2016, http://wiktenauer.com/wiki/Guido_Antonio_di_Luca
345   Achilles Marozzo, trans. William Wilson, "Arte dell' Armi Books One & Two", accessed May 29, 2016, http://www.marozzo.org/marozzo-trans.pdf
346   Antonio Manciolnio, trans. Tom Leoni, The Complete Renaissance Swordsman, (Wheaton: Freelance Academy Press, 2010), 11.
347   Camillo Agrippa, trans. Ken Mondschien, Fencing: A Renaissance Treatise, (New York: Italica Press, 2014),
348   Italians simply used the word sword and it can be difficult to tell the exact difference between what is a side sword and what is a rapier. While the Italians made little distinctions, foreigners did including the English.

principle. Two actions take more time than one. Thus, a thrust would always beat a cut because whoever was delivering the cut had to raise their arm to get their blade prepared to strike, while whoever thrust simply had to extend their blade.

Agrippa used geometry to justify his theories, giving common sense a mathematical addition. For example, if a fighter stands in a narrow stance, he gives the opponent less of a target. By offering the point, he makes a threat. The four guards could be used to protect from all angles of attack. Each point Agrippa made was reinforced by geometrical art or commentary.

Agrippa was so fascinated by geometry that a large part of his book involves a fanciful conversation between himself and a patron on the meaning behind his drawings and how he came up to their mathematical conclusions. This style of teaching through a dialogue and invoking math is similar to Plato's Socratic dialogues, and typical of many Renaissance writings.

The purpose of Agrippa's book was not solely for the duel of honor, however. When describing guards, he is practical in acknowledging why his system might be used for self-defense.

> The reason why they (the guards) are so-named is because anyone who in anger draws the sword he wears at his side, whether because of his own fury or some external provocation of word, or deed, will raise his hand to form a guard.

He goes on and near the end of his work reminds readers not to use what he has taught unwisely.

> While your longing for victory may be such that you are moved to take up the vendetta for some trivial cause, this seems to me to be all pomp and vain exhibitionism…

The art itself is a product of the Renaissance, depicting men in the nude, as well as clothed and in classical costume. The use of naked bodies is to better show body movements, and that style of illustration would continue in the early 17th century.

Agrippa's theories on fencing were revolutionary and were the impetus behind over a century's worth of rapier treatises in the 17th century, even though he was not always mentioned by name. The concepts of gaurds, measure (distance between opponents), tempo (timing) and movement (namely the lunge) were all core ideas that were carried on throughout the 17th century and further defined and explained.[349]

The audience of his work, according to Ken Mondschein, translator of Agrippa's work into English, was the courtier. These were men who sought to impress others and required patronage to climb the social ladder. One way to impress others was to be able to defend one's honor through swordsmanship.[350]

> **Tybalt - What wouldst thou have with me?**
>
> **- Shakespeare**

---

349   Agrippa did not use the word lunge, but the movement is implied. Enough so, that later masters of the 17th century further defined how best to lunge and safely recover.
350   Camillo Agrippa, trans. Ken Mondschein, Fencing: A Renaissance Treatise, (New York: Italica Press, 2014),

Giacomo di Grassi: *Ragione di adoprar sicuramente l'Arme*, Discourse on Wielding Arms with Safety

Little is known of di Grassi, but his style is similar Agrippa's in that he favored the thrust over the cut and adopted guards that kept the point fixed at the opponent. Di Grassi's first book was published in 1570 under the title *Ragione di adoprar sicuramente l'Arme*, but was translated into English and reprinted in 1594 as *His True Arte of Defence*.

The English translation uses, specifically, the word "rapier" to describe the primary weapon. In the native Italian, the word "sword" was used, with no clear definition as to type.

The rapiers depicted in his work were not quite as long or thin as they would become throughout the 17th century and are more in line with what can be called side swords or proto-rapiers. Di Grassi's popularity in England coincided with an influx of Italian fencing masters who had moved to the country seeking employment, much to the annoyance of the established English fencers.

Di Grassi's techniques include the use of the rapier alone and in conjunction with a shield, a variety of bucklers, a cloak and even another sword. Believing his method universal, he also covers the use of the greatsword and polearms.

His system is not identical to Agrippa's, though he similarly favors the thrust and also spends a great deal of time using geometric artwork to back his views. His explanation also refers to antiquity in a way that was popular with Renaissance writing at the time.

> Without all doubt, the thrust is to be preferred before the edgeblow, as well because it strikes in less time, as also for that in the said time, it does more hurt. For which consideration, the Romans (who were victorious in all enterprises) did accustom their soldiers of the Legions to thrust only: Alleging for their reason, that the blows of the edge, though they were great, yet they are very few that are deadly, and that thrusts, though little and weak, when they enter but three fingers into the body, are wont to kill. Therefore I lay down this for a firm and certain rule, that the thrust does many times more readily strike, and give the greater blow against the enemy.[351]

Unlike Agrippa, Di Grassi's rapier depicts three guards to use when using a sword; high, broad and low. All of these guards are point forward.

Artistically, Di Grassi's work has illustrations akin to Agrippa's in that they show a few guards and principles, but unlike Agrippa, the figures within are clothed in Renaissance attire.

Di Grassi's comments on the various weapons and defensive gear can prove enlightening. The cloak being used for defense he claims was never intended and just a happy accident of necessity that has become part of the art. Of the greatsword, he says it is a weapon better used in war to defend the flag or in an urban encounter to keep away many opponents at once. Of the use of two swords, he says it has no place in war but is accepted as an honorable weapon amongst princes.[352]

Di Grassi's audience is not entirely clear, but the context of his work seems to imply self-defense

---

351   Wiktenauer, "Giacomo Di Grassi", accessed May 30, 2016, http://wiktenauer.com/wiki/Giacomo_di_Grassi
352   Ibid.

and duels—and he delves into military matters when it comes to the polearm and greatsword. Like many masters of the 16th century, he appears to be seeking out a universal and mathematical system, applicable with any weapon in any context.

Salvator Fabris: Lo Schermo, overo Scienza d'Arme, On Defense, or the Science of Arms

Salvator Fabris was a well-traveled fencing master from Padua and was employed by their university in his waning years. In the late 16th century, he traveled around Europe and earned a reputation as a fencing master, creating two works on the subject. The first was 1601's *Scientia e Prattica dell'Arme*, a three volume manuscript which he produced while in the court of the Duke of Holstein-Gottorp. Then in 1606, while in the service of the King of Denmark and Norway, he created a slightly revised single volume edition, *Schermo, overo Scienza d'Arme*. This was printed in Copenhagen and illustrated by King Christian IV's court artist, Jan van Halbeeck.

The stories about Fabris are many. In the 1676 reprint of his work, Johann Joachim Hynitzsch introduces Fabris as a Colonel in the Order of the Seven Hearts. He has been indicated as a possible assassin for hire in the struggle between Sigismund, King of Sweden and Poland and his uncle, Charles IX, who had claimed the throne of Sweden for himself.[353] Fabris may have even crossed paths with William Shakespeare.[354]

As a traveling master, Fabris spread his system of fencing across Europe, and long after his death he was praised by others for the completeness of his art and the thoroughness of his approach. Follow-on masters, many of them not from Italy, mimicked his style. Johann Joachim Hynitzsch claimed that Nicoletto Giganti not only copied Fabris, going so far as to claim he plagiarized his work, but also that Giganti did not understand the concepts of fencing.[355] The accusation is a bit harsh and perhaps a result of an unauthorized edition of Fabris published by Jacques de Zeter in 1619 that included Giganti's work within.

Fabris details both what was commonly taught in terms of 17th century fencing in the Italian tradition of Agrippa and his own methods. Fabris' method includes leaning the body forward so that only the head was in danger, rather than the head and body, which was the case when a person leaned back. Fabris also took the four main guards of Agrippa, depicted how most people perform them and then explained how he preferred them including many variations. The thoroughness of Fabris' writings cannot be understated. Fabris deeply explains core fundamentals of 17th century rapier fencing, such as measure, tempo, and how to gain the blade so as to be able to lunge and not be hit. He also discusses improper and unsafe techniques and common situations and how to deal with them. Fabris even gives practical advice on what to do after successfully lunging into an opponent- which is to run the blade through them all the way to the hilt so that they cannot free their sword. All of these concepts are those Fabris says any master can teach, though often improperly. He then introduces what he claims to be a unique way of fencing which is called proceeding with resolution. This method deals with drawing the blade and immediately attacking the opponent without having to spend time gaining their sword.

---

353   Henrik Anderson, "Salvator Fabris as a Hired Assassin in Sweden", ARMA, accessed, May 30, 2016 http://www.thearma.org/essays/Fabris_the_Assassin.htm#.WBFPOPkrKUk
354   Salvator Fabris, trans. Tom Leoni, The Art of Dueling: Salvatore Fabris' Fencing Treatise of 1606, (Highland Village: Chivalry Bookshelf, 2005), XVIII-XIX.
355   Nicoletto Giganti, trans. Tom Leoni, Venetian Rapier, (Wheaton: Freelance Academy Press, 2010), XIII.

Randy Reyes and Adam Simmons of the Phoenix Society of Historical Swordsmanship compare Fabris' stance to that of Capoferro.

The plentiful illustrations in his work are nude or near nude figures, and text and images are used in an equal amount, a departure from the prior century, which was driven largely by text.

Fabris was clear in his work that his methods were for dueling between gentlemen and not for the battlefield. It was only with reluctance that he delved, briefly, into weapons other than the rapier and rapier and dagger. Of the buckler or dagger alone, Fabris said they were not the weapons of a gentleman.[356] Here and there he also has an aside about an unusual situation, such as fencing an armored or multiple opponents.

His influence was profound and others took up his method of fencing including Germans such as Hans Wilhelm Schöffer von Dietz, Sebastian Heußler, Joachim Köppen and Jéann Daniel L'Ange and in the Low Countries Johannes Georgius Bruchius.

NICOLETTO GIGANTI: SCOLA, OVERO TEATRO, AND LIBRO SECUNDO, SCHOOL OR FENCING HALL AND BOOK TWO

A Venetian, Giganti wrote treatises in 1606 and 1608 that were typical of the 17th century rapier theory to come out of Italy. Based on the ideas of Agrippa, Giganti's work describes forming counter-guards to the opponent and lunging with the rapier. As with all Italian rapier masters of

---

356   Salvator Fabris, trans. Tom Leoni, The Art of Dueling: Salvatore Fabris' Fencing Treatise of 1606, (Highland Village: Chivalry Bookshelf, 2005), 263.

the 17th century, the concepts of measure (distance) and tempo (timing) allowed for a proper and safe single-time attack with the lunge.

He is credited as the first to describe the lunge.

> To deliver a lunging thrust, set yourself in a solid stance, better if a bit narrower than wide, so that you may then extend your front foot forward. While delivering the thrust, extend the sword-arm and bend the knee as much as possible.
>
> Here is the correct way to deliver the attack. After getting in guard, first extend the arm, then extend your body forward (in one tempo), so that the attack arrives on target before the opponent realizes it is coming.[357]

The style of Giganti's writing is direct and to the point. While masters from the 16th century, such as Manciolino, included flowery references to antiquity, Giganti almost comes across as terse, warning his readers that he does not like to repeat himself.

His directness makes his work easy to understand and includes such blunt statements as,

> The whole artistry of our discipline consists of this: when you launch an attack, your opponent should be hit.[358]

Breaking from the tradition of Agrippa, and of most other 17th century rapier masters, Giganti does not speak directly of guards; instead he suggests that a fencer adopt a counter-guard to whatever his opponent is doing.

Like the artwork of other 17th century masters, such as Ridolfo Capoferro and Salvator Fabris, the plates depict men who are naked, or near naked, using long rapiers. The rapiers by the early 1600s had become thinner than the sides swords and proto-rapiers of the prior century. These longer rapiers could still be used to cut. Although Giganti considered the thrust ideal, in his second books he gives encounters where a cut to the opponent's leg might be appropriate, and against numerous opponents he suggests cuts toward the face and neck.

Also typical of Giganti's work was the use of the rapier with an accompanying dagger, a trend in Italian fencing that would persist even into the late 18th century. Other items shown in his books are cloaks, shields and bucklers of differing varieties. He also gives a few techniques on how to fence with daggers against all manner of weapons, including a spear.

Giganti does not say, exactly, what his books are for. But reading between the lines, the first book appears to be for gentlemanly dueling, with a few asides, while the second book covers more urban encounters, such as what to do against an opponent who is armored or using a heavier sword, or what to do if set upon when armed only with a dagger.

---

357   Nicoletto Giganti, trans. Tom Leoni, Venetian Rapier, (Wheaton: Freelance Academy Press, 2010), 2.
358   Ibid 4.

Ridolfo Capoferro: Gran Simulacro dell'Arte e dell'Uso della Scherma, Great Representation of the Art and Use of Fencing

Capoferro's work, published in 1610, was fairly typical of early 17th century rapier. The four main guards he suggests are similar to Agrippa's—plus, he provides two additional guards. His stratagem relies on gaining an opponent's blade and lunging. The majority of his techniques are shown with rapier and dagger in hand.

His explanation as to why men should carry swords and learn his art delves into history. Caporferro claims that the Roman Republic was wise because no weapons were allowed except in times of war, but in his day, soldiers were everywhere in Italy and were often the cause of disruption. In other words, the art of fencing was to protect against unruly soldiery.

With palpable lamentation, Capoferro notes that fencing was still a vital skill but no longer useful in war where artillery and the arquebus dominated.

Capoferro cautions against weapons that are too long because they are not fit for civilization and weapons that are too small because they are the kind that are hidden and likely to be carried by murderers.

Like Fabris and Giganti, the illustrations of Capoferro's work depict men who are naked, or near naked, to better display the exact positioning of the human body.[359]

Francesco Alfieri: La Scherma, On Fencing

Published in 1640, with other editions throughout the 17th century, *La Scherma* is a continuation of the Italian fencing method forwarded by Agrippa and carried on by Fabris, Capoferro and Giganti. The rapiers by the mid-17th century were incredibly long, and this can be seen in the illustrations of Alfieri's work.

Alfieri provides commentaries about the masters of old, including praise for Fabris and an insult toward Capoferro. Alfieri also had preferences for certain guards and slightly modified older techniques to fit with what he believed were safer and more scientific methods. For example, he includes a mixed guard, which is neither third nor fourth.

Unlike earlier 17th century treatises, the illustrations in Alfieri are not done in the nude and the men wear typical clothing of the time.[360]

Gentlemen are the audience, and the context is dueling, though additional books were added that included more martial weapons, such as the greatsword.

> They pretend to about all things to regard honor, yet chiefly seek the dishonor of God and of justice.
> - John Rawlinson on the topic of the duel-

---

359   Wiktenauer, "Ridolfo Capo Ferro", accessed May 26, 2016 http://wiktenauer.com/wiki/Ridolfo_Capo_Ferro_da_Cagli
360   Information is derived by a translation gifted to the author.

Adam Simmons and Randy Reyes of the Phoenix Society of Historical Swordsmanship demonstrate the Passata Sotto.

FRANCESCO ANTONIO MARCELLI: REGOLLE DELL SCHERMA, THE RULES OF FENCING

Marcelli's treatise was published in 1686 in Rome for the Queen Cristina Alessandra of Sweden who was living there at the time. His work is another continuation of 17th century Italian rapier fencing using many of the same principles as set down by the likes of Agrippa, Fabris, Giganti, Capoferro and Alfieri.

Where Marcelli's work differs is the use of two-time actions, meaning to parry and thrust, as opposed to the single-time actions that dominated the 17th century. Furthermore, Marcelli's work includes a section on the saber, a weapon he noted as ancient, but lately popular in Italy.

The lunge of Marcelli is also far less wide than that of earlier 17th century masters. This was designed to make the lunge not as long, but far easier to deliver and recover from.

His description of fencing with the saber opposes it to the rapier or the rapier opposed to the saber. He alas, does not give insight on how two men with sabers should fence one another.[361]

Artistically, Marcelli's work is in line with Alfieri. Nude images had given way to artwork showing

---

[361] Carlo Parisi provided the author with a translation of the work. An original can be found at www.umass.edu/renaissance/lord/collection.html

clothed men. Furthermore, the size of text was enormous compared to the images provided, making the work different than prior masters of the 17th century and more akin to the style of the verbose 16th century. Of note, Marcelli, disapproved of the smaller, more fashionable swords that would dominate the next century.

> ... a questionable use is now in vogue and the sword has been made into a small sword, barely longer than one arm. Since this is the new fashion, it happens that, if you wear a small sword and you have to fight in some brawl, with someone who has a rapier or some other advantageous weapon, you have to die for fashion. It happens daily to see fights of this kind, because everyone, friend of his own opinion and of fashion, more so than of his own good, walks in the path chosen by most people, but not by everyone commended.[362]

The Italian method of fencing remained popular into the 18th century, adapting well enough to the small sword, but it would be challenged by various French masters who, like the Italians before them, spread their method throughout Europe.

The Holy Roman Empire

The Germans have the oldest fencing treatise on record, *MS I.33*, which currently resides in London, and have a rich tradition of swordsmanship in the 14th and 15th centuries. Italian methods of fencing spread in the 16th century, but even as late as the 17th century there were still Germans using the cut-fencing of old.

There was no Germany, just as there was no Italy, during the times the treatises were created, and they were written in various places within and outside the Holy Roman Empire. The Empire itself was a loose collection of German kingdoms, principalities, free-cities and bishoprics under the rule of an elected Emperor. Even at their strongest, like Charles V, these Emperors had a difficult time ruling over their Empire. As Voltaire quipped, it was neither Holy nor Roman, nor much of an Empire. That said, the loose nature of the Empire allowed for its long survival and from it sprung a rich tradition of martial treatises.

The context of the early German fencing treatises appears to be a mixture of self-defense and judicial and or sanctioned dueling. Early German works in what is called *Kunst de Fechten* are derived from a mysterious poem, Liechtenauer's *Zettel*, which during the 15th century was fleshed out by subsequent masters.

Fencing was regulated by guilds that held Imperial charters leading to over a century of a German method of fencing. The *Marxbrüder* (or *Brudersschaft von St. Marks und Loewenberg*) and the *Federfecheter* both held such charters. The two guilds were recognized by the Emperor and regulated who was given the title of master or *meister*.

At first, the *Marxbrüder* held a monopoly on the official teaching of arms and they were also the Furrier guild, and included members of other guilds as well. The guild-based nature of the profession

---

362 Translation by Carlo Parisi.

of swordsmanship led to the art being called knightly, while in truth it was run by and directed at the urban middle class. Part of civic responsibility was to the defense of the town or city and prior to the 16th century, the populace was expected to be armed and ready to fight.[363] State-run and mercenary armies eroded this need, which is why the fencing-guilds in the 16th century, throughout Europe, were no longer seen as necessary. They were seem as frivolous hobbies better suited to the marketplace and the masses, a fact openly lamented by Germans such as Meyer and Mair.[364]

Originally, the *Marxbrüder* held tight control over who could be given the status of a master and who could operate schools or fencing events within city-limits. The wait-time to be made a master led to a sub-division within the guild called *Freifechter*, or Free-Fencer. *Freifechters* could ask permission to teach or hold events, such as a *Fechtschule*, which was a form of fencing competition.

These competitions could be risky and death and injury, though lamented, did occur. Samuel Probst was engaged with another in a sportive bout and was following all of the German customs called *Fechten Brauch*. They included no strikes to the eyes, groin or hands and the use of the flat of the blade only. Despite these precautions, Probst struck his opponent's temple with the flat of his *federschwert* and killed him. Though regrettable, it was agreed that it was just bad luck and Probst was not punished.[365]

Cliff Curry, James Harvey Grant, John Patterson, Charles Buschmann, of the Phoenix Society of Historical Swordsmanship, Dylan Smith of Kron, and Steven Gotcher of the Phoenix Society pose after sparring with federschwerts reminiscent of the Fechtschule.

---

363   B. Anne Tlusty, The Martial Ethic in Early Modern Germany: Civic Duty and the Right of Arms, (New York: Palgrave Macmillan, 2011), 10-11.
364   Ibid 215-216.
365   B. Anne Tlusty, The Martial Ethic in Early Modern Germany: Civic Duty and the Right of Arms, (New York: Palgrave Macmillan, 2011), 217.

Members of the *Freifechter* were able to gain Imperial status as their own guild, the *Federfecther*, in 1607, though there is mention of them as early as 1575. The *Federfecther* represented new-blood in the German tradition and introduced techniques that were previously unacceptable among Germans, such as the use of the thrust and weapons such as an early form of rapier.[366] Meyer, a *Freifechter*, refers to these techniques as necessary to learn due to foreign, likely Italian, influence.[367]

The guilds were rivals and the older *Marxbrüder* saw itself as traditional and linked to a chivalric past, while the new upstarts were strange with their modern ways. One *Marxbrüder* wrote a poem decrying the younger *Federfechters*, who he calls goose feathers. In particular he was annoyed by their tendency to write down their techniques.

> A *Marxbrüder* I have become,
>
> Who is angry at the *Federfechters*.
>
> When I thought about it, what a goose feather would be worth,
>
> Nobody would give me for it half a mug of wine.
>
> Why should I give honor to the goose feathers,
>
> Shield and helmet are much better décor for me.
>
> His Imperial Majesty favors *Marxbrüders*,
>
> Who strive for such a chivalrous Art.
>
> For goose feathers and quills,
>
> Are of no use for nightly games.
>
> Because hear ye, feather thin paper [and] black ink,
>
> Should be found only in a scriptorium.[368]

Even as the judicial duel declined in Europe as a whole, it remained on the table in parts of the Holy Roman Empire any time two witnesses contradicted one another. The accusation of perjury could also result in a legally acceptable duel long after such practices had been outlawed elsewhere.[369]

The Thirty Years' War of the mid-17th century broke the Holy Roman Empire in reality, if not on paper. German fencing remained, but Italian fencing in the late 16th century and throughout the 17th century became popular throughout Europe to the point that German masters, unconnected to the guilds, began to emulate Italian ways.[370]

---

366 Customs may have limited the use of the thrust in the Holy Roman Empire, but these were not unknown techniques and early German treatises reference thrusting. A similar trend took place in Poland in the 17th century where in a duel, the thrust was avoided to prevent death and instead cuts were aimed at the head and hands.

367 Kevin Mauer, "Insights into the Fechtschulen of the Marxbruder and Federfechter Guilds", Accessed May 30, 2016, https://docs.google.com/file/d/0B4Wy4VUTvpKKMkRNUHZKOURFWHc/view

368 Ibid.

369 R. C. Caenegem, Legal History: A European Perspective, (London: Bloomsbury Academic, 2004), 105.

370 Domenico Angleo described the German style of fencing with the small sword. The guard was said to be forward weighted, with a bent right leg, and straight back leg, while the sword was pointed at the waist and used to beat and disarm.

MS I.33

The oldest known European Martial Art treatise is *MS I.33* which was crafted, likely, in the early 1300s. The images depict priests teaching students and, in one case, a woman the use of the sword and buckler. The instructions are brief and written in Medieval Latin.[371]

While the image of priests teaching and partaking in swordsmanship may seem strange, it was common enough. Monks engaged in judicial duels with staves and shields. Priests and monks taught fencing in the 16th century, as was mentioned in an off-hand comment by Brantome. Catholic Universities employed fencing masters. And when discussing customs of the late 17th century Kitowicz noted that Catholic Jesuits in Poland taught stick-fencing, called *Palcaty*, as a form of practice for the saber.

Adam Simmons of the Phoenix Society of Historical Swordsmanship with a sword and buckler.

Johannes Liechtenauer: *Liechtenauer's Zettel*, **Liechtenauer's Recital**

The Grandmaster of the German medieval tradition of fencing, *Kunst de Fechten*, is a bit of a mystery. Though he is often cited by later masters, of Liechtenauer there is no known record, nor any original works penned by him. Instead, others reference him, most notably his *Zettel*. The *Zettel* is a poetic form of instructions that is to be recited. In the case of Liechtenauer, the *Zettel* is lacking in details, and without notes, called glosses, it would be unusable when it comes to learning martial arts. The work is entirely text based, giving readers little to work with.

The earliest *Zettel* is found in *MS 3227a*, though dating this common book is unclear. It could have been created in 1389, based on a calendar within, or as late as 1494, when the book was in the hands of Nicolaus Pol. The manuscript itself contains a variety of information, not all of it regarding fencing. Confusing matters further, Liechtenauer is not referenced as the originator of

---

371   There are some other contenders for the 'first' from antiquity, but they are either fragments with little to go on, or images alone. MS I.33 has both images and instructions.

his teachings, making him perhaps just the first to have his insights put to paper. The first mention of Liechtenauer comes from Talhoffer in 1443.

Though even Liechtenauer's existence is somewhat questionable, what is known is that the *Zettel* is attributed to him, and masters, like Talhoffer and Paulus Kal, referenced him. Whatever the truth of the matter when it comes to Liechtenauer, the *Zettel* attributed to him is the bedrock of early *Kunst de Fechten*.

The *Zettel* contains information on the use of the longsword, short sword and mounted combat. A sample of the *Zettel* reveals its cryptic nature.

> He who follows the strokes,
> should rejoice little in his art.[372]

The *Zettel* is purposefully vague so that it would be easy to memorize but, without a master of the system to explain it, unusable. The glosses of other masters help make sense of the *Zettel*. Five different texts included glosses that help explain the *Zettel*, 3227a, *Cod.44.A.8*, pseudo-Danzig, Lew, Ringeck, and Medel.

While Fiore de Liberi wanted his work to be easy to understand with pictures and text, this is not so with the *Zettel*. *Cod.44.A.8* for example indicates the reasoning behind the *Zettel's* cryptic words.

> Therefore he has allowed the Epitome to be written with secret and suspicious words, so that not every man shall undertake and understand them. And he has done that so the Epitome's Art will little concern the reckless Fencing Masters, so that from those same Masters his Art is not openly presented, nor shall it become common.

As for the intended audience, the prologue is written to a young knight, and perhaps this is true, but steadily the urban middle class became interested in the knightly arms especially once guilds took control over the teaching of martial arts.

Hans Talhoffer: MS Chart.A.558

Hans Talhoffer's early life is largely unknown and his first appearance in the historical record involves the abduction and murder of a man. Despite political fallout over this, Talhoffer went on to a very long career as a fencing instructor, working for various nobles. He produced several works, the first around 1443 and the last in 1467. There is some speculation he may have been involved in the earliest foundations of the *Marxbrüder* based on his choice of coat of arms being similar to that of the guild, but no direct connection has yet been found.

Talhoffer's focus appears to be on judicial dueling, barriers can be seen in the art, and he was hired to help train one of his patrons to fight such a duel, though it never took place. Talhoffer remained active, though drifted from patron to patron, selling his services and his treatises.

The art of Talhoffer is of a high quality and, unusually, depicts gory scenes such as the near-

---

372   Wiktenauer, "Johannes Liechtenauer", accessed May 20, 2016, http://wiktenauer.com/wiki/Johannes_Liechtenauer#Treatise translated by Christian Tobler.

decapitation of heads and severing of hands. The weapons involved include longsword, sword and buckler, mixed weapons and dueling shields—and he describes dueling scenarios in and out of armor and mounted combat.

His work was prolific, but shy on text—making it difficult to understand the techniques within, as well as the exact context. Copies of his work were made throughout the 15th century and every century after into the 21st century.[373]

Talhoffer depicted an image of a joust. This is not meant to be a mortal contest, as noted by the type of armor worn and the lances used.[374] While it may appear the knight on the right has lost, the rules for jousts varied. King Alfonso XI of Castile stated that in a joust if one knight broke his lance on another, and the other knight did not break his lance, then the one with the broken lance won the combat. Falling off the horse was, of course, a loss—but seemed to happen less often as jousting became safer.

> ...they all are in agreement, that this knightly art of fencing was in the beginning established with the purpose of serving to the honour, virtue and stimulation to the youth of both high and low birth, and also to the protection and preservation of the fatherland.
> - Paulus Hector Mair

---

373   Wiktenauer, "Hans Talhoffer", accessed May 20, 2016, http://wiktenauer.com/wiki/Hans_Talhoffer
374   Image courtesy the Royal Library of Copenhagen.

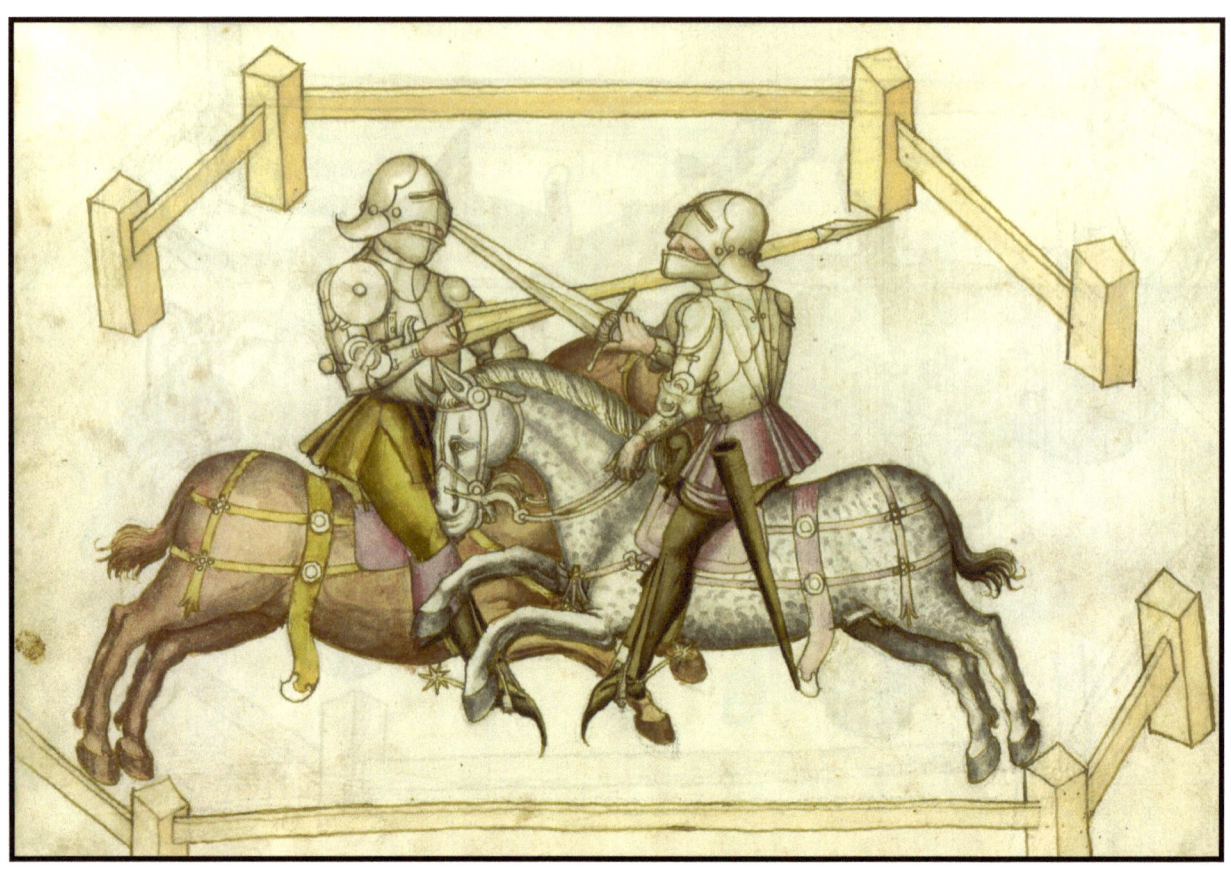

A much more earnest combat is depicted here, with a sharp lance and sword.[375]

Michael Edelson and Tristan Żukowski of the New York Historical Fencing Association. Michael brought the cutting of rolled tatami mats to HEMA. Cutting tatami is commonly practiced in Asian martial arts and the purpose is to better understand the nature of cutting including necessary edge alignment. Photo courtesy of Lauren Dubois.

[375] Image courtesy the Royal Library of Copenhagen.

Ben Blythe of the Phoenix Society of Historical Swordsmanship in the inviting Fool's Guard called Alber.

<u>Cod.44.A.8</u>

Cod.44.A.8, created in 1452, has several authors. One is Peter von Danzig, though the entire work is not his.

The codex includes a gloss to Liechtenauer's *Zettel*, providing insight into the techniques of the German master. From before,

> He who follows the strokes,
> should rejoice little in his art.

With a gloss added by *Cod.44.A.8* much more is revealed.

> Gloss: This is when you come to him with the pre-fencing: then you shall not stand still and look after his hews, waiting for what he fences against you. Know that all fencers that look and wait on another's hews and will do nothing other than parrying deserve such very little joy in their art, since they are destroyed and become struck thereby.[376]

What was hard to discern from Liechtenauer's *Zettel* is made clearer by the gloss. Illustrations are provided, but only for the four named primary guards of German longsword: *vom tag*, *ochs*, *pflug* and *alber*, or, from the day, ox, plow and fool.

Paulus Kal: Allerley Kampf zur Ross und Fuess in und an Harnisch, All Manner of Combat on Horse and on Foot, Both Armored and Unarmored[377]

Paulus Kal was active in the mid- to late-1400s and served in the court the Count of the Palantine, the Duke of Bavaria-Landshut and in the court of the Hapsburg Archduke. He was taught by Hans Stettner von Mörnsheim, of which we know little, and his works are unique in that he references a society of masters who are, supposedly, linked to Liechtenauer, the *Geselschaft Liechtenauers*, or Fellowship of Liechtenauer.

This Fellowship of Liechtenauer includes masters who have known treatises, but the exact details of the fellowship are unknown. The seventeen masters included are from all over the Holy Roman Empire and Poland and include, Liechtenauer, as well as, Peter von Danzig, Peter Wildigans, Hans Spindler, Lamprecht von Prague, Hans Seydenfaden, Andre Liegniczer, Jacob Liegniczer, Ringeck, Hartman von Nuremberg, Martin Huntfeltz, Hans Pegnitzer, Philipp Perger, Virgil von Kraków, Dieterich, the dagger-fighter of Braunschweig, Ott Jud, and Hans Stettner.

Of these masters, Peter von Danzig, Andre Liegniczer, Ringeck, Martin Huntfeltz, and Ott Jud have either surviving treatises, or treatises attributed to them.

Kal's contribution to the Liechtenauer tradition was in the illustration of guards and techniques in a *fechtbuch* penned in the 1480s. This book was roughly divided into two categories for fighting with the longsword, in armor and out of armor, or *bloszfechten* and *harnessfechten*. The artwork provided by Kal and the glosses from other treatises help craft what is early German fencing.

Other additions to Kal's work include a duel between a woman and man, with the man in a hole and the woman armed with a stone wrapped in cloth, a section on sword and buckler and wrestling. Similar art exists in Talhoffer's work as well. Though the two were contemporaries, Paulus Kal makes no mention of Talhoffer in his list of masters.

---

376   Wiktenauer, "Pseudo-Peter von Danzig", accessed May 20, 2016, http://wiktenauer.com/wiki/Pseudo-Peter_von_Danzig translated by Cory Winslow.

377   This was the title stamped by the museum on the cover of the work, not necessarily the title Paulus Kal gave to it.

Kal's work is dedicated to a count but includes the early verses of Liechtenauer, which are directed toward a young knight. Yet, was this so? In the late 15th century, there were numerous fencing schools in the Holy Roman Empire called, *Schirm Schulen*, whose students were likely from the middle, rather than strictly knightly class. These schools were, before the close of the century, brought under the monopoly of the *Marxbrüde*r at which point they took on the name of *FechtSchulen*.[378] While the various masters would use Liechtenauer's work, and reference the art of arms as knightly, the actual audience had become far more urban and common in nature.[379]

JOHANNES LECKÜCHNER: KUNST DES MESSERFECHTENS, THE ART OF MESSER FENCING

An ordained priest, Johannes Lecküchner was also the author of two works, one created in 1478 and another just prior to his death in 1482. The treatises cover the use of a messer, which is a large knife.

The context of the work is not exactly clear. The work is dedicated to a Duke, and indicates in the introduction that many masters of the sword were not so when it came to the messer. While the Liechtenauer tradition is directed at the knightly class, this may not be the case for Lecküchner's work.

Certain concepts used by Lecküchner are similar to those used in the Liechtenauer tradition, sometimes borrowed directly from the longsword glosses, especially the concept of timing. While in the Italian treatises time was eventually categorized with the Aristotelian principles of tempo, in German treatises the terms *vor*, *nach* and *indes* were used, meaning before, after and in the moment.[380]

The second treatise, which shares the same name as the first, includes both text and extensive illustrations. Although the printing press did exist, fencing treatises at this time were still made with traditional methods instead, including hand painting the artwork.[381]

PAULUS HECTOR MAIR: OPUS AMPLISSIMUM DE ARTE ATHLETICA, THE GRAND WORK OF THE ATHLETIC ARTS

Paulus Hector Mair is the only known creator of a treatise to die for his work. He was a citizen of the Imperial free-city of Augsburg and active in the mid- to late-16th century. Within the Holy Roman Empire were cities that operated independently of the territory they were in. Like the various kingdoms within the Empire, they were all, nominally, subjects of the Holy Roman Emperor. These cities were responsible for their own defense, which was managed by the various guilds. This was a common practice throughout Europe. Cellini, for example, was an Italian goldsmith and was

---

378   Kevin Mauer, "Insights into the Fechtschulen of the Marxbruder and Federfechter Guilds," accessed 9 25, 2016, https://docs.google.com/file/d/0B4Wy4VUTvpKKMkRNUHZKOURFWHc/view
379   Ibid.
380   While *vor* and *nach* are easy to define, *indes* is more nuanced. When blades cross, and pressure is felt, that is the time to act, and thus *indes*, or, in the moment.
381   Wiktenauer, "Johannes Liechtenauer", accessed May 20, 2016, http://wiktenauer.com/wiki/Johannes_Liechtenauer#Treatise translated by Christian Tobler.

obliged by Florence, along with all other artists and tradesmen of the city, to reinforce a city gate.[382]

Mair noticed that people's interest in arms was dwindling. He calls the art knightly and says it should be in and of itself worthy to learn for self-defense and yet due to the laziness of men it was being not only neglected, but scorned.

> ...I would have thought it good and advisable, for me to publish this knightly book of honor without any preface, as to the knowledgeable each art can with good reason defend and speak for itself.
>
> But as I become aware and notice, that this manly art of fencing, as other arts besides, which profit the beloved fatherland as useful and honorable, and by the learned are praised for men to study, are by those who out of idleness and neglect fail to respect the good virtues and arts...[383]

To rectify this, Mair created massive tomes that richly compiled the German fencing tradition. Mair did this through personal connections to fencers as well as by purchasing older treatises. His work was incredibly expensive, taking years to finish, and despite the availability of the printing press, was done in the traditional way, by hand—including lavish hand painted illustrations of the highest quality. The first of three versions was completed in 1542.

The material within his grand opus includes longsword, dussack, short staff, lance, halberd, scythe, flail, peasant's flail, sickle, grappling, dagger, the early rapier, the early rapier and dagger, sword and buckler, poleaxe, dueling shields, armored fencing, as well as mounted combat.

The descriptions of techniques and the terminology used are in line with prior German works, but Mair had the German works translated into Humanist Latin, he also included history. While the history is inaccurate, such as claiming Amazons invented the use of the poleaxe, it is a nod to antiquity and makes Mair's tomes a true product of the Renaissance.

Mair also collected pre-existing *fechtbuchs*, such as the Codex Wallerstien and any other work on the use of arms he could get his hands on.

Mair spared no expense in the creation of his tomes, each more expensive than the last and for it he paid dearly. After exhausting his family resources he took to embezzling from Augsburg. This was eventually discovered and Paulus Hector Mair was hung as a common thief in 1579.[384]

> Never disclose your offensive intentions to the opponent- rather, strive to guess the opponent's own tactics. This is because as you encounter each other even-tempered you should make the most of all your designs. But if you fight for your honor, it is laudable to show your designs to the opponent.
> - Antonio Manciolinio

---

382   Jean Chandler A comparative analysis of literary depictions of social violence in two important 16th Century autobiographies, from the perspective of the fencing manuals of the Renaissance. Acta Periodica Duellatorum. Volume 2015, Issue 1, Pages 101–137, 2015

383   Wiktenauer, "Paulus Hector Mair", accessed October 1, 2016, http://wiktenauer.com/wiki/Paulus_Hector_Mair

384   Ibid.

Mair's opus included the traditional longsword, but also weapons that were popular in his day, such as these side swords, which appear to be early forms of rapier. The fencer on the right is of African descent, showing perhaps the cosmopolitan nature of Augsburg, or simply an artist's choice to be unique.[385]

JOACHIM MEYER: GRÜNDTLICHE BESCHREIBUNG DER KUNST DES FECHTENS, A THOROUGH DESCRIPTION OF THE ART OF FENCING

Meyer was a cutler who settled in the city of Strasbourg and was a *Friefechter*. *Friefechters* were free-fencers acknowledged by the *Marxbrüder*, but not recognized as masters.

Meyer, much like Mair, was concerned about the knightly arts being lost and also belittled. Meyer attributed this to the dominance of artillery and the arquebus.

The ignoble gun has arisen and so taken the upper hand, that by its agency the most manly and skilled hero can be suddenly deprived and robbed of his life sometimes even by the pettiest and most timid of men; and often friend as well as foe is hurt and harmed by it.[386]

While in 16th century Italy, private dueling had kept fencing treatises relevant, in the Holy Roman

---

385 https://commons.wikimedia.org/wiki/File:Paulus_Hector_Mair.-_Two_fencers,_one_of_African_descent,_wielding_an_early_rapier_De_arte_athletica,_Augsburg,_Germany,_ca_1542.png Public Domain Art.
386 Joachim Meyer, trans. Jeffery L. Forgeng, The Art of Combat, (London: Frontline Books, 2015), 37.

Empire at the same time, this was not the case, given both Mair and Meyer's dismay at the state of affairs of fencing. Meyer goes on to state that nobles should once again take up fencing and then laments how many current fencers used their art for base needs including gluttony, whoring, lewdness and laziness. Clearly, the knightly art wasn't so knightly! Meyer desired to turn back the clock though, and referenced ancient Greek heroes and noted every noble should learn the art of single-combat to better inspire his soldiers.

Meyer created a treatise for his student and later, a larger, more complete edition for a count, Johann Casimir. Meyer's work is meant to be read completely, much like Fiore de Liberi's *Flower of Battle*, with the concepts from one section being relevant to another. Meyer's work includes the use of the longsword, the dussack, a side sword that is akin to an early rapier, the staff, the halberd and the dagger. Meyer's work is very much steeped in the older tradition of Liechtenauer, but includes a variety of techniques unique to him. Meyer also explains the German attitude toward thrusting. Of early Germans, he says the thrust was used in earnest combat, but by and large Germans did not try to stab one another, even in a sporting context, nor should they- however, outside influences, likely Italian, necessitate the use of the rapier and the understanding of the thrust.

Meyer hosted several *Fechtschulen*, which were martial sporting events. These events were similar to tournaments, but directed at the rising middle class rather than the nobility. Something to note is that while Mair and Meyer both refer to their art as one for knights, neither was a knight himself. The relevancy of the class as the fighting elite was all but extinguished, and by the 16th century the art of swordsmanship was firmly in the hands of middle class guilds and roaming fencing masters. That said, Meyer, like many other masters, flattered his social betters in search of patronage and perhaps a hope that the art might be knightly once again.

Meyer's 1570 treatise, *Gründtliche Beschreibung der Kunst des Fechtens,* was printed on a press and included wood-cuts of a high quality and detail. Akin to Mair, Meyer incurred large debts in the creation of his work. To pay these debts off, he agreed to be a *Fechtmeister* for the Duke of Mecklenburg which was a tremendous financial opportunity. Alas, after traveling during the winter, he died, likely of sickness, shortly after arriving at court.[387]

Meyer was the last of the Liechtenauer tradition. Though his school remained in Strasbourg, when Louis the Sun King took possession of the city in 1681, the school was renamed and taught French methods of fencing.[388]

Erhardus Henning: Kurtze jedoch gründliche Unterrichtung vom Hieb-fechten, Short Thorough Instruction in Cut Fencing

Printed in 1658, Erhardus Henning's work details a form of rapier, or perhaps side sword, fencing that was different from the dominant Italian methods of the 17th century.

The works of prior Italian masters, most notably Fabris, were very popular throughout Europe in the 17th century. As rapiers became the dominant civilian weapon, the thrust became preferred over the cut. A variety of German masters copied or used similar techniques and terms as the Italians.

---

387   Wiktenauer, "Joachim Meyer", accessed May 20, 2016, http://wiktenauer.com/wiki/Joachim_Me%C3%B-Fer

388   Egerton Castle, Schools and Masters of Fencing, (London: George Bell and Sons, 1885), 147.

When Fabris died, according to Hynitzch, the school had gone to German students. Hans Wilhelm Schöffer von Dietz, who was a student of Fabris, recreated his treatise in the German language, adding his own flavor to it. Sebastian Heußler, a student of von Dietz, crafted his own treatise. Johan Gorge Pascha, who created over fourteen works on a variety of subjects, includes the use of the rapier in a style similar to that of prior Italians, including the use of the four primary guards.[389]

Henning, of whom we know little, felt compelled to write a treatise on cut fencing, in which the thrust and cut both had a significant place, unlike most rapier treatises.

His work is entirely text and the audience is unclear. In his introduction he states that friends asked him to write and he is only passing on what he and other learned men knew. Of himself, he says he makes no claim to make a profession at fencing and asks his readers forgive any mistakes he may make.

Henning's instructions are brief and include such advice as to parry with the edge because the flat is weaker, and to cut with little motions so as to not create openings. His instructions are not divorced from Italian methods, and he references the four primary Italian guards.

Questions are presented throughout the treatise, which Henning answers in simple phrases or with terse instructions. Such questions include what to do if an opponent cuts, stands in a guard, counter-cuts, or attacks with cross-cuts like the Poles.

Placing Henning's work is difficult, but it appears to be a blend of older German fencing, married to the dominant Italian theories, or a blend of 16th and 17th century Italian methods.[390]

England

While there was no true Italy or Germany in the 14th century, there was an England. Early English fencing traditions are difficult to pin down through documented treatises. England was not a highly literate culture in the same vein as Italy and the Holy Roman Empire in the 14th century, and it was not until the advent of the printing press and the influx of foreign, namely Italian, fencing masters that English martial arts were put to paper.

Dueling was not as acceptable in England as it was elsewhere until the influx of Italians in the 16th century. Monarchs, early on, had gone to great lengths to limit judicial and private dueling. This ranged from denying judicial duels, denying Passage of Arms, passing edicts, banning fencing schools and levying fines.

Henry VIII, wanting to revive what he saw as England's flagging martial spirit, allowed the creation of a fencing guild in London, similar to that of the Germans in 1540. The Company of Masters of the Science of Defense of London was established.[391]

---

389 Pascha's work includes wrestling techniques, such as how to protect against a thrown beer stein.
390 Erhardus Henning, trans. Reinier van Noort, "Short though thorough instruction in Cut-fencing", accessed May 20, 2016, http://www.bruchius.com/docs/Henning%20translation%20by%20RvN.pdf
391 Jay P. Anglin, "The Schools of Defense in Elizabethan London," Renaissance Quarterly, Volume XXXVII, Number 3, Autumn 1984, 395-396.

The guild was similar to the *Marxbrüder* in its operation, membership and challenges. The guild's purpose was to limit the amount of those who could teach fencing, while at the same time rigorously test any of their members who wished to rise in the ranks. The object was to maintain a high quality and a low quantity, which meant, economically, a pleasant little monopoly.

Four ancient masters controlled the guild; beneath them were men with a series of ranks, including master, provost and free scholar. Students swore oaths of loyalty to a master and in order to increase in rank had to train for a number of years and play a prize, which was a form of fight. This fighting was not a mortal fight, but rather a display of competency that was done in public under the watchful eye of the masters.

The public prizes were organized to raise money. The fighters would, with great ceremony, march to a square or market, and efforts were made to draw a crowd who would toss money onto a stage until enough was gathered that the prize could begin. The guild also made money through charging to teach lessons and requiring membership dues.[392]

Membership in the guild was not the noble elite, but the middle and lower classes. Men of title did not need to form guilds to make money. As had happened in Italy and the Holy Roman Empire, it appears that as judicial dueling declined, it was the middle class that became more interested in teaching and learning how to fence.

The *Marxbrüder* faced the challenge all monopolies do, that of competition. For them, it was the *Friefechter* and later *Federfechter*; for the Company of Masters, it was the Italians. Starting with Italian writings on fencing and followed by Italian instructors who catered to high society, the monopoly of the Company of Masters was eroded. Their charter had been revived by Henry's successor, but there are no records of Mary or Elizabeth I and certainly not the anti-duelist James I doing the same—meaning the guild was operating in a free market.

After Elizabeth's death, the King of Scotland also became the King of England. James I was England's first Scottish king and was dead-set against dueling. Scotland, like England, was not a highly literate culture in the 15th century but produced a greater and greater number of non-martial works in the 17th and 18th centuries leading to the Scottish Enlightenment. While not a product of the Enlightenment, Donald McBane detailed his own, less than gentlemanly, methods of personal combat in the 18th century.

England, meanwhile, relied on foreign influences, and the most famed fencing school in England in the 18th and 19th century belonged to the Angelos, who originally hailed from Italy.

Man yt Wol – The Man that Will

Penned roughly 1440, *The Man that Will* is a poem that loosely describes the earliest known English fencing. The author and context is unknown, and the language is an older form of English.

> The Use of the Two-hand Sworde
>
> The ferste pleyng & begÿnyng of the substansce of ye too honde swerde / ye ferst gronde be gynyth w an hauke beryng inwt ye foote wt a double rownde

---

392   "A Study of the London Masters of Defense", accessed May 30, 2016, http://iceweasel.org/lmod.html

wt. iij . fete howtewarde & as meny homward makyng ende of ye play wt a quarter cros smetyn wt an hauke snach settyng down by ye foote.

Which when translated and interpreted becomes,

The Use of the Two-Handed Sword

The first playing, and (the) beginning of the substance of the two handed sword: the first ground begins with a hawk, bearing in with the foot. (Followed) with a double round with three feet outward and as many homeward. Making (an) end of the play with a cross smitten, (followed) with a hawk snatch, (and finally) setting (the point of the sword) down by the foot.[393]

The exact meaning of the terms and descriptions can be interpreted, though not easily.

Jay Simpson of the Phoenix Society of Historical Swordsmanship poses with a longsword.

---

393   Benjamin G. Bradak and Brandon P. Heslop, Lessons on the English Longsword, (Boulder: Paladin Press, 2010), 155.

THE LEDALL ROLL (ADDITIONAL MS 39564)

Like *The Man that Will*, the Ledall Roll is largely a mystery. Likely created in the 16th century, it is unclear if the author was one J. Ledall or if Ledall was merely a scribe. There is no indication, either, if the instructions are copied, what their context is, or their meaning. As with *The Man that Will*, the Ledall Roll is written in an older form of English and includes terms that have to be interpreted to divine their meaning.

> A quarter fayre before you deliueryde at ??? hande voydyng baek the ryght fote yth an ??? quarter with both hands.
>
> Which when translated and interpreted becomes,
>
> (Begin with) a quarter fair (stroke) fair before you, delivered at the hand. (Then), voiding back the right foot, (attack) with (another) quarter (stroke) with both hands.[394]

As with the *Man that Will*, understanding the meaning behind the text is a difficult process. The most thorough examination of early English longsword can be found in Benjamin G. Bradak and Brandon P. Heslop's *Lessons on the English Longsword*.

GEORGE SILVER: PARADOXES OF DEFENSE

George Silver gives a window into the older systems of fencing as they collided with the new in the late 16th century. In England, the older system was professed by schools, such as the Company of Masters of the Science of Defense of London, and the newer system was introduced by traveling Italian fencing masters.

Silver decries the Italian system, as well as the French and Spanish, as murderous and false. He did not fully understand the dueling mania that was gripping high society and took a logical approach to comparing the English system to that of the Italian. His *Paradoxes of Defense*, published in 1599, explains who was teaching Italian rapier methods in England at the time. He cites three teachers.

The first was Rocco Bonetti, who had come to England 30 years prior to Silver's writings. Silver claims he lived lavishly and taught his rapier methods to the court and high-class gentlemen for exorbitant prices. An English fencer, Austin Bagger, with sword and buckler in hand, stood outside Rocco's house and challenged him.

Silver admits that Rocco was brave and charged into the street with a two handed sword. Bagger was able to get to grips with his opponent and throw him to the ground. Bagger was merciful and did not kill Rocco. According to Silver, whose bias is overwhelmingly negative, Rocco was involved in only one other fight—with a ferryman who used an oar to defeat his rapier.

Vincento Savolio and Jeronimo Bonetti, son of Rocco, were two other Italian fencing masters who also taught the upper class the art of the rapier. Both were insulting toward the English masters, and Jeronimo said that the English, though physically strong, retreated too much.

---

394   Ibid 61.

Silver, his brother Toby and other English fencing instructors sought the pair out, challenging them, going so far as to stride up to their school. Silver claims the two drew their rapiers, hid and were saved by a lovely woman who cried for help. Worse, the rumor spread that the two Italians had defeated all of the English masters of defense.

Vincento Savolio wrote a book on Italian fencing, *His Practice, in Two Books*, which Silver read and said was full of false teachings. In fact, Silver claimed that the Italian method was suicidal at best.

As for Jeronimo, Silver claims he was killed, rather easily, by an Englishman using traditional methods in a sudden duel.

Silver's own methods were traditional English methods. They included concepts such as understanding true and false times and proceeding with the utmost safety. In a quip, Silver notes that two Italians who fight will likely kill each other, but two Englishmen, knowing a perfect defense, will part ways, each keeping their skin.

Despite his complaints about the Italian method, as well as the Spanish, the rapier continued to become the mainstay weapon of England's gentlemen, and Italian methods supplanted the older English ones. While Silver outlaid logical reasons to stick with the sword and buckler, he did not understand that the fashion of the rapier among the gentlemen of Europe was not to be undone by pointing out the rapier's faults.[395]

In the following century, foreign methods would remain dominant and be adopted by the locals. In 1612, Joseph Swetnam[396] introduced his approach to Italian fencing with an acknowledgement that the old methods of England were not relevant.

> Because old weapons lie rusty in a corner, and every man is desirous of the newest fashion of weapons, especially if they seem to be more danger to the enemy than the old, therefore it is my intent and purpose at this time to express and set down both the true and false play principally of the rapier and dagger…[397]

Donald McBane: Expert Sword-Man's Companion

Ben Ker, who compiled McBane's experiences of the 18th century, best summarizes his life,

> Growing up in Inverness and later joining the British regiments, McBane travelled across Europe pimping, dueling, blowing himself up, and performing other incredible feats of a not always admirable nature. The last we hear of him is when he comes out of his retirement in his fifties to fight one last bout in Edinburgh against an uppity Irish youngster, where he defeated his opponent and walked off with barely a scratch himself.

While nearly every fencing treatise was directed at the middle class and above, McBane's experiences and advice come from, literally, the gutter. While his stories perhaps stretch the imagination, his use of the small sword and spadroon is based on his rough and tumble experiences.

---

395   George Silver, "Paradoxes of Defense", accessed May 30, 2016, http://www.pbm.com/~lindahl/paradoxes.html

396   When not writing about fencing, Swetnam busied himself with pamphlets complaining about empowered women.

397   Translation provided by Steven Hick.

Of his upbringing, he says he was trained by many masters and eventually became one himself, teaching others how to defend themselves from all manner of attacks, including ungentlemanly tricks such as sand in the face.

Even though a low-born soldier, McBane understood the concept of honor. When accused of a crime and beaten by his corporal, McBane challenged the man to a duel. He mortally wounded his opponent and had to flee for his life because dueling was punishable by death in the army. His opponent, a gentleman to the end, aided McBane in his escape before expiring. Not all of McBane's opponents were gentlemen.

McBane also fought pimps and random soldiers, sometimes from his own side, and engaged in a variety of adventures that included owning a whore-house and, indeed, getting blown up by a pile of grenades but miraculously surviving.

His advice can be delightfully practical:

> When you have a quarrel with any man, and have not opportunity to decide it immediately, don't trust him within reach unless others be present or near. And when you are going to fight, or returning from it, having got the better, don't trust your adversary behind you…[398]

McBane's work included simple illustrations, and he published it in 1728 after a lifetime of soldiering and adventuring. In his last duel, he used a falchion to break his opponent's arm but excused himself, saying several gentlemen had asked him to do it.

DOMENICO ANGELO: L'ECOLE DES ARMES, THE SCHOOL OF ARMS

Domenico was born in Italy and moved to France to teach fencing. From there, finding high society too costly, he traveled to England, much like the Italian masters of George Silver's era, and like them, set up a fencing school directed not at the masses, but rather at well-to-do gentlemen. Nobles flocked to him and he gained a reputation as a first-rate fencer.

He was challenged by an Irish, Dr. Keys, and fenced him in public, easily deflecting Keys' attacks and responding with his own. Success in the duel only brought more fame.

His school was successful and would last for four generations and be visited by high society as well as soldiers who wanted to learn the art of fencing.

Domenico Angelo's 1763 work on the small sword marks, roughly, when dueling swords were no longer worn for civilian defense and the pistol became the favored weapon to duel with. Fencing was fast changing from a martial art to a sport. This was, however, not an overnight experience.

---

398 Mark Rector, Highland Swordsmanship, (Union City: Chivalry Bookshelf, 2001), 57.

James Harvey Grant of the Phoenix Society of Historical Swordsmanship on guard with a small sword.

Angelo's work was originally meant for the duel and a few cases of self-defense. The work was a collection of illustrated pages with brief directions. The work was reprinted in combination with other material from his son, Henry.

Classical fencing in England can trace its roots to the Angelos, and their praises were still being sung a hundred years after Domenico's arrival in England. When Alfred Hutton, English antiquarian, fencer, soldier and historian wrote his history book, *The Sword and the Centuries*, he lovingly referred to the family of fencing instructors as "our" Angelos.[399]

---

399   Alfred Hutton, The Sword and the Centuries, (Staffordshire: Wren's Park Publishing, 2003 org. 1901), 253-255.

Fencing as depicted by Angelo.[400]

France

Early French treatises on martial arts are rare. There is a treatise on the poleaxe by a Milanese master in the service of Burgundy and little else.

French references to training in the 14th and 15th century is more along the line of acrobatics than fencing, and may have been typical of the time. Boucicaut, who had dueled Fiore's student Galeazzo, had no named master of his own, but rather conducted feats of strength to help him train. Froissart detailed these feats and they included leaping onto his horse while armored, climbing walls, long hikes and striking a wooden log or block of stone with his sword or mace- supposedly very hard.[401]

What may have stood in for French training were copies of Roman writings. *De Re Militari* was a Roman-Era work by Vegetius. There are some scanty references to swordsmanship in the *De Re Militari*, but the focus is largely on military tactics, war, and recruitment. There is also serious debate as to how well read these works were by the fighting classes, or what impact they had.[402]

---

400 https://commons.wikimedia.org/wiki/File:Angelo_Domenico_Malevolti_Fencing_Print,_1763.JPG Public Domain Art.
401 F. Kottenkamp, The History of Chivalry and Armor, (Mineloa: Dover Publications, 2007 org. 1857), 31.
402 Christian Höschler, "Christopher Allmand: The De Re Militari of Vegetius. The Reception, Transmission and Legacy of a Roman Text in the Middle Ages (reviewed by Everett L. Wheeler)", accessed October 1, 2016, http://www.recensio.net/rezensionen/zeitschriften/reviews-in-history/2012/july/the-de-re-militari-of-vegetius

French treatises became more commonplace after the advent of the printing press in the late 17th century. The dominant Italian school of fencing was in many ways supplanted by the French, who varied and changed Italian methods to fit their own. The French lunge was longer than the Italian, and the French were considered the finest fencers in the 18th century.

The French took to dueling, perhaps more so than even the Italians, who supposedly started the craze after the demise of the judicial duel. An increasingly bored and rich aristocracy, combined with steady empowerment of the monarchy, fueled the desire to duel.

Edicts were passed and ignored, starting in 1566 with Charles IX who forbid armed gentlemen from congregating in large numbers, to Henri IV, in the early 17th century, declaring dueling a crime against the king, since it deprived him of officers and state servants. Not that he did much about it.

Louis XIII and his advisor Cardinal Richelieu did much to expand the French monarchy's power, and Louis XIV, the Sun King, embodied absolutism. They both had to contend with duelists who seemed to revel in defying the edicts of their monarchs, even at the cost of their lives. Great efforts were made to curb the practice, and heads rolled, but weaker monarchs, like Louis XV and his son, were not so bold. Dueling crept back into fashion. It would be revolution that curbed dueling in exchange for guillotines, only to see it return, especially in the armies of Napoleon Bonaparte.[403]

Alexander Dumas, author of the Three Musketeers, perhaps best defined France in its dueling hey-day.

> Never fear quarrels, but seek hazardous adventures. Fight on all occasions; fight the more for duels being forbidden, since, consequently, there is twice as much courage in fighting.

Le Jeu de la Hache: The Play of the Axe

The oldest French treatise isn't actually French. *The Play of the Axe* was written by a fencing master from Milan who was in the service of the Duke of Burgundy in the early 15th century. The instructions within the work are written in Middle French, without illustrations, and include techniques to use with a poleaxe, including advice on facing someone who is left handed.

The techniques include trips, plays from the binding of two poleaxes, thrusts and more. They are to the point and practical.

> If again he comes at you with a swing, and you have the *queue* forward. You must move to receive the blow to the right side of your opponent, and from there receive his blow *demy hache*. And at the same time, as close as you can, you must advance your left foot and place it behind his heel really firmly, as you raise his axe which is above yours. And place your *queue* under his chin, and thus give him a jolt backwards to knock him to the ground.
>
> If you fail. You must return on guard. And this should be done quickly.[404]

The author seems to imply the fight is a duel, in that there is one other opponent armed with the same weapon across a field. The intended audience, however, is broad, and in the opening lines the

---

403   Roland Mousnier University of Chicago Press, Mar 1, 1984 p 104
404   ARMA, "Le jeu de la Hache," accessed May 30, 2016, http://www.thearma.org/spotlight/NotesLE-JEUDELAHACHE.htm#.V1ITBPkrKUk May 30 2016

author says that all men, noble or otherwise, should want to live and best learn how to defend themselves. The author also suggests that armor be both physical and spiritual, which fit well in a society where in battle God determined the winner.[405]

From Talhoffer, two armored opponents use poleaxes while within the barriers of what is likely a judicial duel. Le Jeu de la Hache references a similar weapon and situation[406].

Henry de Sainct Didier: Les Secrets du Premier Livre sur L'espée Seule, Secrets of the Premier Book on the Single Sword

In 1573, the only known and/or surviving copy of Henry de Sainct Didier's works was published in French. His surviving work covers the use of the sword alone. As to what type of sword, it appears to be a side sword, the variety most like a proto-rapier, complete with a complicated hand guard. The sword is able to both cut and thrust.

The author was a solider for over two decades and fought at length in the Italian Wars, where he most likely picked up Italian notions of fencing that were Bolognese in nature. His work is similar to Di Grassi's in choice of weapon and style. Like di Grassi, Sainct Didier proposes three guards, a high, middle and low guard, with the point directed at the enemy. Unlike 17th century

---

405   Wiktenauer, "Le Jeu de la Hace", accessed May 30, 2016, http://wiktenauer.com/wiki/Le_Jeu_de_la_Hache_(MS_Fran%C3%A7ais_1996)
406   Image courtesy the Royal Library of Copenhagen.

rapier masters, who suggested only standing right foot forward when using the single sword, Sainct Didier suggests a fencer start off on the left foot. He breaks down attacks simply as a thrust and a cut from the right, a *madritto,* or left, a *riverso*—and he explains how best to defend against them and in return offend.

At the time of his writing, Sainct Didier was in the service of the French King and aware of the methods stemming out of Italy, even using their terms. In his work he introduces a conversation where Sainct Didier explains to a curious pair of fencers why he believes only three strikes are needed, as opposed to other Italian masters who included more. Didier claims that simple is best and that by limiting his defenses and offenses to three forms of striking, a cut from the left, a cut from the right and a thrust, he has a true art that is easier to manage.[407]

Portrait of Henry de Sainct Didier from his own surviving work on the use of the sword. The weapon of the mid to late 16th century was a proto-rapier, capable of thrusts and cuts and not overly long.[408]

---

407   Henri de Sainct Didier, trans. Chris Slee, "The Secrets of the Single Sword", accessed May 25, 2016, http://sleech.info/wp-content/uploads/2012/11/The-Secrets-of-the-Single-Sword-General-Essay1.pdf
408   https://commons.wikimedia.org/wiki/File:Henry_de_Sainct-Didier.jpg Public Domain Art.

Philibert de la Touche: *Les Vrays Principes de l'Espée Seule*, The True Principles of the Single Sword

The 16th and 17th century Italian methods of fencing were translated into French and popular there. In some cases, Italian masters traveled to France, just as they had elsewhere. Calvacabo, a Bolognese fencer, was from Italy but eventually ended up in the court of Henri IV, teaching his son how to fence and providing a French translation of the Bolognese master Viggiani. Calvacabo's own work remained with the French, influencing their attitudes towards fencing. The 17th century Italian masters such as Fabris, Giganti and Capoferro were all known in France, and Italian works continued to be translated and adopted by the French.

Nearing the 18th century, however, the French modified both the sword and the techniques. The long, thin rapier was exchanged for a smaller, lighter sword, directed almost entirely at the thrust. The techniques adapted to the nimbler sword.

Philibert de la Touche's work was published in 1670 and dedicated to Louis XIV the Sun King. Rather than showing mortal combat, de la Touche depicts men using small swords with flexible tips and rounded tips. While fencing without a mask was still dangerous, the intent is more in line with sport and presentation. The Sun King had gone to great lengths to extinguish the private duel, but he was a fan of artistry such as ballet, architecture and fencing.

The techniques of de la Touche are similar to those already advocated by Italians in the early 18th century, but he made changes. In particular, the lunge is extended by stretching out as far and low as possible, to the point that the rear foot, normally planted, extends from the toes.

While the Italians had four primary guards, the French in the later 17th century added more, and instead of using the Italian numbering system of *prima*, *secunda*, *terza* and *quarta*, replaced it with the French form of *prime*, *secunde*, *tierce*, *quarte*, *quinte* and *septime*.[409] French terms replaced Italian. Terms such as the *cavazione*, to disengage the sword and move to the other side, became the dégager.

New French methods include heavier use of the beat, to knock aside the sword, and alterations to the Italian guards and lunge.

The Academy of Fencing masters in 1567 required a provost to use the sword, but also use other weapons such as the greatsword, staff and halberd. Restrictions were lightened in 1644, but the French continued to demand at least the demonstration of older weapons as a means of keeping Italian masters, who did not know these weapons as well, at bay.[410]

The French methods gradually became dominant, not only in the sport of fencing, but also in self-defense and dueling with the small sword. Rapiers, whose length were at times so ridiculous as to earn contemporary commentary, gave way to the small sword throughout most of Europe.[411] With the adoption of the small sword, the French masters rose in popularity, and French methods supplanted older, though long-dominant, Italian ones.

Other French masters continued to develop the use of the small sword, such as Besnard and Liancour in the late 17th century, and their works were influential throughout Europe during the 18th century.

---

409   Egerton Castle, Schools and Masters of Fencing, (London: George Bell and Sons, 1885),139-141.
410   P Brioist, H Drévillon, P Serna, Croiser le fer: violence et culture de l'épée dans la France moderne, XVIe-XVIIIe siècle, (Paris: Champ Vallon, 2002), 87.
411   Thibault makes light of the fact that most men did not know how to gracefully draw their rapiers.

From Philibert de la Touche, a lunge is countered with a volte, or what Italians called an inquartata.[412]

MONSIEUR L' ABBAT: QUESTIONS SUR L'ART EN FAIT D'ARMES, THE ART OF FENCING: THE USE OF THE SMALL SWORD

L'Abbat's work was published in 1696. He had come from a family of fencers teaching in Toulouse since the latter portion of the 16th century. As in del la Touche's work, the use of the small sword was depicted with brief instructions and illustrations.

L'Abbat's lunge is not quite as extended as his predecessor's but is still lengthy. His style of fencing was typical of the small sword and the French methodology.

A key difference in the French method of fencing was the use of the riposte. Italian methods of the 17th century relied on single-time actions. The attack and defense were one in the same, which led to criticism, most notably from George Silver, that it was easy to end up with both fencers being hit. The French worked with a two-time system, where the nimble small sword deflected an attack and then responded—parry and riposte. The Italian and Spanish systems were seen in comparison as too reliant on mathematical principles, lacking in the realism of a back and forth duel.

Other techniques, unique to French fencing, were proposed as well. L'Abbat shows a thrust under an opponent's sword into their side called the *flannconade*.

L'Abbat's work was influential, enough so that in 1734 his work was translated into English and still deemed relevant. Artistically, the images were simplistic and the text brief and to the point.

---

412   https://commons.wikimedia.org/wiki/File:Les_Vrayes_principes_de_l%27esp%C3%A9e_seule.jpg Public Domain Art.

From L'Abbat, the thrust is parried with the use of the off-hand. The swords, as with del la Touche, have swelled tips to indicate a sparring, not mortal, encounter. The lunge is not quite as long as la Touche's.[413]

Spain

Spain was unified in 1492 and had two systems of fencing, the older *esgrima común*, or common fencing, and a newer method, likely based on Agrippa's work, *La Verdadera Destreza*, or the True Art and Skill.

Destreza was an art based on keen geometric principles, both in terms of stance and movement. The Spanish fencer, instead of leaning back or bending forward, stood in a tall, upright narrow stance with an arm extended to create a 90 degree angle. From here, the Spanish fencer calmly circled his opponent, seeking to gain the blade, *atajo*, by touching the opponent's sword, *tacto*. At range, they allowed their opponent to run upon their sword. Up close, they could pass and grapple, ready to deliver a cut.

Destreza dominated Spain as the premier method of fencing and was known throughout Europe. George Silver described it in his *Paradoxes of Defense* in 1599.

---

413   https://columbiaclassicalfencing.com/2015/02/08/monsieur-labbat-on-blade-cant-and-bend/ Public Domain Art.

> This is the manner of the Spanish fight. They stand as brave as they can with their bodies straight upright, narrow spaced, with their feet continually moving, as if they were in a dance, holding forth their arms and rapiers very straight against the face or bodies of their enemies, and this is the only lying to accomplish that kind of fight. And this note, that as long as any man shall lie in that manner with his arm, and the point of his rapier straight, it shall be impossible for his adversary to hurt him, because in that straight holding forth of his arm, which way soever a blow shall be made against him, by reason that his rapier hilt lies so far before him, he has but a very little way to move, to make his ward perfect, in this manner. If a blow is made at the right side of the head, a very little moving of the hand with the knuckles upward defends that side of the head or body, and the point being still out straight, greatly endangers the striker. And so likewise, if a blow is made at the left side of the head, a very small turning of the wrist with the knuckles downward, defends that side of the head and body, and the point of rapier much endangers the hand, arm, face or body of the striker. And if any thrust is made, the wards, by reason of the indirections in moving the feet in manner of dancing, as aforesaid, makes a perfect ward, and still withal the point greatly endangers the other. And thus is the Spanish fight perfect: so long as you can keep that order, and soon learned, and therefore to be accounted the best fight with the rapier of all other.[414]

In *Romeo and Juliet*, there is an idea that Tybalt's fencing is not brave and reckless, as a good Italian's fencing should be, but instead is of the Spanish variety. When Mercutio is stabbed by Tybalt due to Romeo's interference, he says of his foe,

> A braggart, a rogue, a villain that fights by the book of arithmetic!

17th century Italians derided the Spanish system, claiming it could not work in a street encounter, while the Dutch valued it in the form of Thibault, but found it too difficult to master.[415] Two centuries later, amateur historians like Egerton Castle would write Spanish off as overly complicated to no great purpose.

Halfway into the 18th century, the Spanish method remained and was mentioned by Angelo in his small sword treatise as a possible encounter.

> The Spaniards have in fencing a different method to all other nations; they are fond often of giving the cut to the head and immediately after deliver a thrust between the eyes and the throat. Their guard is almost straight, their lunge very small; when they come in distance they bend the right knee and straighten the left and carry the body forward; when they retire, they bend the left knee and straighten the right, they throw the body back well, in straight line with that of the antagonist and parry with the left hand or flip the right foot behind the left.

---

414   George Silver, "Paradoxes of Defense", accessed May 30, 2016, http://www.pbm.com/~lindahl/paradoxes.html

415   Jacopo Monesi and Johannes Georgius Bruchius were contemporaries but had opposite views on the Spanish system.

Their swords are near five feet from hilt to point and cut with both edges; the shell is very large…[416]

The Spanish stance and methodology changed very little from the 16th to 18th century.[417]

JERÓNIMO SÁNCHEZ DE CARRANZA: DE LA FILOSOFIA DE LAS ARMAS Y DE SU DESTREZA Y LA AGGRESSION Y DEFENSA CRISTIANA, ON THE PHILOSOPHY OF ARMS AND ITS SKILL, AND CHRISTIAN OFFENSE AND DEFENSE

The founder of *Destreza* had a geometric approach to fencing. Luis Pacheco de Narváez claimed this was borrowed from Agrippa's, whose approach to Italian fencing broke from the traditional Bolognese style of cut and thrust and many guards in exchange for four guards and a reliance on the thrust. Carranza presented his ideas in a book in 1569, seventeen years after Agrippa.

Carranza used only one primary guard, which used the maximum reach possible to keep the opponent at bay. Like Agrippa, Carranza used geometric principles to justify this new method, which he found scientific. Also like Agrippa, he spent time explaining the mathematical principles behind his methods.

The approach in his writing is conversational, with a group of friends discussing the art of arms. Polemarcho, a character in the dialogue, laments the state of arms at the time.

> To this, in turn, Polemarcho said, the Skill is damaged by men of low quality and humble understanding who use it according to their talent, not to the merit of the Skill. You know already that the art cannot be blamed for the ignorance of the Craftsman. It is evident, as the Divine Plato affirms, that in all the sciences there are many insignificant men of low quality and poor estimation. Especially in the Art we discuss, there are professors of it who are the dregs of the republic. So know well that to be the Skilled Man is not to be it in name.

---

416 Domenico Angelo, The School of Fencing with a General Explanation of the Principal Attitudes and Positions Peculiar to the Art. with Hungarian and Highland Broad Sword and The Angelo Cutlass Exercises, (London: Land's End Press, 1971 org. 1765), 93.
417 Public Domain Art.

In other words, people did not know the true way of fighting, which was not the fault of the art, but rather of those practicing it.

The conversation continues in which the friends, gradually, realize that there is a true skill that is a science and that ignorant men have not learned its lessons.

Adam Simmons and Randy Reyes of the Phoenix Society of Historical Swordsmanship demonstrate the Spanish method in action. Note Randy's upright posture and extended arm as he passes back in response to Adam's lunge.

Contextually, Carranza's work is directed at everyone in Spain who uses weapons. While Agrippa felt his methods mathematically superior to the Bolognese system, Carranza takes this a step further by claiming methods unlike his own were morally wrong because they led to all manner of evils. His student, Luis Pacheco de Narváez, would take this concept even further.[418]

Luis Pacheco de Narváez: Libro de las Grandezas de la Espada and De la Filosofia de las Armas y de su Destreza (revised), A Book of Greatness of the Sword and On the Philosophy of Arms and its Skill, and Christian Offense and Defense

Pacheco was a student of Carranza and would go on to become the premier fencer of Spain. Like Carranza, he sought to do away with older methods of fencing and went to extreme lengths to see this through.

---

418   Wiktenauer, "Jerónimo Sánchez de Carranza", accessed May 30, 2016, http://wiktenauer.com/wiki/Jer%C3%B3nimo_S%C3%A1nchez_de_Carranza

He was challenged to a duel by author Don Francisco de Quevedo, who found the mathematical system of Pacheco and his teacher Carranza not all it was cut out to be. In the duel, Pacheco's hat was removed by Don Francisco's rapier.

Don Francisco would go on to write about a fictional account of the duel in *El Buscón or Vida del Buscón*, while Pacheco would report his opponent to the Inquisition for his book collection. Both men were in danger, however. The Inquisition was intolerant of dueling, even abroad.

Brantome recounted that two Spaniards wanted to duel, but dueling in Spain was illegal. They could not find anywhere to safely duel in Europe and so arranged to fight in Ottoman North Africa. The Inquisition found out and publicly threatened them with the death penalty if they went through with the duel. The men relented and did not fight.

In the case of Pachceo and Don Francisco, they were not punished for dueling, though later Don Francisco would run a man through in a duel and be forced to flee for his life and spend a life, he self-described, as depraved.

Pacheco released his own work on fencing in 1600 and a revised version of Carranza's later in the century. In the revision, Pacheco sought to correct what he saw as mistakes in his master's work. This led to a break in the unified traditions of *Destreza*.

As did Carranza, Pacheco sought to eliminate all other rival system to his own to create a recognized, national system of Spain.[419] This was largely successful as *Destreza* remained dominant in Spain well into the 18th century.

Netherlands

Like Italy and Germany, the Netherlands did not exist as a defined entity until the modern era. The region was known as the Low Countries, and included present day Netherlands and Belgium. The Netherlands had the fortune and misfortune of being wedged between larger powers: France on one side, the Holy Roman Empire on the other and England across the sea. This was good for trade, but also turned the region into a battleground between outside powers. When Burgundy controlled the Low Countries they largely let the cities within run themselves, which encouraged economy and trade.

After Charles the Bold's death in 1477, the Burgundian territories were divided up between France and the Holy Roman Empire. Charles V became ruler over the Netherlands. During this time foreign trade was vital to the Dutch trading cities, such as Amsterdam and Antwerp.

The Reformation struck hard. Charles V's son, who had inherited Spain and the Netherlands, attempted to wipe out Protestantism and establish strong, Spanish rule throughout the Low Countries. The Dutch resented this and with foreign support resisted the Spanish.

The Dutch revolt against the Spanish was part of the larger 80 years war. The northern provinces

---

419   Wiktenauer, "Luis Pacheco de Narváez", accessed May 30, 2016, http://wiktenauer.com/wiki/Luis_Pacheco_de_Narvaez

of the Netherlands had ousted the Spanish by 1581 and in the Peace of Westphalia in 1648 their sovereignty was made official. The Netherlands, known as the Dutch Republic, were an independent entity but not all of the Low Countries were independent. Spain remained in control of the Southern provinces including the city of Antwerp.

The Dutch ability to trade was famous and Amsterdam was, and still is, a major trade city in the North of Europe. The city was also dangerous, with swaggering foreigners butting elbows with local roughs on a continual basis.

Guilds within the Low Countries armed themselves for protection and from there developed guilds dedicated to fencing, the use of the crossbow and handgunners. The fencing guilds were officially established at the end of the 15th and into the 16th century.[420]

Because of the many states with interests in their territory and their extensive trading ventures, the Dutch had access to fencing material from all over Europe. Concepts and ideas from Italy's Fabris and the Spanish *Destreza* system wound their way into the treatises of Dutch masters in the 17th century.

The Dutch also had material specifically geared toward self-defense, including wrestling holds and means to defend against knife attacks—something that occurred all too often in cities like Amsterdam.

Gérard Thibault: *Academie de l'Espée*, Academy of the Sword

Thibault's work is a curious tome of rapier instruction that was lauded in his own time but seen as difficult to perform. Thibault was from Antwerp and used concepts from Spanish fencing but wrote his massive treatise in French. In his formative years he learned the fencing art of *Destreza* in Spain. But he returned to the Low Countries and in Rottedam in 1611 won a fencing competition. He continued to demonstrate his methods, and was invited into royal courts, such as that of Prince Maurice of Nassau.

Though he had his skeptics, he tended to win them over and eventually set to work on compiling his system in a book. Over sixteen engravers were used to create what was to be one of the largest fencing treatises ever created—both in volume and physical size.

The physically enormous book was published in 1630 after Thibault's death and included lavish engravings and detailed instructions. So expensive was the work that individual pages were to be sponsored, some of which never were and have blank "advertising" spots.

While many treatises used illustrations, they tended to show only a single moment of time. A play might be drawn mid-way through, or just after completion. To be as thorough as possible, Thibault's illustrations show numerous aspects of a motion. It is not unusual to have six separate images detailing a single technique. Furthermore, he wrote extensively in the form of two named players performing the techniques.

Thibault covers just about every conceivable situation with the rapier, including rapier against rapier, but also rapier against rapier and dagger, against someone using the methods of Fabris,

---

420   Reinier van Noort, Interview, September 23, 2016.

against a longsword and even against a firearm! Thibault also includes advice on how to properly draw a long rapier, and true to form, illustrates every moment it takes to do so.

Contemporaries were as amazed as they were overwhelmed. Johannes Georgius Bruchius, who wrote the first rapier treatise printed in the Dutch language singled Thibault out as a great master, but lamented that his style of circle-fencing was not in fashion and people did not have the time required to properly study it anymore.

Unlike the Italians of the 17th century, who used a linear method of fencing, Thibault was more akin to the Spanish, using circling motions while keeping the sword-arm extended. Thibault's rapier is held differently than most, and the guard is designed for his specific grip. His footwork is detailed with geometric principles and artwork.[421]

JOHANNES GEORGIUS BRUCHIUS: GRONDIGE BESCHRYVINGE VAN DE EDELE ENDE RIDDERLIJKE – OFTE WAPEN-KONSTE, THOROUGH DESCRIPTION OF THE NOBLE AND KNIGHTLY FENCING—OR WEAPON-ART

The first fencing treatise printed in the Netherlands in the Dutch language was by Johannes Georgius Bruchius in 1671. The book was for the use of the rapier with no other accompanying weapons shown. By this point, the Italian methods of fencing were already well known, and Bruchius acknowledges that much of what he was writing was in the footsteps of Fabris.

The translator of his work, Reinier van Noort, notes that Bruchius' style of fencing is also similar to the German rapier masters such as Sebastian Heußler, Hans Wilhelm Schöffer von Dietz and Joachim Köppe, all of which were in line with 17th century Italian rapier methodology.

While Fabris told his readers his book was primarily for dueling, Bruchius takes a different approach and suggests his work is not for willful murder but for self-defense.

Furthermore, Bruchius took the concepts of tempo, measure and movement, which were already well-established, and combined them. Knowing tempo, measure and movement was not enough, because a fencer had to bring these concepts together in what Bruchius called *Resolutie*, or Resolution.

Structurally, the book involves two named players who perform a variety of actions that are described by text and illustrated with images of men wearing standard attire of the era.

NICOLAES PETTER: KLARE ONDERRICHTINGE DER VOORTREFFELIJKE WORSTEL-KONST, CLEAR EDUCATION IN THE MAGNIFICENT ART OF WRESTLING

The treatise of Nicolaes Petter was published after his death in 1674. The treatise is explicitly for self-defense and is a window to the practical applications of martial arts. While many treatises cover the use of the sword, Petter's book focuses on wrestling.

First, the book laments the death of Petter, but is kind to let the readers know that his student, Robert Cors, was living at the house of his widow and willing to teach at a reasonable price.

---

421 Gérard Thibault, trans. John Michael Greer, Academy of the Sword, (Highland Park, TX: The Chivalry Bookshelf, 2006).

Second, the book starts off in a natural setting, detailing to the reader a likely encounter and why wrestling will be of importance.

> It is common, especially with Hollanders, that every argument, or fight between people, will go to such levels that will end in a physical fight.
>
> It starts with chest-pushing and then turns into fist-strikes.[422]

From there, Petter describes a variety of wrestling techniques that are applicable in a likely street encounter. Petter's book was very much directed at the public at large, not just high society. The detailed artistic plates, engraved by Romeyn de Hooghe, a famous artist of the time, depict numerous scenarios, from wrestling to defending against a knife.

Petter was, in his lifetime, famous for his wrestling prowess, and for over a century his work was republished and remained in high esteem. Copies of his work were translated from Dutch into French, German and English.[423]

Poland

John Patterson and Richard Marsden of the Phoenix Society of Historical Swordsmanship in 17th century Polish attire.

422 Translation by Jerome Blanes.
423 Nicolaes Petter, trans. Jerome Blanes, Self-defense Martial Art.

Poland in the 15th century established itself as a major power in Eastern Europe by uniting with Lithuania and defeating the Teutonic Knights at the Battle of Grunwald in 1410.

In the 16th century Poland transitioned to an elective monarchy that continued until Poland was absorbed by its more absolutist neighbors, Prussia, Russia and Austria at the end of the 18th century.

The Poles had their own system of fencing that used the *szabla*, the saber. Poland adopted European ideas on fencing and dueling, but only applied them haphazardly. The memoirs of a 17th century Polish *szlachta*, or noble, Jan Pasek, give colorful examples of the rough and tumble lifestyle of the time. Pasek engages in several duels, but never attempts to kill his opponents with thrusts. Instead, he tries to cut their hands. Dueling in Poland, while common, and in some ways legal, could also be countered legally. Pasek complains bitterly in his memoirs of the lawsuits that hounded him, most arising from his violent behavior.

While Polish nobles were aware of the Italian customs of dueling, such as sending challenges, they did not always adhere to them. Jan Pasek was once challenged, but rather than await a time and place to duel, rode up to the front gates of his opponent and demanded an apology. This was granted, giving the reader the sense that Pasek had arrived at the man's front door with a veritable army at his heels.

The Polish nobility had immense legal protections, or what they called Golden Freedoms. This included the right to declare a legal war on their enemies or even the king. This was similar to issuing a challenge, but it could involve entire family clans. Furthermore, this was a legal process called an *odpowiedź*.

However, dropping off an *odpowiedź* at the local court was a rather public way of alerting an enemy, and so though the process existed, it was rarely used. Instead, the Poles met as fate would dictate it, and single duels were likely not as common as skirmishes between factions.[424]

There are no known period treatises on the use of the Polish saber. However, by looking at other sources and later works, it is possible to interpret their system and attitude towards dueling. For example, the use of the cut, in particular the cross-cut, can be seen by piecing together historical clues.

Joachim Meyer's 1560 treatise depicts a man in Polish attire using a dussack, indicating some connection. This could have been a student of Meyer's, or influences in the use of the dussack coming from Poland. The cross-cut, for example, appears in Meyer's work, but also in other national treatises.

Erhardus Henning in the 17th century briefly mentions the Polish cross-cutting by name, though in a negative light. After giving advice on how to handle an opponent who comes in with wild attacks, as an aside, Henning adds,

> And here must be noted well that one can also make these same lessons against someone who uses the cross-cuts, which fight is indeed held high by some, but is not at all from the (his) art, but can much more be named a natural or Polish fight.[425]

---

424   Norman Davies, God's Playground, (New York: Columbia Press, 1989), 352-353.
425   Erhardus Henning, trans. Reinier van Noort, "Short though thorough instruction in Cut-fencing", accessed May 20, 2016, http://www.bruchius.com/docs/Henning%20translation%20by%20RvN.pdf

Father Jezierski described the Polish and other European systems by attributing them to dances.

> It seems that, just as merriment has its own outward ways of expression, where the national character is exhibited in various dances, so the movements resulting from anger influence the ways one uses steel.[426]

In the 18th century, Kitowicz made commentary on how the Polish conducted themselves in years past. He includes excerpts on training with sticks, called *Palcaty* (singular *palact*), as well as their attitudes toward dueling. He notes that a walking stick with a war hammer head called a *nadziak* had become popular. Duels with such weapons, however, were incredibly fatal. He noted that with a saber, the usual result was a cut hand, or cheek or ear, but with a *nadziak* people would have their skulls crushed.[427] In the 19th century, Michaeł Starzewski wrote instructions on fencing that are attributed to 17th century methods. Though his techniques have a very 19th century flavor to them, he does note that dueling in the 17th century was performed with cuts over thrusts, sometimes just to the sash that Polish nobles wore.[428]

By considering all the components of Polish culture and the accounts of their swordsmanship, it is possible to interpret their methods.

Richard Marsden and John Patterson of the Phoenix Society of Historical Swordsmanship face one another in the manner of 17th century Poles.

---

426 Translated by Daria Izdebska.
427 Richard Marsden, Polish Saber, (Phoenix: Tyrant Industries, 2015), 38.
428 Ibid 46.

Tim Hall and Casper Andersen wrestling in a finals tournament. Wrestling, called Ringen in German sources, was historically practiced for both amusement as well as earnest combat. Photo courtesy of Véronique McMillan of the Triangle Sword Guild.

Conclusion

The history of Historical European Martial Arts is, quite understandably, vast. Narrowing down the timeframe between the 14th and 18th century limited the scope of this work and yet just one aspect of HEMA's context, such as judicial dueling, or self-defense, could be a weighty tome unto itself.

In broad terms, HEMA's context depends on the time period in question. Early treatises were focused on judicial dueling, the sanctioned duels between nobles and the tournament. However, by the 16th century legalized dueling was largely forbidden, driving the duel underground, where it still retained many of the customs from before, including the use of gloves, exchanging of letters, and the use of seconds and so on.

The private duel, *a la mazza*, as Brantome put it, was the driving force behind many fencing treatises into the later 16th and 17th century. Fabris, celebrated for his complete knowledge of the art of fencing, outright declared dueling the purpose of his work.

Yet, as the private duel was steadily clamped down upon, masters took pains to mention their works were also for self-defense, as Bruchius noted in his introduction, or for sport, as can be seen in late 17th century French material that depicts fencing with swords ending in rounded tips.

Self-defense was a universal application of the martial arts of Europe, where both armed and unarmed combat could be, literally, life savers. Examples exist in some of the earliest writing on martial arts, such as Fiore de Liberi depicting defense from an assassin with a dagger, to the mid-18th century, with Domenico Angelo, who noted how to defend against more urban encounters, such as a swordsman with a blinding lamp. While judicial and private dueling faded away, the motive of self-defense as a purpose behind martial arts remained. However, murder rates dropped rapidly from the 15th to 20th century. Just as Mair and Meyer complained that people saw less value in their arts, 19th century self-defense masters echoed the same sentiment. Egerton Castle, noted in his particular haughty manner, that in his lifetime, the modern science of policing was making the need for self-defense and the wearing of weapons obsolete.[429]

War was generally not the purpose of the treatises, though war lurked ever present in the background. Some masters, like those of the Bolognese school, were seeking a universal method of fencing, one that would be applicable in any situation. As gunpowder's use on the battlefield increased, the learning of martial arts changed. Mair and Meyer both noted, with great lament, that interest in learning martial arts declined because of a greater reliance on gunpowder. Fabris was clear when he noted his work was far afield from the ramparts.

The masters of martial arts were many and varied in their background. Some were knights, others were priests. Some were men who would be sought by the most royal of courts and yet others were eye-patch wearing vagabonds. Some were soldiers and others mathematical theorists. Quite a few were connected to guilds, teaching to the commoners, but harkening back to knightly virtues as they did so. Almost all of them were in search of noble patronage.

Teaching could be informal, with a master-to-student relationship, but it also involved established

---

429 Egerton Castle, Schools and Masters of Fencing, (London: George Bell and Sons, 1885), 3.

guilds and schools, some of which survived for generations under the same family. Universities also taught fencing and the clergy itself continued to teach the use of arms into the 18th century.

National differences were present, with the Italians followed by the French successfully bringing their methodology to Europe when it came to swordplay. However, this was by no means universal. Spain stuck with its *Destreza* and the Polish continued to wear their sabers and cross-cut. Nor was it monolithic. The Germans, Dutch, English and French and Polish all took Italian ideas from the 16th and 17th century and made them their own.

Through it all, myriad and deep as it is, and broad as this work is, a picture emerges—a picture that shows *why* Europeans learned their martial arts. This *why*, when it comes to HEMA, is just as important as the *how*.

Richard Marsden of the Phoenix Society of Historical Swordsmanship with the Polish saber.

Acknowledgments

Researchers, editors, Historical European Martial Artists from around the world assisted in the creation of this work. Without their prior studies, none of this would have been possible.

WIKTENAUER

Wiktenauer is a magnificent researching project directed by Michael Chidester. Without his ongoing efforts much of this work, and the work of many others, would not be possible.

>www.wiktenauer.com

HROARR

HROARR is a website that hosts articles from HEMA researchers and fencers all over the world covering a myriad of topic, from dussacks of the 16th century to Napoleonic escapades as well as modern day trends within the HEMA community.

>www.hroarr.com

RAYMOND J. LORD COLLECTION

The Raymond J. Lord Collection contains a variety of authentic treatises. The collection, managed by Jeffrey Lord continues to do a service to both Academia and Historical European Martial Arts.

>www.umass.edu/renaissance/lord/

The following are deeply thanked for their efforts and contributions,

>Mike Bybee - Photography
>
>Jean Chandler
>
>Michael Chidester
>
>Maxime Chouinard
>
>Trevor Clemons
>
>Tom Farmer
>
>Ksenia Kozhevnikova – Artist
>
>Jessica Marcarelli

Reinier van Noort

Jacob Norwood

Kevin Mauer

Ken Mondschein

Reece Nelson

Cara Patterson - Editor

John Patterson

Mariana Lopez-Ródriguez - Artist

Lee Smith

Henry Snider – Layout

Ashton Warren – Artist

The Phoenix Society of Historical Swordsmanship

For further research consider

Fallen Rook Publishing

www.fallenrookpublishing.co.uk

Freelance Academy Press

www.freelanceacademypress.com

Tyrant Industries

www.tyrantindustriespublishing.com

Phoenix Society of Historical Swordsmanship

www.PhoenixSwordClub.Com

HEMA Alliance

www.HemaAlliance.com

POLISH SABER

Found at Amazon and other online retailers!

Bibliography

Art

- National Library of Wales. Unknown Flemish Artist. Late 15th century. Public Domain Art.
- http://www.strangehistory.net/2013/11/15/the-last-single-combat/ Public Domain Art.
- http://www.bryanskobl.ru/region/history/img/peresv_b.jpg 1914 Public Domain Art
- Bayrische Staatsbibliothek Cod. icon. 393 Mair, Circa 1544 Dbachmann Public Domain Art.
- Talhoffer Image courtesy of the Royal Library of Copenhagen
- Duel with a Dog Public Domain Art.
- Talhoffer Image courtesy the Royal Library of Copenhagen
- Le Duel après le bal masque Thomas Couture 1857. Wallace Collection. Public Domain Art.
- http://www.jarnac-tourisme.fr/images/stories/A_LE_TERRITOIRE/A1_Histoire_patrimoine/A_1_2_Coup_de_Jarnac.jpg May 22 2016 (Swap out possibly)
- Martino Almonte Public Domain Art.
- https://commons.wikimedia.org/wiki/File:Dendrono_-_Der_fechtende_Student.jpg Public Domain Art.
- http://ballads.bodleian.ox.ac.uk/static/images/sheets/30000/25003.gif May 26 2016 Public Domain Art.
- G. Durand - Harper's Weekly, New York: Harper Brothers, Vol. 19, No. 941 (9 January 1875), p. 41; this scan from : Das Wissen des 20. Jahrhunderts, Verlag für Wissenschaft und Bildung, 1961, Rheda, Bd.1 S.439 Public Domain Art.
- http://www.theatlantic.com/photo/2015/11/today-in-history-november-23/417279/ May 14 2016 Public Domain Photograph.
- Digital image courtesy of the Getty's Open Content Program.
- Digital image courtesy of the Getty's Open Content Program.
- Digital image courtesy of the Getty's Open Content Program.
- https://commons.wikimedia.org/wiki/File:British_-_Field_of_the_Cloth_of_Gold_-_Google_Art_Project.jpg Public Domain Art.
- https://commons.wikimedia.org/wiki/File:British_-_Field_of_the_Cloth_of_Gold_-_Google_Art_Project.jpg Public Domain Art.

- http://bibliodyssey2lj.livejournal.com/36774.html Public Domain Art.
- http://wiktenauer.com/wiki/Nicolaes_Petter Public Domain Art.
- Digital image courtesy of the Getty's Open Content Program.
- https://commons.wikimedia.org/wiki/File:Joust_John_Holland_Reginald_de_Roye.jpg Public Domain Art.
- Arnholot, http://www.erfgoedbankhoogstraten.be/php/dia1.php?s=600&trefwoord=dia Public Domain Art.
- Heinrich Wirrich 1571 https://commons.wikimedia.org/wiki/File:Heinrich_Wirrich_-_Proper_description_of_the_Christian_wedding_-_WGA25782.jpg Public Domain Art.
- https://commons.wikimedia.org/wiki/File:Paulus_Hector_Mair_Tjost_fig2.jpg Paulus Hector Mair Public Domain Art.
- https://commons.wikimedia.org/wiki/File:British_-_Field_of_the_Cloth_of_Gold_-_Google_Art_Project.jpg Public Domain Art.
- https://commons.wikimedia.org/wiki/File:British_-_Field_of_the_Cloth_of_Gold_-_Google_Art_Project.jpg Public Domain Art.
- https://commons.wikimedia.org/wiki/File:The_Joust_between_the_Lord_of_the_Tournament_and_the_knight_of_the_Red_Rose.JPG Public Domain Art.
- Digital image courtesy of the Getty's Open Content Program.
- https://commons.wikimedia.org/wiki/File:Battle-poitiers(1356).jpg Public Domain Art.
- https://commons.wikimedia.org/wiki/File:John_hawkwood.jpg Public Domain Art.
- https://commons.wikimedia.org/w/index.php?curid=3508743 By André Koehne Creative Commons 3.0
- https://commons.wikimedia.org/wiki/Battle_of_Grunwald#/media/File:Jan_Matejko,_Bitwa_pod_Grunwaldem.jpg Public Domain Art.
- https://commons.wikimedia.org/wiki/File:Italy_1494_v2.png Creative Commons Share and Share Alike.
- https://commons.wikimedia.org/w/index.php?curid=1177786 Public Domain Art.
- https://commons.wikimedia.org/wiki/File:Francois_Dubois_001.jpg Public Domain Art.
- https://commons.wikimedia.org/wiki/File:Battle_of_Pavia.jpg Public Domain Art.
- https://en.wikipedia.org/wiki/Charles_V,_Holy_Roman_Emperor#/media/File:Charles_V_enthroned_over_his_defeated_enemies_Giulio_Clovio_mid_16th_century.jpg 5-27-2-2016 Public Domain Old
- https://commons.wikimedia.org/wiki/File:Manual_of_the_Musketeer,_17th_Century.jpg Public Domain Art.

- https://upload.wikimedia.org/wikipedia/commons/9/9a/Hohenfriedeberg_-_Attack_of_Prussian_Infantry_-_1745.jpg Public Domain Art.
- https://commons.wikimedia.org/wiki/File:Ms_I33_fol_32r.jpg Public Domain Art.
- Digital image courtesy of the Getty's Open Content Program.
- Digital image courtesy of the Getty's Open Content Program.
- Image courtesy the Royal Library of Copenhagen.
- https://commons.wikimedia.org/wiki/File:Weiditz_Trachtenbuch_031-032.jpg Public Domain Art.
- https://commons.wikimedia.org/wiki/File:VAULT_Case_MS_Fol.U.423.792_11r.png Public Domain Art.
- https://commons.wikimedia.org/wiki/File:Bremer_Soldaten_-_Koster-Chronik_-_17._Jahrhundert.jpg Public Domain Art.
- 1897 The Graphic hand colored wood engraving titled, "Types of Old Swordsmanship: A Duel with Small Swords in 1760." Public Domain Art.
- Digital image courtesy of the Getty's Open Content Program.
- National Central Library of Rome Cod.1324 and Digital image courtesy of the Getty's Open Content Program.
- Image courtesy the Royal Library of Copenhagen.
- https://commons.wikimedia.org/wiki/File:Paulus_Hector_Mair.-_Two_fencers,_one_of_African_descent,_wielding_an_early_rapier_De_arte_athletica,_Augsburg,_Germany,_ca_1542.png Public Domain Art.
- https://commons.wikimedia.org/wiki/File:Angelo_Domenico_Malevolti_Fencing_Print,_1763.JPG Public Domain Art.
- Image courtesy the Royal Library of Copenhagen.
- https://commons.wikimedia.org/wiki/File:Henry_de_Sainct-Didier.jpg Public Domain Art.
- https://commons.wikimedia.org/wiki/File:Les_Vrayes_principes_de_l%27esp%C3%A9e_seule.jpg Public Domain Art.
- https://columbiaclassicalfencing.com/2015/02/08/monsieur-labbat-on-blade-cant-and-bend/ Public Domain Art.
- All Public Domain Art qualifies as Public Domain within the United States due to its age.

Text

- "A Study of the London Masters of Defense", accessed May 30, 2016, http://iceweasel.org/lmod.html

- Agrippa, Camillo trans. Ken Mondschien, Fencing: A Renaissance Treatise, New York: Italica Press, 2014.

- Anderson, Henrik, "Salvator Fabris as a Hired Assassin in Sweden", ARMA, accessed, May 30, 2016 http://www.thearma.org/essays/Fabris_the_Assassin.htm#.WBFPOPkrKUk

- Angelo, Domenico, The School of Fencing with a General Explanation of the Principal Attitudes and Positions Peculiar to the Art. with Hungarian and Highland Broad Sword and The Angelo Cutlass Exercises, London: Land's End Press, 1971 org. 1765.

- Anglin, Jay P., "The Schools of Defense in Elizabethan London," Renaissance Quarterly, Volume XXXVII, Number 3, Autumn 1984.

- ARMA, "Le jeu de la Hache," accessed May 30, 2016, http://www.thearma.org/spotlight/NotesLEJEUDELAHACHE.htm#.V1ITBPkrKUk

- Banks, Stephen, Duels and Duelling, London: Shire Publications, 2012.

- Block, John editor, Scottish Notes and Queries, Aberdeen: 1897.

- Bradak, Benjamin G. and Brandon P. Heslop, Lessons on the English Longsword, Boulder: Paladin Press, 2010.

- Brady Jr., Thomas A. , Politics and Reformations: Histories and Reformations, Boston: Brill, 2007.

- Brezezinski, Richard, Polish Armies 1569-1696, London: Osprey, 1987.

- Brioist, P H Drévillon, P Serna, Croiser le fer: violence et culture de l'épée dans la France moderne, XVIe-XVIIIe siècle, Paris: Champ Vallon, 2002.

- Bryson, Frederick R., The Sixteenth-Century Italian Duel, Chicago: University of Chicago Press, 1938.

- Bury, J.B., The Invasion of Europe by Barbarians, London: 1928.

- Caenegem, R. C., Legal History: A European Perspective, London: Bloomsbury Academic, 2004.

- Caferro, William, John Hawkwood: An English Mercenary in Fourteenth-Century Italy, Baltimore: Hopkins University Press.

- Calmette, Joseph, The Golden Age of Burgundy: The Magnificent Dukes and their Courts, New York: W.W. Norton. 2001.

- Cartwright, Julia Mary, Baldassare Castiglione the Perfect Courtier: His Life and Letters. Volume 2 Toronto: University of Toronto Libraries, 1908.

- Castiglione, Baldassare, Book of the Courtier, accessed May 23, 2016, https://archive.org/stream/bookofcourtier00castuoft/bookofcourtier00castuoft_djvu.txt
- Castle, Egerton, Schools and Masters of Fencing, London: George Bell and Sons, 1885.
- Chambers, Douglas D.C. and David Galbraith, The Letterbooks of John Evelyn, Toronto: University of Toronto Press, 2014.
- Chambers, Robert, Chamber's Journal of Popular Literature, Science and Arts, 1877.
- Chandler, Jean, A comparative analysis of literary depictions of social violence in two important 16th Century autobiographies, from the perspective of the fencing manuals of the Renaissance. Acta Periodica Duellatorum. Volume 2015, Issue 1, 101–137.
- Chauvin, Yves, Memoire dactylographie soutenu devant la Faculte des Lettres de Caen 1969.
- Chisholm, Hugh, Encyclopedia Britannica: A Dictionary of Arts and Sciences, Volume 9 Cambridge: Cambridge University Press, 1910.
- Clephan, Robert Coltman, The Mediaeval Tournament, Ann Arbor: University of Michigan Press, 1919.
- Coleman, Patrick, Rousseau's Political Imagination: Rule and Representation in the Lettre a d'alembert, Geneva: DROZ, 1984.
- "Council of Trent," American Catholic Truth Society, accessed May 18, 2016, http://www.americancatholictruthsociety.com/docs/TRENT/trent25.htm
- Crouch, Dacid, William Marshal: Knighthood, War, and Chivalry, 1147-1219, Abingdon-on-Thames: Routledge, 1992.
- Cummings, Benjamin, The Field of Honor, London: Forgotten Books, org. 1884.
- Davies, Norman, God's Playground, New York: Columbia Press, 1989.
- Derrin, Daniel, Rhetoric and the Familiar in Francis Bacon and John Donne, Teanick: Farleigh Dickinson University Press, 2015.
- "Diary of John Nevely", accessed May 30, 2016, https://archive.org/stream/diaryofjohnevely024466mbp/diaryofjohnevely024466mbp_djvu.txt
- Didier, Henri de Sainct, trans. Chris Slee, "The Secrets of the Single Sword", accessed May 25, 2016, http://sleech.info/wp-content/uploads/2012/11/The-Secrets-of-the-Single-Sword-General-Essay1.pdf
- Eisner, Manuel, Long-Term Historical Trends in Violent Crime, accessed May 20, 2016, https://soci.ucalgary.ca/brannigan/sites/soci.ucalgary.ca.brannigan/files/long-term-historical-trends-of-violent-crime.pdf 87.
- Elema, Ariella, "What Really Happened at the Last Duel," HROARR, last modified March 4 2016, accessed May 27, 2016, http://hroarr.com/what-really-happened-at-the-last-duel-part1/
- Emerson, Catherine, Olivier de La Marche and the Rhetoric of the Fifteenth-century Histo-

riography, Woodbridge: Boydell Press, 2004.

- Fabris, Salvator, trans. Tom Leoni, The Art of Dueling: Salvatore Fabris' Fencing Treatise of 1606, Highland Village: Chivalry Bookshelf, 2005.

- Fallows, Noel, Jousting in Medieval and Renaissance Iberia, Woodbridge: Boydell Press, 2010.

- "A Fechtschule in 16th Century Germany" accessed September 22, 2016, https://fechtschule.wordpress.com/2010/03/13/fechtschule-secret-history/

- "FBI Statistics," accessed May 20 2016, https://www.fbi.gov/about-us/cjis/ucr/crime-in-the-u.s/2015

- "French Fencing," accessed May 30 2016, https://columbiaclassicalfencing.com/2012/11/17/french-fencing-sources-on-using-the-unarmed-hand-to-parry-or-oppose-an-incoming-blade/

- Galas, Matthew, "The Deeds of Jacques de Lalaing: Feats of Arms of a 15th Century Knight," ARMA, accessed May 23, 2016, http://www.thearma.org/essays/Lalaingg.htm#.VG-l3e5V0yUm.

- Galas, Matthew, "Historical-Rule Sets", accessed October 1, 2016, http://hemaforums.com/viewtopic.php?t=664

- Gellius, Aulus, "Stories From Aulus Gellius," Translated by Dustin Simmons, accessed May 10, 2015, http://dustinsimmons.blogspot.com/2013/02/kill-gaul-get-name-titus-manlius.html

- Gevart, Bert and Reinier van Noort, Evolution of Martial Tradition in the Low Countries: Fencing Guilds and Treatises, Boston: Brill, 2016.

- Giganti, Nicoletto, trans. Tom Leoni, Venetian Rapier, Wheaton: Freelance Academy Press, 2010.

- Giganti, Nicoletto, trans. Joshua Pendragon and Piermarco Terminiello, The Lost Second Book of Nicoletto Giganti, London: Vulpes, 2013.

- Henning, Erhardus, trans. Reinier van Noort, "Short though thorough instruction in Cut-fencing", accessed May 20, 2016, http://www.bruchius.com/docs/Henning%20translation%20by%20RvN.pdf

- Henricks, Thomas S., Disputed Pleasures: Sport and Society in Preindustrial England, Westport: Praeger, 1991.

- Holland, Barbara, Gentlemen's Blood, London: Bloomsbury Publishing, 2004.

- Höschler, Christian, "Christopher Allmand: The De Re Militari of Vegetius. The Reception, Transmission and Legacy of a Roman Text in the Middle Ages (reviewed by Everett L. Wheeler)", accessed October 1, 2016, http://www.recensio.net/rezensionen/zeitschriften/reviews-in-history/2012/july/the-de-re-militari-of-vegetius

- Hubbard, Ben, From Spartacus to Spitfires: One-on-One Combat through the Ages, Canary Press, 2011.

- Hutton, Alfred, The Sword and the Centuries, Staffordshire: Wren's Park Publishing, 2003 org. 1901.

- Ireland, William Henry, Memoirs of Henry the Great: And of the Court of France During His Reign, Lexington: Ulan Press, 2012, org. 1923.

- Jones, Michael, Philippa Langley, The King's Grave, New York: St. Martin's Press, 2013.

- Kellet, Rachel E., Single-Combat and Warfare in German Literature of the High Middle Ages, Leeds: Maney Publishing, 2008.

- Kiernan, V.G, The Duel, Oxford: Oxford University Press, 1988.

- Kitowicz, Jędrzej, "On Customs and Traditions in the Reign of Augustus III", trans. Daria Izdebska, (Author given personal copy).

- Kinsley, D.A., Blades of the British Empire, Lulu: 2012.

- Kleinau, Jens P.,"1360 the Law of Judicial Duels in the City of Gelnhausen", accessed May 30, 2016, https://talhoffer.wordpress.com/2013/06/13/1360-the-law-of-judical-duels-in-the-city-of-gelnhausen/

- Kleinau, Jens P., "1444 Two Fencing Masters in Rothenberg", accessed May 30, 2016, https://talhoffer.wordpress.com/2012/12/03/1444-two-fencing-masters-in-rothenburg/

- Kleinau, Jens P., "1478 a Knightly Duel", accessed May 30, 2016, https://talhoffer.wordpress.com/2011/12/20/1478-a-knightly-duel/

- Kleinau, Jens P.,"1487 the Duel between Johann Waldburg-Sonnenberg and Antonio Maria d' Aragonia si San Severino", accessed May 30, 2016, https://talhoffer.wordpress.com/2015/06/19/1487-the-duel-between-johann-von-waldburg-sonnenberg-and-antonio-maria-d-aragonia-di-san-severino/

- Kleinau, Jens P., "What do you do if you are called for the judicial duel with mace and shield", accessed May 30, 2016 https://talhoffer.wordpress.com/2015/04/16/what-to-do-if-you-are-for-the-judicial-duel-with-mace-and-shield/

- Kottenkamp, F., The History of Chivalry and Armor, Mineloa: Dover Publications, 2007 org. 1857.

- LaVaque-Manty, Mika, "Dueling for Equality: Masculine Honor and the Modern Politics of Dignity", University of Michigan, (2006): accessed May 18, 2016, http://www-personal.umich.edu/~mmanty/research/Dueling.PT.pdf

- Lea, Henry Charles, Wager of Battle, In Superstition and Force: Torture, Ordeal, and Trial by Combat in Medieval Law, 95. 3rd ed, Philadelphia: Bodleian Library, 1878.

- Machiavelli, Niccolo, The Prince Mineola: Dover Thrift, 1992.

- Antonio Manciolnio, trans. Tom Leoni, The Complete Renaissance Swordsman, (Wheaton: Freelance Academy Press, 2010), 77-78.

- Marozzo, Achilles, trans. William Wilson, "Arte dell' Armi Books One & Two", accessed May 29, 2016, http://www.marozzo.org/marozzo-trans.pdf

- Marchegay, Paul, "Duel judiciaire entre des communautes religieuses, 1098," Bibliotheque de l'Ecole des Chartes, 1 (1839-1840): 552-564.

- Marsden, Richard, Polish Saber, Phoenix: Tyrant Industries, 2015.

- Maxwell, Herbert, A History of the House of Douglas, London: Freemantle and Company, 1902.

- Mauer, Kevin, "Insights into the Fechtschulen of the Marxbruder and Federfechter Guilds", Accessed May 30, 2016, https://docs.google.com/file/d/0B4Wy4VUTvpKKMkRNUHZK-OURFWHc/view

- Meyer, Joachim, trans. Jeffery L. Forgeng, The Art of Combat, London: Frontline Books, 2015.

- Michaelis, John David, Commentaries on the laws of Moses (Volume 4), Ann Arbor: University of Michigan Press, 1814.

- Mondschein, Ken, The Italian Schools of Fencing: Art, Science and Pedagogy, Boston: Brill, 2016.

- Morgan, Patrick T., "Escrime Classique," accessed May 30, 2016, https://foiled4once.files.wordpress.com/2013/09/montreal-presentation.pdf

- Neilson, George, Trial by Combat, Glasgow: W. Hodge and co, 1891.

- Nicole, David, The Great Chevauchée: John of Gaunt's Raid on France 1373, New York: Osprey, 2011.

- Noort, Reinier van, Interview, September 23, 2016.

- Noort, Reinier van, Lessons on the Thrust, Glasgow: Fallen rock Publishing, 2014.

- Noort, Reinier van, Of the Single Rapier, Glasgow: Fallen Rock Publishing, 2015.

- Ostovich, Helen and Holger Schott Syme, Andrew Griffin, Locating the Queen's Men, 1583-1603: Material Practices and Conditions of Playing, Farnham: Ashgate Publishing, 2009.

- Paris, Bibliotheque Nationale, MS. lat. 5430A, 15.

- Peltonen, Markku, The Duel in Early Modern England: Civility, Politeness and Honour, Cambridge: Cambridge University Press, 2003.

- Petter, Nicolaes, trans. Jerome Blanes, Self-defense Martial Art.

- Powell, George H., Dueling Stories of the 16th Century: From the French of Brantome, London: 1904.

- Reid, Peter, Brief History of Medieval Warfare, New York: Running Press, 2008.

- Rector, Mark, Highland Swordsmanship, Union City: Chivalry Bookshelf, 2001.

- Richardson, Glenn, Generous to a Fault, New Haven: Yale University Press, 2013.

- Rider, Jeff, "The Art of History". God's Scribe: The Historiographical Art of Galbert of Bruges. Washington: Catholic University of America Press, 2001.

- Runciman, Steven, The Fall of Constantinople: 1453, London: Cambridge University Press, 1990.

- Sabine, Lorenzo, Notes on Duels and Dueling, Whitefish: Kessinger Publishing, 2010 org. 1856.

- Schama, Simon, A History of Britain: At the End of the World? 3000 BC - AD 1603, London: BBC, 2000.

- Searle, E., Merchet in Medieval England, Past and Present, 1979.

- Silver, George, "Paradoxes of Defense", accessed May 22, 2016, http://www.pbm.com/~lindahl/paradoxes.html

- Lord Smail, Daniel, "Factions and Vengeance in Renaissance Italy: A Review Article," Comparative Studies in Society and History, 38.4 (Oct. 1996): 781-789.

- Smith, Robert Douglas, The Artillery of the Dukes of Burgundy, 1393-1477, Rochester: Boydell Press, 2005.

- Spierenburg, Peter, A History of Murder, Cambridge: Polity Press, 2008.

- Stevenson, Katie, Chivalry and Knighthood in Scotland 1424-1513, Woodbridge: Boydell Press, 2006.

- Terminello, Piermarco, "Hema Tome", accessed September 20, 2016, http://pterminiello.tumblr.com/post/106061253345/notes-on-preparing-for-a-judicial-duel-from-altoni

- Thomas, Hugh, The Golden Empire: Spain, Charles V, and the Creation of America, New York: Random House, 2011.

- Tlusty, B. Anne, The Martial Ethic in Early Modern Germany: Civic Duty and the Right of Arms, New York: Palgrave Macmillan, 2011.

- Vadi, Philippo, trans. Guy Windsor, Veni Vadi Vici, The School of European Swordsmanship, 2013.

- Vega, Alvaro Guerra de la, trans. Miguel Gomez, "Comprehension of Destreza", ARMA, accessed May 29, 2016, http://www.thearma.org/Manuals/destreza.htm#.V0tvIvkrKUk

- Verbruggen, J. F., The Battle of the Golden Spurs, (Woodbridge: Boydell Press, 2002 org. 1957), 249.

- Virgoe, Roger, Private Life in the Fifteenth Century: Illustrated Letters of the Paston Family London: Weidenfeld & Nicholson, 1989.

- Thibault, Gérard, trans. John Michael Greer, Academy of the Sword, (Highland Park, TX: The Chivalry Bookshelf, 2006).

- "Voltaire," accessed May 20, 2016, http://www.visitvoltaire.com/voltaire_bio.htm

- Wagner, John A. Encyclopedia of the Hundred Years War, (Westport: Greenwood Press, 2006), 107.

- Wiktenauer, "Jerónimo Sánchez de Carranza", accessed May 30, 2016, http://wiktenauer.com/wiki/Jer%C3%B3nimo_S%C3%A1nchez_de_Carranza

- Wiktenauer, "Ridolfo Capo Ferro", accessed May 26, 2016 http://wiktenauer.com/wiki/Ridolfo_Capo_Ferro_da_Cagli

- Wiktenauer, "Pseudo-Peter von Danzig", accessed May 20, 2016, http://wiktenauer.com/wiki/Pseudo-Peter_von_Danzig translated by Cory Winslow

- Wiktenauer, "Giacomo Di Grassi", accessed May 30, 2016, http://wiktenauer.com/wiki/Giacomo_di_Grassi

- Wiktenauer, "Fiore de'i Liberi", last modified August 16, 2016, accessed May 26, 2016, http://wiktenauer.com/wiki/Fiore_de'i_Liberi

- Wiktenauer, "Johannes Liechtenauer", accessed May 20, 2016, http://wiktenauer.com/wiki/Johannes_Liechtenauer#Treatise translated by Christian Tobler.

- Wiktenauer, "Luis Pacheco de Narváez", accessed May 30, 2016, http://wiktenauer.com/wiki/Luis_Pacheco_de_Narvaez

- Wiktenauer, "Le Jeu de la Hace", accessed May 30, 2016, http://wiktenauer.com/wiki/Le_Jeu_de_la_Hache_(MS_Fran%C3%A7ais_1996)

- Wiktenauer, "Paulus Hector Mair", accessed October 1, 2016, http://wiktenauer.com/wiki/Paulus_Hector_Mair

- Wiktenauer, "Joachim Meyer", accessed May 20, 2016, http://wiktenauer.com/wiki/Joachim_Me%C3%BFer

- Wiktenauer, "Hans Talhoffer", accessed May 20, 2016, http://wiktenauer.com/wiki/Hans_Talhoffer

Index

Académie d'Armes, 40

Agrippa, 145, 152-159, 186, 188-189, 205

A la mazza, 34, 144, 151, 197

Alfieri, 37, 158-159

Alfonso XI, 81, 165

Amsterdam, 72-73, 75, 190-191

Angelo, 11, 51, 75-76, 78, 126, 138, 145, 152, 174, 178-180, 187-188, 197, 204-205

Antrauget, 46

Àplaisance, 79

À outrance, 79

Assaulto, 40, 151

Assizes of Jerusalem, 17

Azevado, 17

Bayard, 17, 26

Bolognese, 145, 150-152, 182, 184, 188-189, 197

Boucicaut, 19-20, 22, 180

Brantome, 5, 22, 33-35, 46, 48-49, 51-52, 54, 67, 74, 92, 143-145, 151, 163, 190, 197, 209

Buckler, 10, 30, 40, 63, 68, 77, 104, 128, 134, 136, 138, 150, 152, 154, 156-157, 163, 165, 168, 170, 176-177

Caizo, 33

Calumnia, 18

Capoferro, 33, 37, 135, 156-159, 184

Carranza, 40, 188-190, 211

Cartello, 5, 43

Cartelli, 44

Castiglione, 5, 34, 50-51, 74, 145, 205-206

Charlemagne, 12

Castle, 27, 40, 112, 172, 184, 187, 197, 206

Cellini, 47, 71-72, 76, 169

Châtaigneraye, 23, 28, 33-34

Charles V, 4-5, 14, 23-24, 27, 38, 53, 88, 93, 106-107, 112-113, 115-117, 119, 121, 160, 190, 203, 210

Robert Charteris, 28

Chivalry, 4, 16-18, 24-25, 32, 52, 55, 71, 81, 89, 99, 103, 155-156, 178, 180, 192, 206-210

Claudio, 74

Condottieri, 19, 101, 145

Conrad, 37

Council of Trent, 27-28

Dagger, 4, 18, 46, 48-49, 55, 58, 64-66, 69-72, 75-77, 82, 84, 103, 127, 130-132, 135-136, 138, 146-147, 149-150, 156-158, 170, 172, 177, 191, 197

D'Aguerre, 16-17

Danzig, 164, 167-168, 211

De Caylus, 46

Deeds of Arms, 79, 81

De Fontaine, 16

De la Touche, 40, 145, 184-185

De Soupez, 74

Destreza, 40, 145, 186, 188-191, 198

Di Grassi, 154, 182, 211

Diet of Verona, 25

Dragon, 15, 71, 75, 207

Dussack, 66-68, 132-133, 170, 172, 194, 200

Fabris, 32, 37, 39, 51, 71, 99, 110, 126, 128, 135, 143, 155-159, 172-173, 184, 191-192, 197, 205, 207

Faits d'armes, 79

Fechtbuchs, 26, 170

Fechtschule, 40, 161-162, 169, 172, 207, 209

Federfechter, 38-39, 162, 169, 174, 209

Federschwert, 132, 161

Fiore, 18-21, 26, 35-36, 38, 64, 66-67, 78, 85, 97-98, 129-131, 141-151, 164, 172, 180, 197

Florence, 5, 25, 63, 169

Flower of Battle, 18, 64, 78, 85, 97-98, 130-131, 144-149, 172

4th Lateran Council, 27

Francis I, 4-5, 33, 53, 92-94, 113, 115-117, 120

Frederick II, 25, 120

Freifechter, 39, 77, 161, 162

Galeazzo, 19-22, 147, 180

Galiot, 83-84

Giganti, 33, 37, 71, 75, 78, 135, 143, 155-159, 184, 207

Greatsword, 132, 136, 138, 152, 154-155, 158, 184

Guilds, 37-40, 67, 81, 160-162, 164, 169, 172, 174, 191, 197-198, 207, 209

Gustavas Adolphus, 55

Guy of Steenvoorde, 22, 55

Hamilton, 49, 61, 73

Henri II, 16, 28, 33-34, 91-92, 113

Henri III, 40, 46, 92

Henry II, 25, 46

Henri IV, 40, 54, 56, 113, 181, 184

Henry VIII, 38, 68, 88, 90-94, 114, 173

Henning, 142, 172-173

Herman the Iron, 22

Holmganga, 10

Hutton, 13, 17, 33-34, 37, 40, 55, 83-84, 179, 208

Il duello, 34

Jacques Lalaing, 26

Jacques Le Gris, 23

James I, 16, 32, 44, 56, 89, 94, 113, 121, 126, 174

Jarnac, 23, 28, 33-34, 202

Jean de Carrouges, 23

Joust, 1, 19, 79, 81, 86-96, 113, 165, 203, 207

Judged by Investigation, 25

Kal, 13, 130, 164, 168-169

L' Abbat, 185

Lalaing, 26, 84-85, 207

L'Ange, 36-37, 143, 145, 156

La Touche, 40, 145, 184-186

Laws of St. Louis, 18

Ledall Roll, 176

Le Jeu de la Hache, 181-182, 205, 211

Liechtenauer, 26, 66, 116, 143, 160, 163-164, 167-169, 172

Lincoln, 59

London Masters of Defense, 174, 205

Longsword, 8, 16, 37, 40, 125-126, 129-130, 132, 147-148, 164-165, 168-172, 175-176, 192, 205

Louis IX, 25

Louis XIII, 40, 54-55, 181

Louis XIV, 40, 55, 119-120, 181, 184

Louis XV, 57, 181

Luite ds mortelz ennemis, 82

Mair, 9, 26, 38, 66-67, 78, 89, 124, 131, 161, 165, 169-172, 197, 202-204, 211

Manciolino, 35-37, 40, 143, 145, 150-152, 157

Manet, 59

Marcelli, 37, 136, 159-160

Marshal, 9, 24, 64-65, 80-81, 206

Marozzo, 36, 70, 151-152, 209

Marxbrüder, 38-39, 160-162, 164, 169, 171, 174, 209

McBane, 174, 177-178

Mentita, 53

Messer, 62, 66, 130, 132, 169

Meyer, 26, 38, 40, 68, 142-143, 161-162, 171-172, 194, 197, 209, 211

Mignons, 46

Mohun, 49

Montesquieu, 56-57

MS I.33, 14, 38, 78, 128, 160, 163

Narváez, 188-190

Palcaty, 40-41, 163, 195

Pas d'armes, 26, 83-84

Pas de la fontaine des pleurs, 81, 83

Passage of Arms, 26, 83-85, 147, 173

Petter, 36, 72, 89, 96, 192-193, 203, 209

Poleaxe, 21, 84, 130-132, 147, 149, 170, 180-182

Put to the question, 25

Rapier, 32, 40, 44-46, 49, 51-52, 68, 71, 73, 75, 77-78, 84, 98-99, 103, 114, 126-127, 132, 135-136, 138, 142, 145, 152-160, 162, 170-173, 176-177, 182-184, 187, 190-192, 204, 207, 209

Recet, 79

Ributare, 53

Richelieu, 54-55, 57, 181

Rifiutare, 53

Ritterrecht, 20

Rogito, 43

Rondel, 130

Rousseau, 48, 57-58, 60, 206

Saber, 36, 59-60, 66, 114, 126, 133, 136-138, 159, 163, 194-195, 198-199, 201, 209

Sackville, 32, 44-45, 49, 54

Sainct Didier, 182-183

Salic Law, 9-10, 101

Sastrow, 67

Seconds, 4, 27, 31, 43-49, 55, 60, 72-73, 138, 197

Shakespeare, 51, 54, 71, 79, 153, 155

Side sword, 68, 77, 126, 132-134, 151-152, 154, 171-172, 182

Simon von Stetten, 20

Silver, 51, 98-99, 116, 126, 132, 142-143, 145-146, 176-178, 185-187, 210

Starzewski, 195

Swetnam, 145, 177

Talhoffer, 4, 13, 16, 18, 22, 37, 64, 132, 164-165, 168, 182, 202, 208, 211

Thibault, 40, 135, 143, 184, 187, 191-192, 210

Vadi, 6, 67, 107, 144, 148-151, 210

Voltaire, 58, 120, 160, 210

Wellington, 61

Richard Marsden is a History teacher, holds a Masters Degree in Land Warfare, courtesy AMU and is co-founder of the Phoenix Society of Historical Swordsmanship along with John Patterson. Richard has won numerous medals at Historical Fencing tournaments and so have his students as well as their students. He was President of the HEMA Alliance and holds HEMA Alliance Instructor Certification in Fiore Longsword, Giganti Rapier, and Polish Saber. He has taught classes on various historical fencing techniques at various events in North America. He is also the co-author of over fifty short stories, The Traveling Tyrant series, an RPG expansion for Savage Worlds, War of the Worlds: The Remains, and is the author of The Polish Saber: The Use of the Polish Saber on Foot in the 17th century. He has a loving wife who tolerates his many eccentricities.

Polish Saber
The Use of the Polish Saber on Foot in the 17th Century

Polish Saber - The Use of the Polish Saber on Foot in the 17th Century covers the history, anecdotes and use of Poland's iconic weapon. In matters of honor and personal safety the saber was the Polish nobleman's choice of arms. The concept of the duel, the form and function of the weapon, as well as source material from Poland, Italy and Germany are blended together in an interpretation presented in full-color. The work is suitable for history enthusiasts, Historical European Martial Artists and re-creationists who wish to explore Poland's Commonwealth and the weapon that symbolized its nobility.

Available on Amazon and other online retailers

www.ingramcontent.com/pod-product-compliance
Lightning Source LLC
Chambersburg PA
CBHW040902020526
44114CB00037B/33